Minority Languages and Dominant Culture:
Issues of Education, Assessment and Social Equity

Mary Kalantzis
Bill Cope
Diana Slade

The Falmer Press
(A member of the Taylor & Francis Group)
London • New York • Philadelphia

UK   The Falmer Press, Falmer House, Barcombe, Lewes, East Sussex, BN8 5DL

USA   The Falmer Press, Taylor & Francis Inc., 1900 Frost Road, Suite 101, Bristol, PA 19007

First published 1989

British Library Cataloguing in Publication Data

Kalantzis, Mary
    Minority languages and dominant culture: issues of education, assessment and social equity.
    1. Linguistic minority student. Education.
    I. Title   II. Cope, Bill   III. Slade, Diana
    371.97

    ISBN 1-85000-628-8
    ISBN 1-85000-629-6 pbk

Typeset in 10½/13 Garamond by
Chapterhouse, The Cloisters, Formby L37 3PX

Jacket Design by Caroline Archer

Printed in Great Britain by Taylor & Francis (Printers) Ltd, Basingstoke

Minority Languages
and
Dominant Culture

02

Contents

Introduction

In an era of extraordinary movement of human populations it is hard to escape cultural and linguistic diversity. This book is about the relationship of minority immigrant languages to mainstream culture, and the particular ways in which the institution of education handles linguistic diversity. Its main focus is on Australia, including a discussion of the development of Australian languages policy in Chapter 3 and a report in Chapters 4 and 5 on a major piece of empirical work we undertook, investigating German and Macedonian language maintenance in the Wollongong-Shellharbour region of New South Wales.

The book, however, is not *about* Australian languages and education. Rather, it is a more general argument, using Australia and several other countries as examples, about the general phenomenon of minority language use. Chapter 1 discusses the issues theoretically, contrasting simple pluralist and holistic models of the place of minority immigrant languages. A celebratory and conservationist approach to the differences characteristic of some versions of multiculturalism, it is argued, is clearly inadequate. An holistic model is more able to account for language shift, and to consider the linguistic logistics of access to mainstream society for immigrant groups. Chapter 2 develops these arguments, examining key educational debates about 'semilingualism' and immigrant children in Sweden, bilingual education in Canada and language rights in the United States. The Australian situation is analyzed in Chapter 3, again, not as a national description, but as a lead into the key question of whether multicultural education and the teaching of minority languages should be concerned with the maintenance of cultural and linguistic difference, or access to mainstream society, or some combination of these two objectives. By this point we hope we are beginning to give some practical educational answers to the problems posed by the sociology of language in Chapter 1.

Chapter 5 provides a detailed report on the research project we conducted into German and Macedonian language maintenance in the context of migration. Preceding this, Chapter 4 serves the dual function of discussing the language testing methodology we used in this project and applying the conclusions about language and pedagogy we reached in Chapter 3 to the vexing and complex area of language testing in a multilingual context. The aim of this examination and application of testing was to push the debate about minority languages beyond immediate politics of attitudes and maintenance to a consideration of the relationship of minority to majority, official languages in the development through education of linguistic skills for effective social participation.

Key Questions in the Australian Setting

The 'community' language movement in Australia has now been in full swing for over a decade. Under the umbrella of a pluralist multiculturalism, one of its key tendencies has been to make all languages appear to be of equal prestige. Since all people and groups are supposed to be equal in our plural or multicultural society, at least at the level of 'ethnicity', English must also be considered to be a language just like any other in the Australian context. English too is a 'community language'. It is revealing that the groups we surveyed did not see things this way.

One has to question seriously what this term 'community' means and how useful a descriptor it is. For example, are those post-1960s migrants of Greek background, who live in the outer western suburbs of Sydney and work in factories and shops, of the same community as those pre-war migrants of Greek background who live in the eastern suburbs and work as professionals? Are they of the same community as those who were born in Australia and live in the southern suburbs and work as public servants? Are they of the same community as the aged group who migrated from the Greek island of Lesbos and are now institutionalized in an old people's home? Do they speak the same Greek? Which community do they actually belong to? Are their language needs similar? In what senses can we talk of a Greek 'community language' linked to a Greek 'community'?

The notion of a 'community language' begins to break down when one asks questions like this. This is even aside from the technical issue of varieties of usage and speech communities. The crucial question is, what is a 'community language'? How real is the 'community' or does its use convey a certain type of 'ethnic politics'?

The development of the concept of 'community language' is a recent one that complements the push by certain groups to get jobs, services and special funding allocations. This is the stuff of 'ethnic politics', but how useful is the notion of 'community language' in formulating language policy? At the most general level, practical policy decisions can only be made on the basis of numbers, and, given the range of languages used in Australia today, numerical size is a problematic criterion for policy decisions. Furthermore, barring more detailed analysis of language usage, language communities can only be measured by place of birth or parents' place of birth — a very crude indicator of language use and variety. When reference is made to English as a 'community language', the term loses all clarity. Difference within difference and parity of difference are all we are left with, despite the fact that English is, and will remain within the foreseeable future, the language of general communication and the language of access to education, jobs and power in Australia.

The only way to understand fully the concept of 'community language' is to place it historically within the framework that gave it birth: in the supercession (in Australian official policy) of assimilation by cultural pluralism. The language question cannot be seen as separate from broader questions of sociocultural policy. Which languages are to be maintained and why? Which languages are to be used where? Which are to be serviced? In what ways? It is the decision to accept a sociology broadly of cultural pluralism in Australia at a government level that has opened up the language question.

The maintenance of languages other than English in Australia should not be seen as a major issue in relation to the conservation of those languages for posterity. An exception is the Aboriginal languages, where it is probable that these forms of communication will disappear if some action is not taken. However, there is no fear of the other languages spoken in Australia fading away and needing to be preserved for the sake of their very survival as languages *per se*. Preservation is occurring in their place of origin. The issue of maintenance in Australia should be primarily about something that is going on in Australia; communication in the home, communication between different groups, communication with the rest of the world, self-expression, success and optimizing social opportunities. How are these things achieved and what is their relationship to language variety? None of these social goals has simple implications for the formulation of language policy. Communication at home for some families that have migrated to Australia is in many instances fraught with conflicting, and far from familial, values and aspirations. Communicating in a hybrid form of the language of origin, which is the result of shifts and borrowings for many transported languages, has its limitations and frustrations. But these frustrations are not just at the level of words and syntax. Words alone are not enough when one is straddling two worlds, as parent or child, for example. The issue of maintenance is fraught with complexities.

Likewise, in the case of intergroup communication, culture clash cannot be overcome just by learning another language. The imperatives and meanings of culture cannot simply be shared or understood at the symbolic level of language, but only through the living practices for which that language is a tool. One will not necessarily understand or become more tolerant of, say, individualism among longer established, English-speaking members of the middle class simply by learning its words. The claim that language embodies culture is very vague, and the claim that culture can be taught through language is tendentious at best. Culture and life shape language as much as language reshapes life. Language is a tool of social interaction. Any language has the potential to be transposed onto mainstream culture. What goes with language is constructed in social, living circumstances. Its semantic range, function and form are products of social circumstance. We will elaborate upon these arguments in Chapter 1.

At the level of communicating with the rest of the world, the issue for the language question is the same as it always was for what was called foreign language learning — languages usually take uneven forms without a living context. The dilemma of language maintenance is that the living context of languages other than English in Australia is a shifting one, and the language forms which sometimes develop are ones which are not always readily applicable or functionally successful in their place of origin.

At the level of self-expression, success and access to jobs and power, the language question is exceedingly complex. The situation is different for different groups of different ages. One has to question particularly the link between language maintenance and passing in other school subjects or getting a job. How the latter is best facilitated is not something which lies within the parameters of the current community language debate, with its emphasis on 'self-esteem', 'prestige' and 'rights'. It is, rather, to do with the relationship of language, cognition, intellectual formation and access to social goods. Language, therefore, must not be fetishized for its forms, as it often is at the moment. It is not merely an artefact, the face of 'ethnicity', the embodiment of tradition. It is a human tool with social functions. Of course, the latter, more general consideration encompasses the former considerations. The problem is one of emphasis: to put immediately political issues up front as the most important rationale for language servicing is to weaken the case, particularly in a time of general economic stringency, where moves to self-help are seen as alternatives to government intervention. This is aside from the theoretical sloppiness encouraged by a reflexively political impetus to research and social practice.

So far, Australia has had a problematic experience even with the only foreign language considerable effort and resources have gone into teaching: English as a Second Language. How will the education system cope with the demands placed on languages which mainly stem from immediately political motivations? One of the pressing problems connected with children of some non-English-speaking backgrounds is their underachievement at school. This is not just because assessment procedures are culture-bound. Nor is it the case, of course, that whole schools can have populations of children with lower natural abilities. Language policy debates must put these issues at the top of their agendas. In particular, how are language, cognition and success at school related? What variety of language is being maintained by the community, and what is the extent and nature of its vitality?

1
Minority Languages and Dominant Culture: Theoretical Propositions

The language question arises partly from the current view of contemporary industrial societies as pluralist. As a consequence, declarations are made that we live in societies that are 'multicultural' and 'multilingual'. As the government's role in modern society is in part to service society to ensure its smooth reproduction, a claim can then be made that the state must service this plurality in its decisions and in the way it allocates public funds. This chapter explores the nature of this stated plurality in order to assess its requirements, particularly in relation to the language question. This is done through an examination of some cultural-linguistic dynamics in modern industrial society.

Plurality is made possible by what is sometimes termed the core, dominant or mainstream culture. Culture, following the cultural anthropologist's conception, is a whole way of life, not just aspects of high culture or folk culture. There is plurality in modern society, but we need to comprehend another unifying dynamic which transforms this plurality and makes it its own. The process of unification is uneven, and thus the drawing together of different people, ideas and material culture occurs in such a way that the unifying mechanisms are often obscured. This unification, however, does not mean an inevitable end to plurality even in the long term. Indeed, plurality (visible as cosmopolitanism and in the dynamism and variety of cultural phenomena) is an endemic part of industrialism. But unification sets limits to, as much as it guarantees, plurality.

Some people negatively call the unifying process assimilation. Because they view culture narrowly as 'ethnicity', rather than as a whole way of life, they claim that assimilation in a place such as Australia is into a hybrid, ethnically defined Anglo-Celtic-ness. But it is, in a sense, an historical accident that Anglo-Celtic-ness is the dominant medium through which industrial society/culture is organized in Australia. In Japan it is Japanese, but what remains of traditional, pre-industrial Japanese culture is incorporated and commodified in a similar way to those vestiges of pre-industrial Anglo or Celtic culture which remain in modern Australia.

The plurality that exists in modern society is not always a diversity of equals. When one considers languages, one has to assess function in terms of power and self-determination. The linking of languages to the question of maintaining cultural differences in a pluralist society then becomes problematic. It will remain problematic so long as we uncritically propound a simplistic sociology of pluralism.

Historically, one of the initial concerns in the language question was that of language as a tool of self-determination or access. The emphasis, as a consequence, was on initiation into the majority language as a second language, and later on transitional bilingual programmes. More recently another line of argument has emerged, about cultural variety and cultural and linguistic maintenance as virtues and social or educational ends in themselves. This is often informed by a simple pluralist sociological framework, and earlier programmes are sometimes condemned for having assimilationist assumptions. Presently, the two lines of action, the one towards social empowerment and the other towards cultural maintenance, sit together in tension in government policy. As a result of this tension, many of the assertions and claims made under the umbrella of the language question are contradictory and indecisive. Thus it is important to examine closely some of the unspecified premises in the debate on the language question, while at the same time pointing to another paradigm that might be more fruitful as a basis for research and policy deliberations.

Languages in Culture: Theoretical Implications

Two major movements in the modern world are important as historical background to the language question. One is a massive internationalizing and universalizing trend, produced through the mass media, transport, labour migration, tourism, industry and trade, the spread of technology, multinational corporations, academic and scientific exchange and so on. This movement is not entirely new to the past two centuries, but it is unprecedented in its scale. The other movement is a concomitant of the first. In the process of this universalization there has been a thrusting together of a huge number of differences among commodities, people and ideas. This dual process of the modern world, and its unprecedented scale and rate, has to be kept in mind when considering the modern phenomenon of 'multiculturalism'. And modern it is, despite some claims that multiculturalism has always existed because people of different backgrounds and languages have always lived in proximity. The drive to structure and service this diversity by government is new. The concept of 'ethnicity' as a bargaining tool is also new, although its origins and goals are complex and unclear.

Complaints abound from all quarters of the globe, and are increasing, that multiculturalism as a concept, policy or practice, is fuzzy and problematic. The severest complaints come from both the left and the right of the political spectrum, but their misgivings, even though they often seem to coalesce, emanate from different perspectives. The left complains that it is a tokenistic sop, ducking fundamental questions of socio-economic justice. The right sees multiculturalism as subverting and unified cultural and economic nationalism. Multiculturalism, it seems, is the domain of the middle ground of so-called liberals, at a time when liberalism is on the defensive. It is important, therefore, to redefine the substance of the phenomenon and its demands. However, one obstacle to this goal is the fact that mainstream academe has largely ignored the multicultural phenomenon; and the limited, top-down, state interventionary nature of multiculturalism adds a further complication.

Multiculturalism and Pluralism: A Critical Overview

Many countries have made cultural pluralism a policy in some form or other, including Australia, USA, Canada, UK, Sweden, South Africa and the Soviet Union. The various forms are not all equally valid or similar in approach, but the historical problem to which each has responded has been fundamentally the same. In different ways, the expansion, growth and wealth of each of these countries have depended upon the quick integration of peoples from a variety of backgrounds because what is asked of them is the same — to participate in the same culture: modern, industrial society. Or, at least, they have to stay 'different' (for example, structural racism and socio-economic location) in order to be integrated into the same new structure. The diversity that exists in modern nation states is part of the becoming of the modern nation and the rise of the so-called 'core culture' of industrialism as a way of life.

It has been a powerful tendency of modern industrial culture to make the experience of life uniform. From the beginning of the industrial epoch, imperialism, colonialism, economic expansion and the internationalization of labour, capital, commodities and technology have had this effect. Industrialism has had the means and the need to fling together people from the remotest parts of the world, and thus bring into contact previously parochial cultural forms and processes of socialization. The consequence has been diversity — but what sort of diversity is it? How does the universalizing dynamic transform and, in some respects, maintain diversity? Is the incorporation of diversity really plurality in any structural sense, or is it a redefining of the larger face of a single culture? Does this trend serve the requirements of a new nationalism in some instances? Does the emphasis on diversity successfully deny the universalizing pressures, in theory or in practice? Can it possibly allow government to retreat from service provision to meet the general goals of participation and equity? It is necessary to examine these wider perspectives before considering how different groups of people and different nation states are responding to the diversity that has become a feature of all industrialized nations.

Language is the most obvious and prominent feature of this diversity. It is also one of the easiest to promote because it does not necessitate any particular social practices but, in its various registers and forms, it can be the vehicle for a great many social practices. There is always a powerful link between language and culture, but, as a tool in an abstract sense, language is open. Any particular language can have very different cultural contents, according, for example, to various socio-economic contexts of use. It is much easier to consider maintaining and servicing a group's language in its nominal national or ethnic sense than many of its underlying social practices, which might threaten or contest the social-structural arrangements for reproducing life in the immigrant setting. Languages can be viewed as artefacts, primarily of personal, symbolic importance. This is in keeping with industrial culture's special emphasis on individuals and their psychology, self-respect, identity and so on. A political response to language can then be presented as a formal statement of equality. But the relation of language to culture, particularly in the immigrant situation, is very complex. A more sophisticated theorization of the complexity of culture and the development of multiculturalism is required — one that takes into account generational, regional, class, occupational and gender factors in a more holistic way.

So the two great movements of industrialism, at first glance movements in contradiction with each other, have served to unify and homogenize life, yet also to throw together and tolerate diversity. For every inroad industrial forms of life — wage labour and commodity consumption, weekends and mass media — make into traditional life-styles, the traditional has its feedback into industrial society, throwing together workers of diverse backgrounds and putting Indian clothes or Turkish food into the markets of metropolitan industrialism. In the words of James Banks, both 'traditionalism and modernity co-exist in modernized and modernizing nation-states and individuals are capable of having multiple identifications' (Banks, 1983: 230).

But crucially, the traditional/diverse and modern/universalizing do not sit together as equals. We need a theory which specifies their relations in order to understand properly the nature of migration and the place of minority languages. However, much of the research in the area of minority languages lacks rigorous sociological premises. Lewis is representative of the most commonly proffered type of theory of linguistic pluralism.

> The moral dilemma of a plural society is to promote advantageous contact while simultaneously maintaining the separate languages and the speakers' pride in them . . . . The use of a child's language is something to which he is morally entitled . . . . Language is not only a means of expression and communication, it is also a symbol of one's cultural and ethnic affiliation . . . . [No] individual can possibly achieve a personal identity or mature satisfactorily unless he has assimilated at least some of the core elements of the culture of his ethnic group or nationality. Having assimilated these elements he may be critical of them and disown others. But he is inextricably attached to the group and its culture; the one thing he cannot afford to do is to isolate himself from that tradition, for if he does he is not merely rootless, he is defenceless against anarchy . . . . The task of bilingual education is to maintain the traditional cultures, to further the development of the broad national culture as well as our understanding of it, and finally to provide the conditions whereby each type of culture reinforces and supports the other. (1981: 389–93)

Why do we need traditionalism to prevent restlessness and anarchy? How do traditionalism and 'national culture' reinforce and support each other? In the emotive tone of this passage, answers to these questions are simply asserted, doing little justice to the complexity of the situation. Is assimilation to one's ancestral culture always and unequivocally a moral good?

For the purposes of argument, we will draw a caricature of a simple pluralist model of language in culture (see Figure 1.1). This simple pluralist multiculturalism sees modern industrial societies as akin to a cultural-linguistic fruit salad bowl, with cultures and community languages floating about like bits of fruit, happy to be ingredients in the great cuisine of modernity, yet mutually distinctive and tolerant. From this description flows a moral prescription: that we should learn to tolerate, enjoy, maintain and reproduce this cultural-linguistic diversity. But there are serious deficiencies in this moral pluralism, this view of a multicultural, multilingual society.

First, even impressionistically, it is a trivialized view of what culture is. In schools and the media, for example, the iconography of the multicultural is exotic food, clothing or dance, and perhaps some multilingual signs; it is nice and colourful to preserve a variety of languages and cultures. But this is to neglect other, deeper issues. Seen as communicative tools, for example, it is simply not true that there is a colourful equality to languages here. Language and society cannot be separated. Language is always an integral part of the social process and, as such, most obviously in terms of effective social participation, the dominant language of state and public participation is more than equal to other

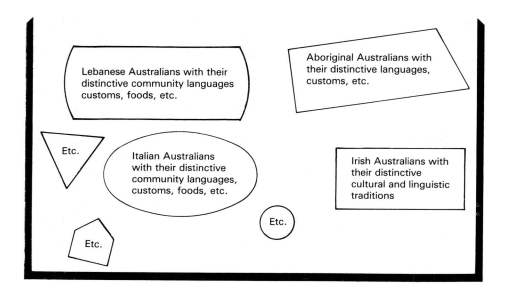

Figure 1.1 The Australian Cultural Fruit Salad Bowl

languages in any particular national or local context. Even the most ardent pluralist, keen, for the sake of appearances, to stress equality by calling the dominant language equally a community language, is hesitant to deny this. Less obviously, not all languages as they are used, including some forms of the dominant language (such as some working-class English usages) function as communicative or cognitive tools adequate for full and effective social participation beyond certain circumscribed social and domestic arenas (see below). Simple pluralism, in its attraction to the colourfulness of linguistic diversity, frequently fails to analyze the language forms and linguistic prerequisites for equal social participation and access to the full range of possible forms of social and cultural interaction.

Second, simple pluralism's fetish for difference not only leads to a superficial working definition of culture, but can often be unself-consciously conservative or even racist. It is not that conservatism qua conservatism is always a bad thing, but that simple pluralist multiculturalism is often unreflectively so. Preserving 'communities' is not a good for its own sake, as if peoples should be preserved as museum pieces, so that they are not lost to posterity. 'Communities' are always mixed, contradictory, conflict-ridden and by no means socially isolated entities. Active cultural re-creation, if people so wish, might involve consciously dropping one language in preference for another or abandoning some cultural tradition or other — such as sexism. If we are going to preserve, it has to be for more than preservation's sake. Moreover, there is a double racism to preservation for its own sake. Communities often fight for their own self-preservation — 'Be careful who you marry; good girls are ... and speak ...' — but there is often an intrinsic prejudice in preserving one's 'community' by marking its boundaries negatively against an unacceptable 'outside'. A simple pluralist multiculturalism can easily condone, and even actively foster, the reproduction of ethnic chauvinisms.

There is, moreover, a certain structural racism to the educated, successful, liberal multiculturalist, who delights in plurality yet ignores the fact that it is precisely someone else's difference that often disempowers them. Plurality in industrialism is not always among equals. Making people feel good about their cultures and languages, by officially viewing them as nice pieces of the national mosaic, does nothing about the structural inequalities written through this same plurality. Besides, there is a rash presumption in thinking that people unproblematically want to maintain the diversity they have, when immigrants almost invariably aspire to the all but universal goals (within industrialism) of a good job, a good education, a good house and so on.

Third, behind the trivialized view of culture, the implicit conservatism and unconscious racism, is a hidden agenda of assimilation. If we do not talk about survival strategies in Australia, and dwell only on colourful plurality, we can conveniently neglect elementary issues of social welfare measured in the material terms of the necessities of survival in industrialism. A smattering of 'community languages' as a token to our multiculturalism can be at the expense of taking effective pedagogy (measured in social outcomes) very seriously. By addressing ourselves to what appear to be plural needs and relevance, we can neglect the singular features and processes of power in industrial society, and the general skills needed to succeed or to be able to choose. It is not that assimilation does not happen. It is a fact that remains hidden, and one is inevitably assimilated as part of the general social system: wages, housing, welfare, taxes, laws — as one of its minions with a relative lack of power. The plurality story is often an ideological illusion, with a hidden agenda of assimilation which does not allow some fundamental cultural processes to be examined (since, according to the theory, assimilation is not supposed to be happening). As we convince ourselves about plurality, a certain structural and cultural integration goes on, but this is just commonsense and not part of our theory.

Fourth, a frequent implication of simple pluralist multiculturalism is that culture is little more than the traditional or the exotic and the domain of minorities. What is culture for longer established residents? Surely not Elton John, Kentucky Fried Chicken or Eyewitness News? Most of us, regardless of our origins, receive and participate in this culture. Intuitively, it is hardly the stuff of multiculturalism. If culture, as seems to be the case for simple pluralism, is just those things of diverse traditional origin which can be multi in today's society, for longer established residents, such as 'Anglo-Celtic' Australians, this must mean it is made of things like Yorkshire pudding and Irish ditties. Anything else is a product of the international culture of industrialism. Perhaps, realistically, many longer established residents will be unable to dredge up any such culture. But most importantly, this culture is principally a matter of private choice.

Generally speaking, the traditional and the colourful can most easily find their expression at the weekend rather than during the week, in leisure rather than work, in the domestic rather than the public arena. Of course, this is not universally and simplistically the case: there are also the permutations of the local shop or on the factory floor. But all such manifestations of cultural variety are within structural limits. This is not to deny diversity as a necessary and integral part of society, but to conclude that the arguments for pluralism mask the very processes that limit diversity and self-determination.

The space in which cultural diversity can find its expression is shaped in a way uniquely characteristic of industrialism. Cosmopolitanism does not mean that the traditional can co-exist with impunity beside the universal structures of industrialism; it defines spaces and makes the traditional part of its own culture. Cosmopolitanism and variety are thus attributes of industrialism itself. It is rather like the tourist shop where the characteristic social relations are universal to Western industrialism (entrepreneurship, wage labour, commodities), yet the products sell and the place has an attractiveness precisely for its colourfulness and fetish for the striking, the unusual, the traditional, the different.

The dominant 'official' language serves as *lingua franca* for the culture of industrialism in any particular context — hardly just another language among the 'communities' of the nation, but the accidental language of the common culture of industrialism. Parents may well tell stories to their children in the dominant language or in minority languages on one side of the week/weekend, work/leisure, public/private divide. But it rings rather hollow to say that the dominant language is just another community language, when the everyday divide of dominant from minority languages is so all-pervasive. This is not to deny the importance of communication in the domestic arena and the private sphere, or its psychological function as a link to family or group identity and solidarity, but even at this level, using language principally in these limited spaces influences its function and character.

Towards an Holistic Understanding of Language in Culture

Against the deficiencies of simple pluralism, we propose an holistic theory of culture in Australia. This is a far from unusual proposal, being based on a broad, cultural-anthropological understanding of culture. We have written at length elsewhere about the meaning of 'culture' for 'multiculturalism', reviewing the literature and debates in the area in detail (Kalantzis and Cope, 1980, 1981, 1984). Here we simply present a review of these research findings.

It is the simple pluralist or 'spaghetti and polka' view of culture that is unusual, being pragmatically and no more than intuitively associated with those things brought from a variety of traditions which can, without threat to the fundamental structures of industrialism, be happily 'multi'. Minority languages (in their proper place), food and dance, fit as quite acceptable cultural variety. Some bits of cultural peculiarity even sell well. But Lebanese peasantry and Polish communism are cultural forms which are out of the question in an industrialist First World context.

Of course, culture is more than what can neatly fit within the narrow, pragmatic conception. It also includes everyday life practices which might conventionally be called political, economic or structural. 'Peasantries', 'communisms' and 'Western industrialisms' are aspects of culture, as much as food and dance. Even those practices that the simple pluralists find so attractive do not exist independently of wider social pressures. We propose an alternative view of culture which analyzes the dynamic relationship of different levels of cultural activity. These are, first, those activities which express the essence of culture and human-ness; second, those variable in history but singular and universal in Australia today (manifest as Western industrialism); and third, those life practices which can exist in variety in the spaces made by Western industrialism in Australia today.

The Characteristics of Language across all Human Cultures

When we ask what culture is for, we find certain things which unite all people as humans. The cultural anthropological definition of culture was initially developed, in part, in a theoretical quest to distinguish humans from animals. Humans characteristically learn their particular forms of social interaction. This means that humans, uniquely, have the ability and freedom to create and change their cultures or social worlds, and not just be bearers of social roles, for whom a blueprint (as with ants) is laid out in their genes.

There are no primordial cultural differences and no cultural gaps which ultimately and irretrievably thwart communication. The extraordinary translatability of languages, even if word does not always precisely correspond with word, is but one piece of evidence to support this proposition. Although particular cultures and particular societies are not biologically predetermined, there is a certain common human inevitability to culture and society. From birth, humans are unable to survive independently. It is this universal fact of sociality that creates the impetus for cultural formation and transmission. All humans have to live in systems of social sharing to satisfy fundamentally common basic needs. This is not to say that all cultures satisfy needs as well as they could, but to claim that these needs are the reasons why society and culture exist. These form the basis of universal human standards by which cultures can be judged. Material deprivation, the anti-social maltreatment of one person by another, or insufficient food to eat, for example, are not to be judged by each person's particular cultural standards, but by universal human standards in the essence of what culture is for.

Simple pluralist multiculturalism commits a crime of omission in its obsession with difference alone and, in line with its sentimentalism, in its concern only with such differences as can pleasantly exist in variety. This crime of omission has special implications for analyzing linguistic variety. Languages are not simply to be described in terms of their variety. All, in the nature of culture, are communicative tools. There is something very ordinary, mundane and pragmatic about this fundamental similarity of function which is lost to pluralist analysis so captivated (*qua* pluralism) by the differences and so concerned for their preservation.

If a socially relevant communicative capability is a need in the very nature of human existence and human culture, we can critically assess the extent to which this need is satisfied for different groups in different social contexts. This might lead us beyond uncritically lauding linguistic difference, to an assessment of what is required to be linguistically competent and effective in different social settings. One is compelled to make this sort of emphasis about the nature of language to redress the loading on difference that predominates in the pluralist model of culture, particularly in relation to educational practice. To reduce language to its function and utility, however, is not to ignore the subtleties and variety of form and meaning that it develops in real life practice, but to attempt to push thinking on the matter into a direction that might form a more balanced basis for analysis and policy.

What, then, is language as a basic, common, functional human factor? Other animals use signs — languages of sorts — but human language has a qualitatively different character in its relation to thought and meaning. Only humans have theoretical and practical thought with which to comprehend and mould nature; to act self-consciously and communally, to transform nature to their own ends. There is, according to Vygotsky, a qualitative leap from the total absence of consciousness in inanimate matter to sensation in animate entities; and the leap from sensation to thought is of the same magnitude.

> A frightened goose suddenly aware of danger and rousing the whole flock with its cries does not tell the others what it has seen but rather

contaminates them with its fear . . . . Communication by means of expressive movements, observed mainly among animals, is not so much communication as a spread of affect. (Vygotsky, 1962: 6)

There is much more to human communication than exchanging signs. This is evident even in the word.

A word does not refer to a single object but to a group or to a class of objects. Each word is therefore already a generalisation. Generalisation is a verbal act of thought and reflects reality in quite another way than sensation and perception reflect it . . . . There is every reason to suppose that the qualitative distinction between sensation and thought is the presence of the latter of a *generalised* reflection of reality, which is also the essence of word meaning; and consequently that meaning is an act of thought in the full sense of the term. (Vygotsky, 1962: 5; emphasis in original)

In theorizing about the nature of language in human culture in general, the question then arises of whether language and thought shape the human world or whether language and thought are reflections of the world. It is not possible to give this question a simple answer.

In one sense, reality (social practices and environments) determines thought and language. Needs are satisfied in forms socialized upon the young by the particular natural and human ecosystem into which they happen to be born. The particular patterns of thought and language are determined by existing natural and social circumstances. Languages are pragmatic solutions to practical problems of survival: problems which are solved differently in different patterns of social organization. But, in another sense, languages, as already existing parts of each overall solution to the problem of existence, reproduce particular forms of society in each newly emerging individual. As Piaget pointed out, a small child might use words which stand for complex generalizations or syntactical relationships (such as 'because', 'if', 'when', or 'but'), before they grasp their thought-full import in terms of understanding the full nature of causal, conditional or temporal relations — concepts which adult humans use for social survival. Languages are ready-made social tools with which children learn to shape nature, social relations and meaning in the same ways as their mentors. Children in socialization inherit languages with which to make their natural and social worlds. Intrinsic to such a learnt process (as opposed to one genetically programmed) is the possibility of conscious re-creation of social relations, relations with the natural world and meaning in general, but only on the basis of critical resynthesis of forms of thought and action that have been inherited through socialization. In both these processes — sociality being the pragmatic basis of language and language making sociality, in it specific forms — humans are equally created and creative. Culture and language have historic roots, but history is always in the process of being made and remade.

A number of important consequences follow from this trans-human characterization of language, neglected on one side in the language question of multiculturalism: the side with a fetish to preserve linguistic differences. First, in our human natures, language is a very practical thing, which can be critically evaluated for its subjective and functional efficacy. Sentimentalism about difference clouds adequate analysis. Second, as a learnt (as well as useful) thing, language can change. This is more than to restate the cliché that languages are dynamic, but to affirm that conscious social re-creation might involve changing languages fundamentally. Given the predominant usefulness of language, there is nothing inherently lamentable in the disappearance of languages or discourses or linguistic genres of past generations. If this occurs for practical reasons, willed with or against history by its users, so be it. Third, we are not simply bearers of cultures, languages and histories, with a duty to reproduce them. We are the products of linguistic-cultural circumstances, actors with a capacity to resynthesize what we have been socialized into and to solve new and emerging problems of existence. We are not duty-bound to conserve ancestral characteristics which are not structurally useful. We are both socially determined and creators of human futures. We may wish to struggle against structural cultural pressures on the basis of ancestral cultural experiences, or we might wish to reject ancestral cultural experience because of its agreement or dissonance with structural cultural pressures.

Language is both determined by our social and natural being and creates or re-creates relations in our natural and social worlds for us. Such considerations are critical in the immigrant experience when our response to intergenerational cultural dissonance, to be genuinely helpful, should not be based on an unproblematic advocacy (for pluralism's sake) of maintenance or preservation. We should not prejudge the validity of a whole range of cultural-linguistic options. There might be strong reasons in terms of association, desired community or even the perceived logistics of 'getting ahead' to let an ancestral language drop. On the other hand, language maintenance might be a means of feeling a particular strength through community, or of galvanizing support against the established structures of industrialism, or of gaining respectability and legitimacy within those broader structures, or as a transitional educational tool in acquiring a second language and continuing one's educational progress uninterrupted in the immigrant setting. All of these are uses which equally might justify actively maintaining or changing ancestral language. Language maintenance, however, is not a value in itself. In terms of the nature of culture, language has a usefulness (its real, common value to all humans) which means that maintenance or abandonment could be equally valid choices in a given set of circumstances.

Language and Cultural Variation

The foregoing description of a first level of culture encompasses those common, universal things that make us all human. At a second level, there are important differences in patterns of social organization, and these differences are to be found in the ordinary taken-for-granted institutions through which basic human needs are satisfied: ways of everyday life, work and welfare, social structures, economic and political institutions and so on. At this level, there is not real plurality of cultures in today's industrial societies. But what sort of differences could possibly be found at this level if one were to retain the meaning of culture as a whole way of life? We can begin with the division of traditional from modern society, used in so much of the literature of the social sciences. Within each of the categories 'traditional' and 'modern' are significant divisions, between hunter-gatherers and peasant agriculturalists, and Western industrialism and existing communist industrialism.

There are some very important implications arising from viewing this realm of life as culture. We will take Australia as an example to demonstrate these implications. Although there is no diversity of culture at this level in Australia today, there are two major cultures in Australian history and perhaps two cultures within the lives of many families who have migrated to Australia.

The two major cultural forms that have existed on Australian soil are traditional Aboriginal culture and the one that has become dominant during the two centuries since 1788. Traditional Aboriginal hunter-gathering life could hardly be more different from the Western industrialism that has developed since the first European settlement. The difference is certainly at a much more profound level than the one which just recognizes the difference between, say, today's Italian-Australians and Greek-Australians, or the difference between witchety grubs and sausages. It is a bit late to profess pluralism and multiculturalism now, when the fundamental everyday hunter-gathering culture has been all but destroyed by a history of systematic non-pluralism.

Even today, serious offers of genuine pluralism are rarely made. At best, there is a tokenistic respect for such Aboriginal culture as can now exist in plurality without hindering the basic economic intentions of the post-1788 culture. When it comes to the Aborigines, it is very handy to restrict our understanding of culture and dominant social values in Australian history to happy theories focusing on those things that happen to be comfortably multicultural in Australia today. It is nice to see Aboriginal art in galleries, but let's not deceive ourselves that this means we are preserving Aboriginal culture, in which, before European domination, production of such a thing as 'art' for 'sale' was inconceivable. Cultural phenomena can be misconstrued to be unproblematic expressions of cultural diversity and cultural maintenance. Simple pluralist multiculturalism, as many Aboriginal community leaders themselves recognize, can misread the injustice done to the Aborigines, and misinterpret the amount of plurality really allowed in Australia today. Attempting to 'maintain' Aboriginal languages by recording them, and setting up schools which teach them to people on reserves, in paid employment, or recipients of welfare payments, is hardly an unproblematic contribution to preserving traditional Aboriginal culture. It certainly creates jobs for linguists and educators; that is, in the extension of the activities of mainstream culture. Preservation of Aboriginal languages is worthy and necessary, but this alone is not enough to redress an unjust history.

There have also been two cultures at this level in the lives of many migrants to Australia. For example, many people have experienced quite traumatic breaks from peasant-agrarian life to Australia's Western industrial society. Often, in some vague way, they willed the break when they migrated. At this second level, people newly born in Australia and migrants when they arrive have to adjust to learning the everyday tactics of existence in Australian industrial society. This is neither to condemn nor to approve, but to state the fact. If we think of a family migrating to Australia from a village-agricultural culture, there is no practical possibility of them continuing the same life. Besides, historically, people have not migrated to maintain the conditions of village-agricultural society in Australia, that is, to maintain their culture at this second level. They have migrated to leave situations which they might have found socially/culturally unsatisfactory or limiting, for a new culture. This is not to imply that they have simply made a cultural choice in migration. Migration is often a necessary strategy for reasonable survival. But, to the extent that altered or improved conditions of life are expected, willed or worked for, there is a process of conscious cultural re-creation in and for a new context.

A hypothetical person from village-agricultural society might find him/herself at first in a factory. This is a vastly different physical (indoors) and technological social institution, and a very different way of spending the larger part of one's active life. Even if our ex-villager had (very improbably) decided to go counter-cultural and set up a 'traditional' style commune, he or she would still have had to work in a Western industrial society in a Western industrial way to earn the income to buy the land (unlike the family lands and inheritance systems of peasant societies). In an industrial society, the cash economy takes on a greater role and importance. A person needs money to rent or buy any housing at all. If one is not working for payment, one has to have some other monetary support such as welfare payments.

Work itself does not directly provide the things you need, as it had in the village. You have to go to shops or supermarkets to spend the wage earned in your specialized job. Then, how does one relate to one's boss and trade union? How does one use the welfare and health systems? New concepts uproot old ways of mentally organizing the world. New ideas of time have to be learnt: to work by hours and minutes instead of the sun and seasons, to divide the week (work) from the weekend (family), instead of having work and family life constantly interrelated. Arrangements of land and property ownership (and no one proposes that we should be multicultural about these) are often alien, beginning with the fact that rent or ownership has to be worked for and bought rather than granted by inheritance or marriage. Dowry and traditional inheritance systems break down. Where, in our so-called multicultural society, do we find the human geography of a Greek, Lebanese or Laotian village? We might find some shadows, but that is not the same. And what happens to the extended family in the face of the demands of occupational mobility? Do migrants from village-agricultural cultures resist consumerism and its structural implications? How easy is it to avoid buying washing machines when it is now necessary for a wife to work in a job too? What are the implications for a daughter's independence when she gets a job? What happens if you do not master the particular abstract thought needed for basic survival and social interaction (prices, banks, traffic lights, etc.)?

In some fundamental senses, then, migration to Australia is inevitably going to involve a cultural leap or break if migrants come from a significantly different culture. At this level, Australia is not a multicultural society. Some people might argue that it is not the job of multiculturalism to concern itself with culture in this sense, even if some of the most elementary welfare issues of migration are to be found here. But the problem with simple pluralism is not just that some of the most important questions are missed. It is that de facto assimilation to a single culture is just assumed. It is 'common sense' that new immigrants and most contemporary indigenous peoples will have to live up to many of the values and demands of industrialism simply to survive, let alone succeed. There can be flurries of colour but, by and large, only within spaces made for them by industrialism (commodities, the weekend, the realm of the private and so on), or within limits defined by industrialism. Simple pluralist multiculturalism has a hidden agenda of assimilation, simply because this is not discussed. Apparently, it seems so obvious that it is not worth discussing. We should stick to being multicultural about the culture that it is possible to be 'multi' about. We can forget about the cultural break inflicted upon indigenous peoples from the outside, and the cultural break in many immigrants' lives. It might be nice to have a multiculturalism which has a convenient blind-spot for such issues, but it is not true to cultural reality and people's own experiences. It is convenient to keep underlying assumptions about assimilation at this second level hidden so as not to interfere with our idea that modern industrial states genuinely allow cultural diversity.

At first glance, this generalized cultural theory has little bearing on language. People bring or keep languages irrespective of social and structural factors. They might have to learn the dominant language of Western industrial culture in any particular context, but other languages can simply be maintained in the spaces made or left by industrialism for diversity. Minority language recordings can be bought as commodities in shops, or we can speak our ancestral languages in the private space of the home or the communal in the space called 'leisure'.

This diversity is, of course, a truism. But the truism is doubly deceptive. First, the diversity is not that of equals. No one is seriously proposing a thoroughgoing multiculturalism at this second level of culture: multilingual banking, computing, parliament, law and taxation, such that one could become professor of computing or head of state without a knowledge of the official or dominant language. Nor would instituting such a multilingualism be a rational use of resources. But so long as multilingualism is not taken this seriously, languages other than English will be structurally (although certainly not personally) unnecessary. They may be attractive phenomena, but they will be relegated to the world of the private and the domestic, or to interaction with compatriots.

Second, not all languages as they are spoken in pre-migration social situations and after arrival in Australia perform the same socio-historical-cognitive functions. From one pattern of social organization to another (culture at level two), languages, both in form and cognitive and functional content, differ profoundly. Languages, transferred to a new context, might have to change profoundly to become adequate to that context. For example, language genres perfectly functional to peasant-agrarian social situations might not be adequate for equitable social participation in industrial culture. This might not be true for other registers in the same language which might be perfectly functional in the halls of power of the host country, if only that were the *lingua franca* or even the common language of a particular institution.

First languages stretch and change to accommodate the social process of migration when the break for a particular person or class of people is substantial. For example, even if an ex-villager continues to use his or her mother tongue in the factory and at home in Australia, the language has to deal with issues and activities of the new mainstream culture at level two, and traditional values and practices must be reinterpreted in new circumstances. This can have an effect on the content, meaning and vocabulary of the mother tongue. Culture and language are never simply maintained. A change in structural context requires new cultural and linguistic solutions to be developed.

Language within an Industrial Society

At a first level, language is a common cultural attribute to all humanity. At a second level of culture, there are fundamental differences between patterns of social organization, reflected in fundamentally different semantic fields and linguistic genres. At level two, there is only one culture in present-day First World societies: Western industrialism. But at a third level, these societies are indeed diverse. As a result of migration, there is a multitude of types of cultural practices: different types of food, clothing, celebration, music, dance, language and so on. There is no denying that this enriches contemporary life. Simple pluralist multiculturalism's subject matter — culture at this level — is very worthy of emphasis. Whereas language is a communicative tool at level one and there is one dominant language of elementary social institutions and power at level two, at level three language is something whose sounds we can enjoy, and which touches sentiments through shared meanings — yesterday's songs or a mother's turn of phrase. Language conveys special meanings and significance. At this level, but at this level alone, the dominant language is just a 'community' language, itself used in a series of equally valid genres and registers, and no intrinsically better or more useful than any other in this respect.

The problem with simple pluralism is that it considers culture and language only at level three. We wish to deny none of the pluralist propositions that people should be enabled to maintain languages because they like them, or because variety of this order is an important value and a human right. Nor would we deny the more academic arguments about the psychological aspects of language in family interaction, identity or the symbolic significance of language as an instrument of solidarity for minority groups. We simply wish to point out that the picture is larger and more complex than being one of linguistic diversity. The arguments about rights and needs cannot be abstracted from the processes in which languages function and interact.

The Dynamic Interaction of Levels in an Holistic Understanding of Culture and Language

In sum, we have proposed a three-level, holistic model of culture (see Figure 1.2). It is impossible to understand the dynamics of culture, even if our only interest were in culture at level three, unless it is examined holistically. One can only understand particular elements of culture in the context of culture as a whole way of life and the interrelation of different levels of culture. It is possible to extend the diagram of an holistic model of culture to explain migration, in order to discuss language in migration. Again, we will illustrate the theory with an Australian example (see Figure 1.3).

Level 3

> Differences in custom, self-expression, ways of behaving, e.g., food, dance, languages, celebrations. There is cultural diversity at this level in Western industrial societies which we should all value.

Level 2

> Major types of political-social-economic-cultural arrangements, with different, culturally appropriate forms of cognition, genres and semantic fields represented in language as a practical tool, e.g., hunting and gathering, feudalism or peasantry, Western industrialism. At this level, First World societies today only have one culture: Western industrialism.

Level 1

> Things common, in the very nature of culture, to all human cultures. What culture is for. Language as communication.

Figure 1.2 An Holistic Model of Culture

Culture/Society 1 ⟶ migration ⟶ Culture/Society 2
(e.g., rural Lebanon)   (e.g., Western industrialism as practised in Australia)

Level 3

> Expression of culture which can be transported by immigrants. Origin of these practices can be explained in relation to culture at Level 2. The extended family (for example), or arranged marriages, are integrally linked to the structure of peasant society (Level 2) with its particular patterns of work, land ownership, etc.

> Of the cultural practices transported by immigrants some (e.g., food types) are relatively easy to maintain, while others (e.g., arranged marriages) are no longer necessary in industrial culture, but are maintained by the conservative forces of tradition and ideology. Some practices are eroded away as the influences of the new structures at Level 2 creep in. Conflicts emerge between the desires of the older and younger generations. It is a pity if some cultural practices disappear, but it is perhaps a good thing, in terms of cultural freedom, if other practices alter.

Level 2

> Everyday life — peasant-agrarian-village complete with traditional structures and arrangements.

> Immediately and unavoidably immigrants must deal with a completely new everyday life more in keeping with Western industrialism.

Level 1

> The reason for culture/society. Standards of social/cultural judgment.

Figure 1.3 An Holistic Model of Culture in Migration to Australia

For the purposes of analyzing language in migration, we will examine what occurs at levels two and three. Our argument is that language forms performing one function in a peasant-agrarian place of origin will not remain unproblematically adequate upon migration. This is not just because the language is different, but also because it is functionally and semantically inappropriate to manipulating a very different world. (Migration in the other direction would equally involve linguistic inappropriateness.) Before elaborating upon this point, we reiterate: we are not talking about whole national or regional languages. A long-term, middle-class, industrial city dweller, speaking a language with the same name, might go through no such cultural break at level two, upon migration to another industrial social context. Their language in its place of origin might be fundamentally different from that of village dwelling farmers. This difference might be superficially manifest as snootiness, but such an impression belies the importance of profound underlying linguistic-cognitive differences, genres and semantic fields. Even upon migration, the existence of such differences within languages with the same name helps to explain the very different structural positions of immigrants and suggests that there is no necessary 'community' among compatriots.

These observations should not be taken to imply that there is an unbridgeable gulf of difference and that it is impossible to acquire other forms of a language or a completely new language for a new set of socio-linguistic purposes. Nor is it a statement about contextual appropriateness, or a judgment about linguistic worth, or an implication of a hierarchy of genres. Luria conducted empirical linguistic research into precisely the problem of socio-linguistic context, examining speakers of the same language in non-industrial and newly emerging industrial social settings. The profound linguistic changes he observed reflected 'not only new fields of knowledge but also new motives for action' (1976: 13). He noted, for example, new forms of perception, generalization and abstraction, theoretical or hypothetical patterns of reasoning and problem-solving and so on. This contrasted with pre-industrial linguistic forms and modes of reasoning, which were graphic, more directly practical and analogical.

At this stage, we wish only to hint at directions in which research is sorely needed: research which has been neglected in the pluralist reluctance to analyze the differential functioning of languages in different social settings and the effects of the thrusting of peoples and languages from one setting into another. Given the relative lack of research into this problem, we can only point in the direction of the problem in very general terms. In one of our earlier studies, a child from rural Lebanon, for example, was able to draw a picture of his social world in such detail that all the connections in his social world — relatives, houses, the church, fields, work, education, play — could be portrayed visually as a coherent whole. He then attempted to draw his social world in Australia.

Although genuinely trying to force himself to perform the same task he had for his village, to conceptualize his Australian social relations in the same way, he was unable to get beyond a limited street map, with the majority of the connections relevant to his life remaining indeterminately off the page (Kalantzis and Cope, 1981: 73–4).

Modern industrial societies are large and complex in historically specific ways, such that effective understanding and manipulation necessitate a particular sort of abstraction: map-reading, detailed laws and regulations, intercommunication through telephone or mass media systems. Large, structural relations need to be perceived if one is not to be completely marginalized. For all of this, a new language is required, not so much in terms of meanings and functional content. For example, providing translation services for taxation, for the law, or even mounting multilingual courses explaining social institutions, presupposes that all immigrants, irrespective of their particular life-history, had the appropriate semantic framework for manipulation of these new life forms in their place of origin. For the middle-class, educated, 'modern' city-dwellers, that might be the case. But for a very substantial proportion of many immigrant groups, this is not always so. Indeed, it frequently becomes the case that some new immigrants move between domestic interchange in their first language and the use of the host country's dominant language to explain new institutions, technologies and social relations, rather than take on the forms of their language of origin which express and manipulate life in advanced industrial quarters in their place of origin. (This, incidentally, raises the question of which form of language should be taught and for what reasons: the language precisely as spoken in the social situation of origin, this language with modified ring-ins from the dominant language as it is used within the minority community in the immigrant context, or its 'standard' form as appropriate to social situations in 'developed' socio-economic settings in the country of origin.)

We have made no claim that dominant languages have any privilege as languages for industrialism, other than, in each case, a fortuitous historical one. In Australia or Canada or the United States, for example, English happens to have been the tongue of the pioneers of industrialism and, even internationally, much of its vocabulary has found its way into other languages along with the drive of industrialism's commodities and social relations. But English itself has a history in which, even if many of the words are the same, its pre-industrial and industrial usages are profoundly different. One very interesting line of research would be to trace structural parallels in the history of the English language, to the history of other languages from industrial to pre-industrial settings, and to language in the migration process.

The foregoing analysis only draws in a small part upon the work of Vygotsky and Luria. Our interest in these two writers stems from the fact that they indicate important problem areas, generally neglected and directly pertinent to analysis of language in migration from one pattern of social organization to another. We do not accept their analysis unreservedly. First, neither Luria nor Vygotsky provides adequate sociologies to explain how and why the different forms of language and thought they describe are apt and useful to different social structures. Second, they parallel linguistic phylogenesis with linguistic ontogenesis. In other words, they claim that children, in the process of linguistic-conceptual development, go through the same process that occurs historically with the transition from pre-industrial to industrial forms of life and cognition. This amounts to a harsh judgment of forms of thought and language which were perfectly adequate for adults in satisfying their biological and social needs in pre-industrial patterns of social organization. There is no necessary inferiority to language as a communicative tool in either situation, even if one were to make judgment, one way or the other, about pre-industrial life in general. We suggest that the contrast between pre-industrial and industrial thought and language does not parallel the ontogenesis of adult language in the socialization of children in industrial society.

At level three, also, important things happen to language in the migration process. With reference to the diagram of culture in migration (Figure 1.3), there are cultural practices which are readily transportable. This is what those working with a simple pluralist model celebrate. But even culture at this level cannot be understood except in dynamic relation to level two. Some cultural practices, such as domestic language usage, are relatively easy to maintain, even though, perhaps, they are not fixed and indefinitely necessary in terms of mainstream social survival. But these same practices, just because they are necessary for survival, can as easily be eroded away, in a fashion that would probably be structurally impossible in an immigrant's place of origin.

Minority immigrant languages might be maintained, and there are many strong arguments supporting their maintenance. But the very space they inhabit, the functions they perform and their consequent social character are defined by the industrial culture of level two. They predominantly become languages of domestic, private or leisure time usage. They need not be that way and, as we have already said, are mostly not like that in their countries of origin. But with the particular place they have in industrialism, they frequently (especially for second generations) become that way. So the key informant report in Chapter 5 that returned Macedonian-Australian children in Yugoslavia as a general rule do very poorly in school says something about the sort of Macedonian language that children learn in Australia, given the spaces it is able to inhabit here. Moreover, because languages other than English become unnecessary to everyday survival in the long term, they are sited in such a way that strategies for their maintenance have to become self-conscious rather than inevitable and unexceptional. One might wish for a society in which a plurality of languages were to be used equally in every sphere of life, but no one has seriously proposed this. The success of multilingualism of the variety presently advocated ironically requires different spheres of language. It is this paradoxical requirement that produces the quandary of language maintenance.

Moreover, the pluralist celebrates diversity at level three as if the diversity were a truly independent realm and a diversity of equals. Our duty, it follows, is simply to maintain languages as they are for the sake of their preservation. As we have argued, this is not an easy or even possible task, and there are specific pedagogical consequences flowing from whether one views language from a static pluralist point of view, or holistically, as part of a dynamic social process.

In an holistic view of the situation, there is nothing necessarily problematic about the goal of multilingualism so long as it does not simultaneously involve reproducing structures of inequality in which some linguistic forms are in practice adequate to social participation, and others not. This does not deny that there are different spheres of social participation, for which there are different languages or forms of language. Pedagogically, then, our primary task is to assess their general social function. This applies equally to the role of the dominant language. We must be careful not to limit our view of social function in such a way that tokens or gestures seem adequate, in the hope, perhaps, that regardless of the linguistic outcome, some psychological sense of self-esteem or tolerance of others will come simply through institutional approval of a language. Whether it be the dominant language or minority languages, our motives should be more than sentimental or aimed merely at conservation. Our interest in teaching minority languages should be based on long-term pedagogical objectives and not short-term political genuflection. If the language question is reduced to a reactive political level, it can only lose credibility.

The difficulty with much research on the language question is that its premises about culture and society are left vague. They tend to operate at level three (that of visible diversity), without situating that diversity in a wider context.

2
The Language Question: Key Debates

This chapter develops the main arguments and issues raised in Chapter 1. Its focus is particular debates thrown up by particular national circumstances. It is not an exhaustive description of approaches to linguistic diversity or the politics of multilingualism in education in each of the various countries. Rather, it uses incidents and debates that have emerged at various times in each context to develop some of the major points arising from Chapter 1. We focus on debates about the 'semilingualism' of children of minority language background in Sweden, debates about bilingualism and cognitive development in Canada, and the issue of language rights in the United States. In Chapter 3, we go on to discuss the Australian situation, not so much with a view to describing a national context as to use the Australian experience to suggest some practical educational resolutions to the key issues raised in Chapters 1 and 2.

The 'Semilingualism' Debate in Sweden

At an international symposium on multicultural and multilingual education in immigrant countries, the Swedish Minister for Immigration Affairs, K. Andersson, declared in his opening address that 'Sweden today is a multi-cultural and multilingual society.' This was so, he maintained, because 'one million inhabitants of the total eight million are of foreign origin.' Similar claims to plurality are made by all the countries examined in this chapter.

In Sweden explicit recognition of this fact came in 1975 when Parliament established three goals for immigrant and minority policy: equality, freedom of choice and cooperation. The policy had implications for the servicing of languages particularly, and in May 1976 it was followed by the Home Languages Reform Bill. Although aimed at the pre-school level, it had repercussions for the rest of schooling.

The well-developed welfare state of Sweden has a long-standing commitment to responding to disadvantaged groups in its population. The influx of Eastern European refugees and migrant labourers put this commitment to the test in the 1970s. Moreover, the Swedish practice of comprehensive free education for all had to take into account new social pressures and demands, especially in urban areas where, in some cases, over 50 per cent of the population were of recent immigrant origin. As the Minister for Immigration Affairs attested, the children of these people faced 'greater difficulties than other children and young people as far as education and employment was concerned.' The goal of the legislation of the 1970s was equality of opportunity and the emphasis was initially linguistic. Most recently, however, there has been a shift in emphasis towards issues related to 'culture' and 'ethnicity' generally.

This shift is predictable in the light of our earlier statements about the politics of 'multiculturalism'. If socio-economic conditions are such that genuine equality of opportunity shows no signs of being achieved for some groups in society, some other solace has to be sought. Esteem for and equality of cultures in a narrow, simple pluralist sense, which relies more on words than substantial funding, therefore, provided an emphasis which seemed convenient.

Against this, however, is one of the most significant, albeit contentious, Swedish contributions to the language question. In 1968 Nils Hansegard claimed that children of non-Swedish-speaking background were disadvantaged because often they suffered from what he popularized as 'semilingualism'. That is, they were not proficient in their mother language nor the mainstream tongue of their new homeland. (The Swedish use the word 'home language' to refer to the languages used by migrants and their children who do not speak Swedish as their first language.) This concept has been hotly disputed in academic circles, in Sweden and elsewhere, and often rejected as a useful one in the analysis of the linguistic situation of children from non-Swedish-speaking immigrant background (Oksaar, 1979; Ohman, 1981; Hyltenstam and Stroud, 1982).

Nonetheless, given the facts of academic underachievement and the over-representation of children from some migrant backgrounds in unemployment figures, the notion cannot be ignored altogether (though the situation for Sweden's migrant population is not so serious in socio-economic terms as in other countries). Lambert (1983) uses the term 'psycho-linguistic limbo'. Similarly, we have used the term 'cognitive void' to describe a situation in which the home language is not continued with growing sophistication past entry to formal schooling either at home or at school, and in which the initial experience of formal schooling does not adequately prepare students for proficiency in their second language. In the mainstream context, immigrant children, when they arrive at school, are expected to pick up the language around them. Peer group modelling, at this stage, however, has real problems associated with it, given that the basic structures for the new languages have not yet been established. In the initial years it is often the case that children appear to be operating in the playground and classroom context with similar proficiency to native speakers. But as they proceed into later years and no conscious attempt is made to respond to their linguistic needs, situations can occur where they are labelled uncreative or lacking in ability, when in reality the problem has been one of uneven linguistic development.

The home situation of some children of non-mainstream language background compounds this problem. It is not unusual for such children to limit their home language interactions to a domestic range and to switch extensively between two languages. Furthermore, the role models of their home languages can change as parents incorporate words, structures and meanings from the mainstream language into their own (Gaarder, 1977).

The consequence of these processes can be what Hansegard (1979) has called 'semilingualism'. This is a situation in which children's ability to express themselves and manipulate the world around them through language is hampered. The ensuing frustration can have ramifications beyond language. This is not, however, a static situation. Language learning is a life-long process. In the recent rush to theories of 'pluralism' there has arisen a notion that the mutations of a home language in its new context form a coherent new form of the home language, equally solid and functional in the changed circumstances (Oksaar, 1982). But against such theoretical optimism one has to place the stark fact that only 67 per cent of children of immigrant background who finish the compulsory nine years of schooling go on to upper secondary school compared to 86 per cent of Swedish-speaking children (Robinson, 1981: 156).

Given this latter scenario, we would suggest that the earlier Swedish contribution of the concept of semilingualism should not be thrown out of the window altogether, simply because it seemed to stigmatize those of migrant background and possibly anyone with an accent. Nor does the dismissal of the notion on the grounds that it is a generalization not based on empirical research (Oksaar, 1983: 22) weaken its descriptive power. Rather, it requires that this generalization be subject to research and testing in a systematic, longitudinal manner. In the modern world, formal language skills of speaking, reading and writing are the means to certain sorts of futures and power. Schools cannot make decisions to deny the full range of options to students just because only a few realistically will need them. Certainly those academic researchers and policy-makers who have mastered the pinnacle of mainstream language have little right to dictate that others should not have to, even if it is in the name of pluralism.

The immigrant groups in Sweden come from over 130 nationalities and none is particularly large. The Finns make up 45 per cent of all immigrants, but only 2 per cent of the entire population. (The figure increases to 4 per cent if those that are naturalized are included.) The next largest groups come from West Germany, Yugoslavia, Greece and Italy. There are also small numbers of

Lapps and Gypsies. Of the one million students in compulsory school in 1981–82, grades 1–9, 87,000 were from other than Swedish language background. About sixty different home languages are taught in schools, and about 64 per cent of students with a home language other than Swedish participate.

The type of home language programmes offered varies. The more common ones are two to four lessons per week in the home language, incorporated into the mainstream curriculum. These start in kindergarten and continue through to upper secondary school. In some instances some selected subjects are also taught in the home language. There are also bilingual composite classes. These classes consist of half Swedish-speaking students and students from one other home language. For 60 per cent of the curriculum these students are separated and taught in Swedish or the home language respectively, and for the other 40 per cent of the curriculum they are reunited as a class group. The home language teaching classes reduce to 30 per cent of curriculum by grade 3 and then remain for three to four lessons per week for the rest of schooling. The other significant type of home language programme can be described as monolingual mother tongue classes. In these classes Swedish is not introduced until grade 3, minimally, and then usually with only two weekly oral classes. The general idea is that students will make a transition to Swedish classes by grade 7.

In 1978–79 the Swedish National Board of Education studied 7000 students participating in home language classes in mainstream and maintenance models in grade 9. They found that there was no significant grade point average difference between Swedish students (3.3) and minority language background students (3.2). There was, however, a great variation among different nationalities, with the French and Czechs scoring 3.6 and the Turks and Danes 2.9. It was also found that a command of Swedish was crucial for school achievement, and therefore also for future education and success in the labour market (Ekstrand, 1982: 146).

A study by Skutnabb-Kangas and Toukomaa (1976), however, reinforced the concept of 'semilingualism'. Their research found that students from non-Swedish-speaking backgrounds did poorly at school and that low-achieving Swedish as a second language students could not become properly bilingual. They advocated the segregation of the migrant child until firm patterns had been established in their home tongue.

Peterson's study of all immigrant students who applied for upper secondary education in the city of Malmo by the end of the school year 1977–78 found that a student needed at least eight years of residence to obtain a grade point average equal to that of a native student. When he checked his student sample along social cleavages, he concluded that upper-class immigrant students performed below native students, middle-class immigrant students performed exactly the same as the Swedish middle class, while immigrant students from the lower class performed significantly better than Swedish students from the same social class. This finding seems to contradict Skutnabb-Kangas and Toukomaa's results, but we need to ask what descriptors of class Peterson used. If it was primarily income brackets, this might say little about background, connections, propensity and facilities to assist students, and so on. For example, those of the 'upper class', of immigrant background, if based on income indices, might still not have the so-called 'cultural stock' of their native upper-class counterparts. On the other hand, 'lower-class' migrants suffer doubly in their decision to move, and their commitment to upward mobility for their children would be much stronger than their class counterparts.

The generally positive results that many of the Swedish studies have revealed must in some part have been contributed to by the fact that education in Sweden is, from pre-school, comprehensive, free and open to all. And all students have access to intensive Swedish language teaching for as long as they need it.

One problem area has been the debate over the monolingual mother tongue teaching programmes where Swedish is not introduced until late in the junior school. The main demand for these types of classes comes from the Finn minority. There is some evidence that students involved in such programmes tend to do poorly in secondary school (Wieczerkowski, 1971; Kuusinen *et al.*, 1982; Magiste, 1979). The findings of these studies were not only that students did poorly in high school but that native-like proficiency could not be reached in the mother tongue. Also the positive segregation required to create monolingual home language classes was challenged as creating a negative social effect and accused of not adequately preparing children to cope and deal with the mainstream society in which they lived (Ekstrand, 1982: 157). On the other hand, there is research that shows the superiority of mother tongue class students in a range of areas.

Predictably there are criticisms of both sides of the debate, particularly around issues of research methodology. The numerous studies investigating the success of the varieties of language classes in Sweden remain contested, contradictory and unclear as to the significance of language teaching and language maintenance. More often than not, it seems, features other than language learning were more significant in levels of academic achievement and social success — particularly the socio-cultural environment outside the school. Given the function of language as a vehicle of communication and the pressure of the mainstream culture in which a migrant language is situated, the more ambitious goals of home language maintenance appear unrealistic. Increasingly the reasons for failures in language programmes have been put down to the fact that too much emphasis was put on language proficiency, and the culture of the children of migrant background ignored. Despite twenty years of experimentation in a variety of language programmes, opinion remains divided. In academic circles with an interest in multiculturalism, despite disputes about strategy, there are few opponents of the notion that home languages other than Swedish have to be catered for. It seems that migrant organizations, too, seek support for mother tongue maintenance in their new homeland (Skutnabb-Kangas, 1983: 134; 1988).

However, official authorities, bureaucrats and politicians do not always agree, despite national legislation. The liberal and conservative parties, in particular, oppose the mother tongue classes. The need to preserve Swedish unity and the issue of resource allocation and maximum social benefit become arguments for dissenters. There are no clear surveys to reflect what parents and students think, although there is some evidence that they are not always in agreement with what pressure groups would claim. Dissenting groups of migrants are not as organized as those lobbying for the servicing of home languages (Skutnabb-Kangas, 1983: 134).

The training of appropriate numbers of teachers in the home languages and the creation of suitable teaching material have proved to be slow processes, and this has handicapped the general progress of the different language programmes. The large allocation of resources needed to maintain and extend language programmes no longer seems forthcoming, despite Sweden's historically and politically strong commitment to the social democratic welfare state.

Nor has the debate about 'transition' or 'maintenance', 'segregation' or 'integration' models been resolved either politically or, in terms of educational and social goals, by the research conducted so far. The position taken by different theorists depends on their vision of what sort of Sweden there should be and what sort of Sweden there is most likely to be. Given the small and diverse numbers of migrants and the pressures of industrial culture, it seems that 'transition' and 'integration' are the more likely outcomes. The proximity to their homeland for many of Sweden's minorities, however, does allow for the linguistic variety to persist. Economic uncertainty in the 1980s in Sweden was accompanied by the return of many to their homeland. It is felt that their 'freedom to return' needs to be facilitated by official policies on the maintenance of home languages across generations. In Germany this consideration is the basis for some language maintenance programmes. In the case of Turkish guest workers and their children in Bavaria, teachers are recruited from Turkey and students undergo complete Turkish schooling in expectation that they will return. Thus a policy of language maintenance can be a two-edged sword (Rist, 1983: 44).

Debates about Bilingualism and Cognitive Development in Canada

Canada also declares itself to be a multicultural society, but the language question there has had a clearer focus. Like Sweden, Canada has experienced post-war economic and social expansion via migration from various parts of Europe and, more recently, from Asia. But it has a history of older migration that established large and distinctive linguistic groups of French and English speakers. The politics attached to the demands of the French in the face of English dominance are much more assertive and politically explosive than the so-called 'ethnic' demands of later immigrants. The issue of language is one of the battle grounds on which the contest is fought.

Both English and French are official languages in Canada. The legal basis of these linguistic statuses and rights originates in confederation and the passing of the British North American Act in 1867. They were reinforced by a Language Act a century later. The English mother tongue population, however, is twice the size of the French mother tongue population. In consequence, they have occupied a larger portion of public offices and, for a while, tried to impose English as the compulsory language of instruction in schools. The Francophones struggled constantly against such legislation in those provinces where it was imposed. Their goal has always been to stem the influence of the English language and to establish French language schools. Bilingual education has had a long and uneven history in Canada.

The political and social impetus for what has occurred in Canada's language experiences is very different from Swedish and Australian circumstances. But there are some interesting and paradoxical points of commonality in the basic debates that are useful to consider.

On the whole, the Francophones, for obvious political reasons, continue to press in the direction of monolingual schooling in French. Some Anglophones, on the other hand, for reasons which include the threat of French Canadian secession, yet from the relative security of their language dominance, have embarked on experiments in bilingual schooling. The most famous is the St Lambert's immersion programme. St Lambert's is a school situated in a suburb of Montreal in the province of Quebec, where the majority population has always been French speaking. In the 1960s the threat of a possible separation of Quebec from the rest of Canada and a strong movement to make French the working language of Quebec induced a group of Anglophone parents concerned about the fate of their children to reconsider the language education they were receiving. They felt that the traditional method of teaching French as a foreign language was inadequate. From this concern arose the development of the French immersion programmes in 1968.

There are now about 115,000 students who participate in a variety of immersion programmes. While they only represent 3 per cent of the school population, these programmes have made a great impact on research and thinking in language education. In Montreal about 20 per cent of the Anglophone student population participate in early immersion programmes. The programmes typically involve the segregation of Anglophone students who are immersed in a school situation where only French is used as the medium of instruction and interaction.

> A French immersion class is not primarily a language class. It is a class in which subjects other than French, such as mathematics, history, art and physical education, are presented in French. . . .Teaching [is] *in* French not teaching *of* French. The intention is that the new language is to be learnt by use while learning something else and not by formal instruction. (Stern, 1984: 4)

The types of programme offered vary from what is called early immersion to late immersion, depending on the grade in which immersion starts, and full immersion and partial immersion depending on how much of the curriculum interchange is conducted in French. The home language (English) is usually introduced in grade 3 and then the programme develops year by year until it has become, by the end of the primary school, a fully bilingual programme.

From the nearly twenty years of experience in this sort of programme, a number of claims are made for immersion.

1. There is a need to immerse Anglophone students in the language and culture of the dominant subgroup so that social co-existence and mutual understanding can be enhanced (Lambert and Tucker, 1972; Swain, 1974; Genesee, 1978–79).
2. Immersion most resembles natural language acquisition and contributes to the making of successful bilinguals (Lambert and Tucker, 1972; Swain, 1974; Genesee, 1978–79; Barik and Swain, 1975; Tucker, 1980).
3. Those who participate in immersion programmes perform better academically than their monolingual Anglophone peers in both English and other subjects by the end of grade 4 (Tucker 1975; Barik and Swain, 1978; Lambert and Tucker, 1972).
4. The learning of a second language does not pose a threat to the student's sense of cultural identity nor affect the maintenance of the mother tongue (Swain, 1982).

The Canadian research findings on immersion programmes thus appear to disprove both the traditional view that early bilingualism can hamper educational and social success and the Swedish notion of 'semilingualism'. Moreover, it is maintained that such programmes contribute to society generally because they are the means whereby more caring and sensitive students, more suitable for a multicultural world, will be produced (Lambert, 1983). An attitudes profile of the early St Lambert's project found that students' attitudes towards French Canadians, English Canadians, European French and self were essentially similar and positive. In contrast, French Canadian students tended to rate their own ethnic group higher than English Canadians or the European French (Swain and Barik, 1978).

But, as some of its critics point out, the Canadian immersion model is paradoxical. Despite its so-called contribution to a multicultural society, it has served the élite better and is successful mainly with middle-class students (Clift, 1984: 66). Much of its success and attraction for the children lies in the fact that French is not only a major international language but its use enhances job opportunities in education, the bureaucracy, politics and other professions in Canada.

The placing of students in a school environment not of their mother tongue, not giving them any language instruction in their first language and expecting them to pick up the second language by participating in regular school activities, is not only a description of what many theorists and educationalists programmes but a description of what many theorists and educationalists complain happens, with detrimental effects, to children of minority backgrounds in the lands their parents have migrated to. In the latter situation, varied descriptions, testimonials and research exist pertaining to the psychological damage and educational disadvantage such an experience can produce (Lambert, 1983).

Lambert describes the Canadian immersion programmes as 'additive'. In other words, Canadian Anglophone children are able to 'add' to their linguistic capabilities another skill, because they do not lose their first language in the process. On the other hand, the bilingual experience of children of migrant background is 'subtractive' because the first language has fewer arenas for extension; the second language experience therefore swamps the first, and the child loses language skills. This, however, is an insufficient explanation as it only looks as the situation from a linguistic point of view. The socio-economic influences and the power dimension behind different language groupings cannot be overlooked. Languages might be, as Lambert claims, equally 'precious' in their own right, but the 'preciousness' has little vitality when it is of necessity primarily a private affair or not one of the tools of empowerment (Lambert, 1983: 99).

On the technical side, critics of the French immersion programme claim that, although the proficiency of the Anglophone children in French appears to be equal to native French speakers in school tests (Lambert and Tucker, 1972), in everyday interaction their French is hesitant, avoids difficult structures and is full of grammatical and vocabulary errors and pronunciation difficulties (Harley and

Swain, 1977). More seriously, although younger students appear to be very successful, there is a declining rate of success as students get older. By grades 8 and 9 there is evidence of regression as the dominant language makes its inevitable demands and English pervades all out-of-school life (Bibeau, 1984: 45). Furthermore, in a survey conducted by Mourgeon, Brant-Palmer, Belanger and Chichocki (1980) of the Francophones in Ontario (who are a small minority community, not speaking standard French), less than 50 per cent responded that they mostly, or always, used French with their children. In spite of attending Francophone schools, some students of this background were not able to master standard French by grade 12.

There is some pressure currently in Canada for the extension of some type of immersion or bilingual programmes (in some cases trilingual) to minority groups such as Greeks and Germans. The Heritage Programme, begun in Ontario in 1977, funded the teaching of languages other than official French and English for up to two and a half hours per week in the primary schools. The results of projects sponsored under this programme have been generally presented favourably in terms of language learning and self-esteem, but they do not seem to have contributed to an improvement in academic performance in general (Bhatnagar, 1983: 71). It is not surprising that Lambert says one of the main problems to be overcome is parents' resistance, and the need to convince them of the educational and social value of such schemes (Lambert, 1983).

Some research has been done to disprove the contention that bilingualism is most successful with middle-class students. Bruck *et al.* (1971) compared working-class students in grade 1 and 2 immersion programmes with a comparable group of native English-speaking students and native French-speaking students. They tested achievement in maths and overall cognitive development. Their findings, though tentative, claimed to demonstrate that English language students of working-class background in immersion classes did as well as the comparable socio-economic groups, though they were not on a par with native French-speakers in French. Their conclusions were that immersion programmes were just as appropriate to them as middle-class students. (One cannot help but wonder what the results would have been had the children been compared with middle-class students).

Public opinion, however, has not travelled as fast as the academics would have wished. Pressure groups have formed to argue against the extension of immersion classes. Workplace tensions, job competition, dissent about which language to use to report which event in the media, issues of language prestige, fears of a French takeover with assistance from an interfering government, are erupting in some English-speaking circles. These broader political issues complicate and vex the language proposals and experiments in Canada (Clift, 1984: 66).

Quebec's resistance to cultural and linguistic pluralism is an additional problem. In order not to compromise the status of French, there is a refusal to introduce English as a second language early. It is argued loudly that continued and reinforced state intervention is needed to preserve French in Canada. Quebec is moving in the opposite direction to English-speaking Canada on the language question. Canada is left with a situation where plurality and bilingualism are supported at the national level, but by some only in order to ensure spaces of non-plurality and monolingualism at a provincial level.

In the light of these developments one needs to question the Canadian contribution to the language question, and in particular its claims that academic superiority results through the cognitive advantage of bilingualism, and that social cohesion has been created through exposure to other languages.

In examining the first of these claims, the work of Cummins has the most significance. Research since 1960 has found a link between bilingual and cognitive development, at least for some types of bilinguals. Peal and Lambert (1962) first attempted to correlate bilingualism positively with intelligence. Their research with 10-year-old, middle-class Canadian students found that bilinguals performed better on verbal and non-verbal tests than their monolingual peers. Pursuing this line of argument, Cummins and Gulutsan (1974b), testing grade 6 bilinguals, found that so-called balanced bilinguals achieved better oral use and were more divergent thinkers than their monolingual peers.

Barik and Swain (1975), using IQ data gathered over five years from pupils in grades Kindergarten to 4 enrolled in French immersion classes and those in regular English classes, found that there was no significant difference between the two groups. There was, however, a significant difference between 'high' French achievers and 'low' French achievers in IQ, particularly in analysis and in following verbal instructions.

Research by Owen (1981) with 4- to 6-year-old pre-school children on their ability to label and relabel objects, and Quinn and Wersk (1980) with 11-year-olds on their ability to formulate hypotheses in science problems found in both cases that coordinate bilinguals (who learnt the two languages simultaneously) performed better. But at the other end of the educational scale work by Mestre and Gerace (1981) on the academic success of Hispanic bilingual college students in technical fields showed lower proficiency than monolingual students on comprehension, word problem-solving, language and algebraic tests. Monolinguals outperformed bilinguals in every test. In both the positive and negative findings, bilingual language proficiency correlated with mathematical performance. An important factor related to the latter results is that the Hispanic bilingual college students come from significantly lower socio-economic circumstances than the monolinguals.

Cummins has developed criteria to describe variations of bilingual proficiency. Although his schema is essentially a linguistic description which does not adequately take into account broader sociological factors that produce varied results, it is useful to consider. His work generally suggests that advantages and disadvantages of bilingualism depend on the way people become bilingual and the level of language proficiency achieved. For his schema, coordinate bilinguals (those exposed to two languages from a very early age and who learn two distinct coding systems) have a cognitive advantage. Compound bilinguals (those who learn their second language through translation from the dominant first one) do not show any cognitive advantage.

The positive results of research like the above can be explained in part by Cummins' (1979) Developmental Independency Hypothesis which posits that the level of second language competence of a bilingual is attained partly as a function of the level of competence the child has developed in the first language at the time of exposure to a second language. (So the subjects of the Canadian immersion programme would need to be proficient in the first language before being immersed, though some results say this need not be the case.)

Furthermore, Cummins' Threshold Hypothesis maintains that, in order to avoid deficiencies and to allow the potential beneficial aspects of becoming bilingual to influence cognitive growth, the child must attain a threshold level of linguistic competence in the first language. On the basis of Cummins' hypothesis, it could be speculated that students who score poorly in bilingual tests would not have passed through the threshold level of proficiency in their first language to be able to perform well in a second language (Cummins, 1984; Cummins and Swain, 1986).

It is possible to find empirical research in Canada, as in Sweden, that proves almost any sort of position on bilinguals. At the bottom of this problem is the complex dilemma of interpreting a number of pieces of research between which the statistics and findings are rarely comparable. Not only are there linguistic considerations, but there are also issues of environment, socio-economic status, psychology, teaching programmes, cultural attitudes and gender-specific issues. One thing that does seem to come out of most of the research is a greater awareness of the necessity within research to control such variations, in that socio-economic backgrounds and general environments outside the school influence language proficiency as much as what goes on within the school.

None of this overview of the research findings would necessarily lead one to say that there is a limited role for schools in the area of bilingual education. But we would suggest that the arguments about cognitive superiority and bilingualism are not the most vital ones, nor the most generally applicable arguments for school involvement in language learning. We can only conclude that under certain conditions, such as coordinate bilingualism in students of middle-class background, it seems there is some cognitive advantage. But in many other situations of bilingualism the overall effect does not seem so positive. For example, children who were not born in Canada are generally underrepresented in high academic streams (Wright, 1975; Deosaran, 1976). Socio-economic status in such cases, it seems, did not contribute to variance, as much as language use (Feeney and Hartmann 1977; Bhatnagar, 1980).

This point is important when a significant proportion of an immigrant population is situated in lower socio-economic brackets and in linguistic environments that do not contribute to the development of balanced, coordinate bilingualism. The pressure of work on the parents, sibling linguistic role models, the pervading influence of the media in the dominant language, and the changing form of the mother tongue for parents (with increased borrowings from the dominant language) in many cases is not conducive to the development of balanced bilingualism, as it often is in the case of middle-class English-speakers in Canada seeking linguistic and cultural enrichment through the learning of French. According to Cummins' hypotheses, students who do not have ideal environments to become either ideal monolinguals or ideal coordinate bilinguals will fall behind in either or both languages and will not be able to succeed academically. As a basic requirement for academic success, they need threshold levels of achievement in one language.

The lower limit of ideal compound bilingualism, at which linguistic development is hampered, occurs when children are removed from their first or home language environment and taken to a second language in such a way that development in their first language is slowed down or interrupted. In such circumstances proficiency levels at school appear to rise initially, and even become the same as native speaking peers. But as the children progress through the school grades, their proficiency level splits away from their native-speaking peers and remains below it. Coordinate bilinguals, on the other hand, begin and continue learning their first and second languages independently and consistently. Because they do not need to go through the translation procedures of compound bilinguals, they can use forms of language which are unique to each. These students thus have cognitive advantages as they can then transfer these abstract skills to other subject areas (Cummins, 1984; Cummins and Swain, 1986). Is it bilingualism *per se*, however, that provides these advantages? Perhaps one could suggest that learning music or chess or any other abstract form of interaction might give students similar cognitive advantage. The more critical question, though, is what in fact contributes to cognitive disadvantage and how language might be linked to it.

There is an implication in Cummins' theory that bilingualism, to be advantageous, needs to have been commenced early, at least before a student goes to school. If not, given the amount of language that has already been learnt, compound bilingualism is all that is possible. The emphasis in schools, therefore, would have to be initially on attaining threshold proficiency in one language — ideally in the mother tongue and with the subsequent introduction of the second language. The results, however, could only go as far as the upper limits of compound bilingualism.

The leads us into the next important debate in the language question — transition or maintenance? We will discuss this in the context of the experience in the United States of America. But before we do that we need to pick up on the second general claim of the Canadian experience that bilingual programmes contribute in a special way to societies whose population is of diverse cultural background in that they provide one of the keys for mutual understanding and harmonious co-existence.

There is no substantial evidence that language programmes are the only, or even the best, way to achieve this goal — particularly given that in Canada only 3 per cent of children are participating in them. A much more important chan- nelling of resources for this goal might be into mainstream social education aimed at all children equally. The aim would have to be to enable children to become literate about how they become and function as social beings, through programmes where their differences are not separated out, reified and turned into 'precious' objects, but examined in terms of their historic development and as part of a process of socialization or enculturation that all humans go through, whatever the variation of form. Differences in languages would then be under- stood as creative responses to the same basic human needs. But differences are not simply relative in their impact and effect. Languages can be seen as tools responding to human needs: material, spiritual and emotional. Their success in meeting these needs will then become primary rather than the 'preciousness' of the 'different language' *per se*. Too often there is a slipping and sliding in emphasis on this count which comes essentially from an inadequate and poorly thought-out theory of modern societies and their cultural phenomena.

Such a goal would require an abandonment of the loose, preaching manner in which today's socio-cultural orientation of multiculturalism operates. The danger is that the loose framework of pluralist cultural theory — the so-called cultural mosaics or fruit salads that some theorists and educationalists refer to — only serves to mystify and ignore differences that in fact lock people into unequal situations. Schools have a primary responsibility to contribute to assisting all children to acquire the skills needed to be able to reflect on their own cultural becoming and their society at large. This requires, as a very basic precondition, general language proficiency in the dominant language. That there are numerous ways of doing this is indisputable, but in a period of contracting resources it is important that priorities are chosen with clear sight and with a view to maximum benefit. In both its directions, cognitive superiority and social harmony, the Canadian experience has only problematic lessons to offer.

Language Rights in the United States

The transition/maintenance debate in the USA reflects the movement of the language question from proficiency in English to 'rights', and parallels the trend from policies of assimilation to policies of pluralism. This is in theory at least, because in practice, as described earlier in this chapter, the assimilation/pluralism division in contemporary society is complex and often made simplistic by overly narrow and optimistic theories. Such theories almost deliberately miss the double dynamism of the modern world to universalization as well as to diversity. This is not to deny the important battles people fight in the name of difference, but only to suggest that, in terms of education and pedagogy generally, the necessary blurring of concepts for political ends and social service does not give adequate direction for effective practice.

The blurring and fudging of concepts in order to get an edge of any sort can lead to problematic reactions. The US government over the past decade has in fact cut funding for first language education other than English. In a speech in 1981 President Reagan accused bilingual programmes of deliberately impeding the acquisition of English among minority groups, thereby limiting their vocational preparation (Forster, 1982: 292). His administration maintained that the government has no place in intervening in the private cultural choices of individuals. The public purse, it is argued, could not and should not be expected to provide people with private language options (Rist, 1983: 56). But for the first time federal funding has been extended to support private alternative education which emphasizes 'back to basics' in the three 'R's, morality and nationalism. The more recent focus of government intervention on the issue of language instruction, therefore, has been limited to 'transitional' language programmes designed to enable students to transfer to English as successfully as possible. Kutcher (1980) claims bilingualism is a crutch which only serves to lengthen dependency of students on their native tongue. Quigg (1979) is also of this opinion.

This position reflects a clash with current academic opinion and some 'ethnic organizations' which have moved to a position over the last decade of advocating 'maintenance' programmes over 'transitionary' ones. Maintenance programmes involve the students' first language at all levels of schooling as a language of instruction. Typically they also involve the students' cultural background as a subject area in the curriculum. Those who advocate bilingual and bicultural education are committed to the idea that America is a multicultural society. In their view the traditional assimilationist, melting pot theory of American society did not work, and languages represent the significant diversity in the USA today. They are suspicious of transitionary bilingual programmes and accuse them of contributing to the outdated and outmoded assimilationist trend that did not meet the real needs of the diverse population of America (Simoes, 1976; Blanco, 1979; Edwards, 1981). So a number of very complex educational, political and ideological factors are tied together, and slippage from one to another has caused much confusion in educational practice.

The issue has been made all the more complicated by the 'English Only' movement in the late 1980s. Perhaps the most notable incident in this push has been the approval of Proposition 63 which amended the Constitution of the State of California to make English the 'official State language'. By 1988 a total of thirteen states had established English as their official language, with similar moves afoot in over thirty other states and also for the amendment of the Federal Constitution. Bilingual education is bearing the brunt of much of the 'English Only' movement's criticism. Spokesperson for the debate in California, former Senator S. I. Hayakawa, publicly summed up his position in these terms: 'We have embarked unwisely upon a policy of so-called ''bilingualism'', putting foreign languages in competition with our own. English has long been the unifying force of the American people. But now prolonged bilingual education in public schools and multilingual ballots threaten to divide us along language lines.'

If one takes an historical perspective various factors have to be considered as contributory to the renewal of the language question in the USA. In 1958 the National Defence Act made special funds available to schools and colleges to improve educational outcomes. The impetus for this Act was a fear that the USA was slipping behind the USSR in a number of areas. This concern put languages back on the educational agenda (along with maths and science) as an area needing special attention and upgrading. Simultaneously a trend from another direction coupled with this concern to open up other aspects of the language question. In 1963, as a result of Cuban immigrants fleeing communism for the USA, a number of bilingual schools were set up in Miami. These schools set an example, provided a new model and stimulated renewed interest in language education.

The 1960s became a period of general upheaval. The civil rights movement and the anti-war movement challenged the myth of the American way. At the educational level the so-called 'progressive' movement put a renewed emphasis on the individual, on disadvantage and non-conformity. A 1960 study of students of Spanish background in California, who were 14 years or over, found that 50 per cent had not gone beyond eighth grade, compared to 25 per cent of the total population. Of the total population, 20 per cent had completed one or more years of college, whereas only 7 per cent of children of Spanish background had attained this level of education. This study also noted that the Spanish population of the southwest did not fare economically as well as the general population (Blanco, 1979: 457).

The American Dream, it seemed, was not possible for all. A combination of these factors led to the passing of the Elementary and Secondary Education Act by the US Congress in 1965. In 1968 Title VII of this law became known as the Bilingual Education Act. These Acts made funding available for programmes designed to serve the 'needs of limited English speaking ability' students. Unlike Canada, therefore, the primary emphasis of language learning became, not teaching another language to students of the dominant language group, as might have been the expected result of the Defence Act, but the teaching of students who had limited abilities in English through their mother tongue so they could gain knowledge and skills necessary to make the transition to English successfully (Kjolseth, 1972).

In 1974 funding of the 1965 Elementary and Secondary Education Act was extended beyond bilingual education at the local level to adult education, pre-school education, teacher training, teachers' aides and so on. Title VII also provided funds for Materials Acquisition Projects, Dissemination and Assessment Centres for Bilingual Education and Oral Materials Development Centres. It also provided for teacher training and in-servicing.

The Federal Government's initiating role in appropriating funds for bilingual education has subsequently generated significant legislation at the state level, and in some ways it can be said that the strategy has been a top-down one supported by funding which is insecure in the longer term. But it did open up spaces for claims by groups to be made, and to snowball. A significant and symptomatic consequence was the 1974 Supreme Court claim in the case of *Lau vs. Nicholls*. The court declared that 'the failure of the San Francisco school system to provide English language instruction for approximately 1800 students of Chinese ancestry who do not speak English denies them a meaningful opportunity to participate in the public education program and thus violates section 601 of the Civil Rights Act of 1964, which bans discrimination based on the grounds of race, colour, or national origin; in any program or activity receiving federal financial assistance' (Blanco, 1979: 458).

The federal legislation and the court decisions on language set the basis for the so-called 'compensatory' bilingual programmes which were transitional in their goals. The progressive educators' emphases on the individual and non-conformity, self-esteem and identity were to be realized through the incorporation of the child's cultural background as well as their language into schools. This side of the argument grew and studies began to link low achievement to cultural factors (Fishman, 1977; Paulston, 1978). The white, Anglo-Saxon middle-class education that dominated schools was accused of being inappropriate to the special needs of minority groups and those of non-English-speaking backgrounds. One needs to ask, though, if these children were ever in situations that really did effectively facilitate the mastering of dominant skills and knowledge.

This would have required more than just a disjointed attempt at compensatory education in limited areas. Were these children prepared for assimilation in terms of sharing social power, prestige, wealth and mobility? Perhaps it could be argued that assimilation did not work, not because migrants or minority groups did not aspire to mainstream American culture, but because they were locked out of it in many instances.

There are about five million 'limited English ability' children in America today. The language situation for these children is very complex. There are those who are recent arrivals from Cuba, Haiti, Mexico and, most recently, South-East Asia. Some within this last group, particularly the Vietnamese, are showing an eagerness to take on US culture and language as quickly as possible, while the dropout rate for the Hispanic group continues to remain high (Rist, 1983: 44). There are those children born in the USA whose first language is not English, such as those of Puerto Rican, Mexican and Portuguese backgrounds. There are children from Greek, Italian, French, Chinese and German backgrounds born in the USA who learn the mother tongue and English together and often unevenly. There are those of a variety of backgrounds, including indigenous native Americans, who have no skills in the language of their ancestors. There are also those children who are monolingual speakers of non-standard English, such as some black American groups. And there are monolinguals who desire to add another language to their linguistic skills for vocational or personal reasons. The variety of linguistic experiences extends far beyond these categories and the number of languages and dialects runs to three figures. The movement of emphasis towards 'rights of maintenance of difference', rather than rights of participation in mainstream society, has put new pressures on the US educational system.

The funding of bilingual education began at $75 million and has now reached $160 million. Language education, from the beginning of the 1980s, has become the largest single funded project in the budget of the Federal Department of Education. This level of funding is more than matched at state and local levels. Currently seventy-three different language groups are served in all but six of the states; 75 per cent of programmes funded are in elementary schools and 25 per cent in secondary schools. The tertiary sector, however, has been slow in responding.

The type of programmes offered varies. Most are transitional, involving English as a second language and another language. There are some maintenance programmes involving bilingual instruction and bilingual curriculum. Some of these are what has been termed 'restorative', in that they aim to restore language and culture lost in the process of assimilation. Another type of programme is called 'culturally pluralistic', in which all options of culture and language curricula are open to all students.

One of the most significant debates that has evolved from these programmes is the appropriate methodology for teaching language in general. This debate is a general one in terms of the conflict between the growing 'back to basics' movement (both in content and method) and the open, progressive, experiential, process-oriented movement in teaching of the 1960s and 1970s. But it also has specific ramifications for the language question. The issues of language, cognition, achievement and identity highlighted in both the Swedish and Canadian experiences are inextricably tied up with the vexing question of methodology. One of the weaknesses of the language movement in the USA has been in materials, training and methods. The disparity and uncertainty in these areas mean that research on the language question relies as much on opinion as scientific research. Making policy has been much easier than implementing it.

It it not good enough to explain the emphasis upon issues of 'cultural identity', on one side of the language debate, in terms of an antipathy to the pressures of assimilation. The argument against compensatory and transitional aspects of the language question, and for enrichment and group cultural-identity maintenance aspects, has not been clarificatory. On the one hand, it serves to confuse social inequalities with cultural differences, while the élite reproduces its social and educational position as ever. It also begs the whole question of the purpose of segregation and desegregation. Does cultural maintenance mean a return to segregation in the name of pluralism? The result of this trend is a claim that compensation for the disadvantaged is demeaning because it makes their 'difference' appear inferior when, in fact, it is just a matter of variety in a multicultural society. So we end up with 'rights' of the individual. How does this translate into practice and how does it fit into the situation of contracting government intervention and funding?

The non-existence of a genuinely equalizing melting pot process can be understood as much as a failure as a matter of resistance, particularly given the unequal way in which difference is linked to culture. One has to examine closely the concept of 'ethnicity' in this regard. Why has it become a focal point? What bargaining powers does it really bring? What analytical strength does it have as a social descriptive category? Such questions necessarily lead us to an examination of cultural pluralism. What sort of plurality exists and is possible in modern US society? In Chapter 1 we tried to respond to this question, and our answer was that the plurality that exists is part of the dynamic of the singular mainstream culture of industrialism and is not an indicator of structural difference.

How does this reflect on language maintenance and language shift? English will remain the vehicle of power and empowerment in the USA, and while other languages used in the United States can perform certain social functions, they will survive. Such functions include the family and psychological comfort. Despite a level of maintenance for immediate personal purposes, however, there has been a shift occurring at both the level of the mother tongue and transfer to English. These shifts cannot be ignored by unclear moralistic or optimistic de-clarations of the multicultural nature of contemporary American society. In fact, the issue of shift is critical. As Fishman (1976) and Gaarder (1977) note, if members of a particular speech community are able to use that language and another different language equally in all places, the need to be bilingual wanes. They argue that the only possibility for sustaining bilingualism is in a situation of diglossia, that is, where each language has a separate sphere of use.

But, as Fishman also points out (1977), this means that schools cannot be relied upon to contribute to language maintenance. It is the speech com-munity's responsibility primarily to facilitate maintenance by requiring and using its language in specific spheres. As mentioned earlier, given the pressures for learning the more politically powerful mainstream language, it is difficult to ensure this will happen. Fishman (1976) has to argue that it is the role of those who believe in the richness that diversity offers society to manipulate community support for bilingual education to establish power bases and lobby groups in order to extract political support and funding and then to ensure its use in their community (at the very least).

No one disputes at a general level that bilingualism or trilingualism, or indeed, knowing as many languages as possible, is useful, enriching and rewarding. In the immigrant experience, however, those who do not speak the dominant language often come from a background where they might have gained little formal literacy. In their new homeland many are slotted in at the bottom in social-economic terms. The language question for such groups cannot effectively be primarily a matter of esteem, pride or cognitive superiority. Gaarder (1977) calls an aspect of such goals 'folk bilingualism' which results not from choice, but from economic necessity. For those who have achieved a socio-economic status which provides them with the skills and know-how to manipu-late social structures to their advantage, language can become an issue of enrich-ment or a precious additive; be it the mother tongue or a foreign language. Gaarder (1977) calls this 'élite bilingualism'. There is also the question of rede-fining the status and participation of indigenous groups deprived of their tradi-tional material cultural bases.

Much of the research and theory in the American setting seems to slip backwards and forwards from different empirical situations to make generaliza-tions. The issue has become more political than pedagogical. This has a specific effect on programmes, materials, training and research. If Kjolseth, Fishman and others are right, the prime facilitator of language maintenance is the speech community itself. Otherwise, there will simply be foreign language learning, with all its limitations.

Cohen's (1970) finding that most children of non-English-speaking immigrants achieved low academic results does not seem to have been reversed by language experiments. While there is no absolute homogeneity in speech communities, particularly in socio-economic terms, some groups continue to do poorly. Cardenas (1982: 16) claims that the dropout rate of children from minority background is up to 50 per cent by the time they reach grade 12. Critics of the language innovations maintain that in the long term there will be a loss of native mastery without any improvement in English (Gaarder, 1977; Kjolseth, 1972). MacNamara's work in the United Kingdom supports this. The implications of these arguments are that energy and resources are being misdirected and that the goals of compulsory education should be the raising of general school achievement. Fishman, Paulston and others, of course, would disagree. They place great importance on social harmony and mutual respect, which they believe to be outcomes as valuable as school achievement. But open resistance is growing among some groups in America to having different language programmes, such as the Puerto Ricans of New York and the Crow Indians (Lewis, 1981: 317). Bilingual programmes must raise achievement levels in order to remove themselves from controversy (Forster, 1982: 297; Lambert, 1983).

3
Linguistic Pluralism or Social Equity?
The Language Question in Australia

In this chapter we use Australia as a case study to develop the arguments that have emerged theoretically in Chapter 1 and in the discussion of key debates in Sweden, Canada and the United States in Chapter 2. Our purpose is not to chronicle the development of language policy and educational practice in Australia but to use the Australian example as a medium through which to examine some of the critical issues of policy and pedagogy in the relation of minority languages to dominant culture.

We begin by examining the politics of language, focusing particularly on the difficulties of an approach which gives precedence to immediate political considerations over long-term pedagogical ones. The chapter describes the development of national languages policy in Australia in the 1980s, and the public attacks that have been made, if not so often on languages policy itself, then on multicultural education in general and the broad social consequences of an immigration programme that continues to bring about increasing cultural and linguistic diversity. To meet these criticisms, we present in the next part of the chapter a brief sociology of cultural and linguistic diversity in Australian education, arguing that there are some very specific needs resulting from four decades of mass immigration that require specialist educational servicing. Multicultural education is simply a necessity in a context like this. Some forms of multicultural education, however, have proved cost-ineffective, tokenistic or even counter-productive. Returning to the alternative sociological paradigms describing cultural and linguistic diversity which were introduced in Chapter 1, we contrast language curriculum strategies founded on a simple pluralist model of culture with approaches more concerned with the role of education in fostering social equity and founded on an holistic understanding of language-in-culture in an industrialized social setting.

The Politics of Language

When we examine the situation in Australia, we come up against an edifice of ill-thought out pluralism and mainly small-scale empirical research with limited application. With a smallish academic population and limited research and development funding, the language question in relation to the issue of plurality has become primarily the province of the political side of multiculturalism. Advocacy-type claims have drawn selectively on overseas results to put their case.

> The most basic issue is a philosophical one, namely, what kind of society do we want? That is, if Australia is in fact a multicultural and multilingual society, and it can be shown that schooling predominantly reinforces dominance in one language, one cultural interaction style and a monocultural pattern of rewards, does the education system want to perpetuate this system of dominance? (Robinson, 1981: 56)

> Not every individual can be bilingual, but he can share in the other aspects of culture and cultures in our society, as well as acquire a positive attitude to the very notions of Australian multiculturalism. There is no denying that the best way to understand another culture is to acquire, or at least to learn something about, its core value. Since in many cultures the cores are linguistic, the learning of a particular ethnic or community language by members of other ethnic groups represents cultural pluralism at its deepest and most meaningful level. (Smolicz, 1981: 9–10)

Some have cautiously hinted at associated problems:

> . . . if there is any common ground that is shared by the so-called multicultural programs it must be that they do not take seriously either languages or cultures. . . . At its worst, it represents a trivialisation of language and culture and is, therefore, counter-productive of its own aims. . . . But the most serious defect, I believe, is that, even with good multicultural programs, there is no guarantee that schools can bring about attitude changes. (Horvath, 1981: 39–40)

> In its public life and institutions Australia is not a multicultural and multilingual society, and reforming the language curriculum in schools is not likely in itself to change this. (Quinn, 1980: 44)

When proponents of the folk view of Community Language teaching spell out what they mean, it goes something like this: 'We need school programs in Greek so that non-Greek Australians will be able to talk in Greek to Greeks living in Australia' . . . . I must confess that I find this sort of thinking, which appears to be quite common, unfortunately naive. For one thing, the amount of language that is taught in school programs is not all that great. But even if it were adequate, there is a more important consideration: the folk argument assumes that knowing the language of another group readily promotes social interaction with that group . . . . Even supposing that a non-Greek Australian manages to learn enough Greek at school to speak the language easily, does he thereby have ready access to Greek social situations? I doubt it. (Quinn, 1981: 88–92)

Others, opposed to the insubstantiability of multiculturalism, dismiss all its proposals.

It is difficult to see how multiculturalism can be stopped, but it is imperative that it should be. Week after week, public money is wasted on its distorted priorities. The Victorian Education Department, which has virtually abolished all teaching of Latin and classical Greek, and which makes Asian and South East Asian languages available in very few schools, boasted in July through a Ministerial Press Release that it was now introducing modern Greek in selected primary schools to prepare children for a multicultural society. While no education is entirely worthless, the teaching of 'community languages' to primary school children in Australia in 1980 must be pretty close to it. So far as educational priorities are concerned, it surely can only be explained in terms of political opportunism. (Chipman, 1980: 6)

Given how political and emotional the whole question is, one might be inclined to despair about there being a way through it. In educational terms, despite mandatory multicultural policies in some states, it seems that fiscal stringency and growing public uncertainty about the concept might edge out the still nebulous multiculturalism. Although the rhetoric of multiculturalism is official policy in the late 1980s, represented symbolically by the Office of Multicultural Affairs in the Prime Minister's Department, areas of policy implementation such as multicultural education are under increasing pressure to justify themselves in social and economic terms.

With few linguists involved in discussing the language question in terms of a sociology of plurality, either at the theoretical level or at the applied level, a pattern of reliance on overseas research for policy deliberations has developed. Yet the Australian context, though in broad outline not unlike those of Sweden, Canada and America, is different in empirical detail. As Clyne (1982) points out, there is no single major minority language in Australia, such as Spanish in

America, French in Canada and Finnish in Sweden. So, given the enormous number of languages that exist in Australia, the numbers speaking each language, the geographical dispersal of speakers and the variety of levels of use and function generally, responses at the level of policy and educational programming are vexing.

Clyne, in keeping with the spirit of pluralism, suggests that this situation only means that it is not bilingualism that is appropriate for Australia, but multilingualism, and not just for children of migrant background, but for all people in Australia. This is despite the tendencies he notes that the younger generation or second generation of non-English-speaking background use more English, particularly amongst themselves, and to intermarriage. He suggests 'promotive government policies', much akin to Fishman's suggestions, so that language becomes a resource in contributing to the elimination of 'xenophobic' attitudes among 'Anglo-Celtic Australians' and 'ethnocentric ones' among 'other ethnic groups' (Clyne, 1982: 148). Despite these assertions, we have come across no empirical evidence that language can be used as an effective resource for the process of intervening against racism and prejudice.

At another level, and equally problematic, is the development of the concept of 'community language' within Australian research and popular usage. This has two ramifications. First, there is the question of methodology. Here, the debate is between the appropriateness of standard forms as opposed to their particular forms in the immigrant context. Second, there is an attempt to ascribe equal status to all languages in keeping with the philosophy of pluralism. English, according to this view, is simply a 'community language' too. In both cases, language is reified and made into an object, thereby removing it from its social function and effects. One of the dangers in the latter tendency is the emergence of an idea that to aim at native-like proficiency in English for those of non-English-speaking background is to deny the enlightenment of contemporary multicultural practice (e.g., Gray, 1984).

Moreover, the use of the concept 'community' here tends to sidestep the importance of social variables and replace them with ones of 'space' and 'language', defined loosely. This is at the expense of analyzing the multiplicity of factors which combine to make up the social process. Linguistic life histories might not simply be objects of celebration. In complex relation to other social factors, such as socio-economic ones, certain types of linguistic variety might serve to compound social disadvantage.

More recently the term 'community language' has been replaced by the broader acronym 'LOTE' or Language Other Than English. This partly reflects an economic emphasis on, for example, the most efficient development of languages of trading significance to Australia, such as Asian languages. It includes in its scope the teaching of 'languages of economic importance' (Lo

Bianco, 1987) as foreign languages and the development of first language abilities in these particular languages among non-English-speaking background (NESB) students. The interest in this case is less on language learning as a community relations exercise than building upon existing language resources in the community to Australia's optimum economic benefit. On the other hand, there has been a growing tendency to link the language question with a notion of 'rights' (Jayasuriya, 1988). This term, however, does not have the strength it has in the United States. A proclamation in policy of people's rights to maintain their language and culture need not necessarily mean very much at all.

It is a vague emphasis on 'maintenance' that in Australia also propels the language question to the sphere of cultural diversity. The most significant work in this area is on Aboriginal languages. But since these are oral forms, the work to maintain them through the construction of written forms and literature is paradoxical in terms of the argument of maintaining traditional culture. In practice, it is not so much a matter of maintenance but of transformation of the function of language and the establishment of new power relationships. Bilingual education for Aboriginal students is seen by some of its advocates as a movement away from former misguided assimilationist policies. A few studies that have evaluated the results of such bilingual programmes claim that there are certainly advantages in terms of cognitive development and language skills, but not an increase in general academic achievement (Buschenhofen, 1983: 12). Also, despite the valiant efforts at bilingual programmes, the dropout rate and non-attendance levels of Aboriginal children remain high. One must also question which culture the process of formal schooling serves. The serious maintenance of traditional culture does not need bilingual programmes in schools but the material/structural basis for its reproduction. In other words, the question is never raised of maintaining culture at the second level in our cultural model by many minority language maintenance advocates. Aboriginal people need land and legal space with absolutely no strings attached if they wish to reproduce their lives in a way which is traditional in any strict sense. This is not said in ignorance of the fairly unavoidable pressures of modern industrial society and its historic encroachment, but to point out some murkiness in the arguments about language maintenance.

The cognitive advantage of maintaining a mother tongue through schooling is undisputed, but if the skills acquired in the school have limited relevance to life outside school, their vitality will be limited. Transitional goals, using bilingual methods to transfer to English, on the other hand, are often considered to be doing an injustice to culture in terms of the pluralist framework. But it has to be considered that it has been the failure of assimilation through exclusion at a structural level, as well as resistance, that has made English appear irrelevant as a central goal for many Aboriginal students. But, to struggle for their rights and for self-determination, Aboriginal people need the language power and the skills of the culture that impedes their self-determination. Prejudice and injustice are not simply linked to language, nor reversed through the restoration of language.

The issues are equally murky for other minorities and their languages in Australia. The most pertinent research here is that on ethnic background, language competence and academic achievement (Marjoribanks, 1979; De Lemos, 1975; De Lemos and Di Leo, 1978; Taft, 1975b; Taft and Cahill, 1981). Generally, the conclusion from such research is that an inadequate introduction to and use of English, together with socio-economic factors, hampers academic achievement. Children of non-English-speaking background tend to have high aspirations and stay at school longer, but they are often not as successful as their monolingual peers in academic performance and therefore reap fewer of the benefits that might flow from that.

Taft and Cahill (1981: 36–7) describe research that found that children from non-English-speaking background liked school more than their native English-speaking peers and that girls from middle-class Italian or Greek background did better than their native English peers. They found this intriguing. But perhaps it is not so intriguing when one considers that, for some of these children, school is the main contact with dominant Australian life and, for girls particularly, may often be even liberating. Also it can offer the opportunity of deviating in some respects from their parents' culture or background, in terms of career aspirations and a desire to be a part of the culture of modernity, such as rock music, the cinema, peer group entertainment, gender role blurring and so on.

With regard to language specifically, it is also the case, as Clyne (1981a: 32) points out, that for many children of non-English-speaking background the language of the parents in practice becomes more like a second language. The proliferation of community 'ethnic schools' cannot be seen as an expression of the desire to 'maintain' languages *per se*. Research shows that one of their main roles is to ensure the reproduction of a social group, to provide an area for mixing with one's own and to discourage, for some groups, intermarriage. This ironically contradicts the spirit of pluralism.

As our study confirms (see Chapter 5), both the short- and long-term effect of immigration to Australia from non-English-speaking societies is often uneven English and mother tongue development, and this has an effect on academic achievement generally. As the Campbell report on English as a Second Language (1984) points out, ESL teaching does not always overcome this problem.

> ...With respect to the issue of the effectiveness of the E.S.L.
> Programs, the safest verdict should be something akin to the Scottish

'not proven'.... It's one thing to be aware of, and sensitive to the problems and quite another to be able to do something constructive about them.... The majority of mainstream teachers in our schools are unable to intervene very effectively in the teaching of non-English speaking background students. (Campbell *et al.*, 1984: 97, 89)

Further down the complex track of cause and effect are strong indications that the unemployment rates for some young people of migrant background are significantly higher than their native English-speaking peers. This is particularly the case with those belonging to the more recently arrived groups (Morrissey *et al.*, 1984; Hugo 1987; Castles, Morrissey and Lewis, 1987).

The language picture is complex with many different scenarios that need considering. These include:

1. older new arrivals eager to learn English and hampered at school if this is not achieved quickly;
2. younger new arrivals entering school with no English but with a sound command of their mother tongue;
3. Australian-born children entering school with limited English and uneven mother tongue proficiency;
4. students of all levels who have made a transition to English and have lost mother tongue skills;
5. students wanting to learn another language as a foreign language.

This is only a simplified summary of a number of possible situations for children in Australia, from Aborigines to most recently arrived refugees. It does not even begin to consider other critical variables such as socio-economic background, gender or ethnic differences. From our study it was clear that esteem and identity came with succeeding at what school required and with the possibility of getting a job. Students were less concerned with language as an artefact or symbol of identity.

There is not sufficient research into the so-called community language programmes that have arisen with the rise of multiculturalism to be able to generalize about their impact or success. Methodology and issues of segregation are still peripheral, as the main goal seems to be to achieve acceptance of the extension of language servicing as much as possible. There is a danger that heading off without a clear framework can weaken the whole movement. It is important, as McLean, Horvath and others have maintained, to return the language question to serious educational arenas. We would maintain that as long as the language question is tied up with the social theory of multiculturalism in its simple pluralist form, it will not find a sound foundation for decision-making. Language policy has to be removed from this level of politics. The emphasis needs to be shifted towards linguistic competence for social participation. The Campbell report also makes a proposition along these lines:

> We believe that multiculturalism should be freed from its special relationship with E.S.L. to exert a more pervasive influence upon the curriculum, and that E.S.L. should be strengthened by its inclusion within a coherent language programme, comprising, as well, English as mother tongue, language across the curriculum, bilingual studies, and 'foreign' languages. (Campbell *et al.*, 1984: 100)

The development of a national languages policy is an attempt to resolve these difficulties, but, as we will go on to discuss, it has been hamstrung by the politics of its beginning and politicking for survival amid severe financial cutbacks and flagging government commitment.

Language Policy in Australia

The move towards an explicit national policy on languages has been a slow laborious process. Through to the early 1970s the implicit (and often not-too-implicit) policy rationale behind Commonwealth funded migrant settlement programmes, such as the Child Migrant Education Programme, had been cultural in linguistic assimilation or integration through the learning of English. By the mid-1970s, however, it was becoming blatantly obvious that the old policy of assimilation/integration was not working. A plethora of government reports showed, for example, that immigrant students of non-English-speaking background (NESB) were educationally disadvantaged. At the same time larger concerns pressured government towards a shift in policy: assimilation or integration at a cultural and linguistic level was simply not occurring, specialist servicing (such as language services) was increasingly needed as the proportion of the population of NESB increased; return migration to the European economic miracle was a serious economic drain which needed to be reduced, and 'ethnic' organizations and lobby groups were emerging and possibly even constituting a 'migrant vote' (Kalantzis and Cope, 1984; Castles, Cope, Kalantzis and Morrissey, 1988).

In many ways the Labor years of reform represent a culmination of the project of integration, even though they also laid some of the groundwork for the emergence of a policy of cultural pluralism. Al Grassby, Labor Minister for Immigration until 1974, spoke, not of cultural difference, but of a unified 'family of the nation' and of equal economic opportunity for all Australians. In the late 1970s, however, the conservative parties came up with a very different approach to the undeniable 'problem' of mass immigration.

The concept of 'multiculturalism' itself and the particular programmes that emerged by the early 1980s were pre-eminently the product of the Fraser period of Liberal-National Party conservative government and its acceptance and implementation of the Galbally report (1978). Its manifestations were the Special Broadcasting Service, the Australian Institute of Multicultural Affairs and the Multicultural Education Program, to name just a few prominent examples, the last two of which are now defunct and the first of which almost became defunct. The typical emphasis of Fraser-Galbally multiculturalism was a move away from Labor's fundamental conception of social policy for immigrants: from a social analysis based on the concept of disadvantage to one based on the concept of cultural difference. For Labor, being an immigrant was primarily a subset of more general lines of socio-economic division. For the new Fraser multiculturalism, ethnicity became a critical new form of social categorization. Cultural dissonance rather than social justice was seen to be the problem that government policy most needed to address.

In the area of language policy and practice, Fraser multiculturalism manifested itself in a move away from almost exclusive concern in the Labor reform years with better English language provision to a new emphasis on cultural diversity and linguistic maintenance. In many important ways this was a progressive development. One's ancestral language is frequently an important fulcrum of communality, a rallying point for political and social solidarity, of psychological comfort in the home, of heartfelt aesthetic power or a conveyer of specific meanings related to self and identity. But the move to this particular policy of cultural pluralism also involved a retreat from Labor's reformist vision of a just and united society. Issues of social justice were replaced with a celebration of colourful cultural differences. The project of 'initiation to core culture' (to recycle the terminology of the 1973 Karmel report on education) was replaced by self-esteem programmes in which one would end up feeling good about one's cultural difference. The problem with the Fraser model of multiculturalism was that cultural differences are often not simply worthy of celebration, but embody relations of social inequality (Kalantzis and Cope, 1984, Castles, Cope, Kalantzis and Morrissey, 1988).

In the area of language learning, we saw the rise of so-called 'community' language education programmes. But with limited rationales of self-esteem and cultural maintenance and inadequate funding, this meant, on the one hand, tokenistic short-term programmes in which students often poorly learnt a few words of domestic interchange and a little bit of 'culture', and, on the other hand, the removal of some educational responsibility to the semi-private sector in the form of meagre subsidies to community-run 'ethnic schools'.

Critics of this simplistic pluralist approach to the language question came to argue that 'community' language learning would never become a serious and useful educational endeavour until it concerned itself with language, not just as a means to cultural maintenance, but as a tool of social access as well. This would necessarily involve transitional bilingualism (learning mainstream subjects in one's mother tongue, with a gradual transition to English to that lines of cognitive development were not disrupted by language break) and teaching 'community' languages with the same degree of intellectual seriousness as traditional 'foreign' languages. Indeed, funding for tokenistic 'community' language programmes with restricted cultural aims might well have been better spent on improving specialist English as a Second Language (ESL) teaching. Two important developments in the 1980s have attempted to overcome some of these difficulties: the 1984 *National Language Policy* from the Senate Standing Committee on Education and the Arts, and the 1987 *National Policy on Languages*, written by Joe Lo Bianco.

The *Report on a National Language Policy* of the Senate Standing Committee on Education and the Arts was published in October 1984, after several years of committee deliberations. A mark of its comprehensiveness was that it received general acceptance both from those involved in ethnic politics and from some of the staunchest opponents of the principle of multiculturalism. Even Lauchlan Chipman, longtime vocal critic of multiculturalism, was able to bring himself to write in Quadrant that 'the issues it deals with are important, and by and large it deals with them competently and sensitively' (1985).

The stated purposes of language study in the report include language skills required for effective communication with non-English-speakers, development of an understanding of other cultures, maintenance of ethnic (including Aboriginal) languages and cultures, the development of cognitive and general linguistic capacities, and the development of personality and a sense of individual identity. It would not be possible to argue, except perversely, against the legitimacy of any of these purposes. We would argue, however, that critical differences in policy and practice will emerge if emphasis is put on different goals, or even if all goals are accepted, but they are prioritized on the basis of what immediately appears to be most practicable (Senate Standing Committee, 1984: 136–9).

The first purpose in the above list is direct communication, though in the particular phraseology employed the matter under discussion is somewhat narrower: communication with non-English-speakers, principally by first language English-speakers or first language speakers of a language other than the second party in a communicative situation. This might be informal (such as between linguistic groups in Australia) or formal (such as interpreting services). This, we would argue, is not one of the strongest rationales for maintenance of languages other than English, because English in the longer term could be an adequate *lingua franca* of direct communication, while the use of interpreting and translation services can be a matter of shorter-term adjustment in a period of transition to adequate English usage for formal or institutional communicative situations. There is a strong argument that we need a body of people trained well enough to perform these duties professionally, but, failing radical linguistic pluralism (which the Committee does not advocate), this purpose does not necessitate a broad-based, comprehensive policy of maintenance of languages other than English, even though such a policy might be desirable.

The second stated purpose of language study is that there is value in the 'language learning experience as a means of developing sensitive and tolerant cross-cultural attitudes'. There is nothing to deny the validity of this proposition in an ideal set of circumstances. But, as we have pointed out above, there is no empirical evidence to support such a proposition. Even if the claim proved to be valid, language learning to a level of genuine reading and communicative competence (to the extent of genuinely understanding the other person's particular culture through learning their language assumptions, values, kinship structures, aspirations in the Australian context and so on) might not be the most cost-effective means of achieving the more general social goals. There are other more direct strategies to these ends, such as bringing issues of multi-culturalism, non-racism, social participation with cultural diversity and human rights explicitly to the fore in school curricula and the media. Furthermore, even a very high-level language learning, such that the full profundity of cultural practices can become evident through the texts of a language or in communi-cation, will not necessarily endear all aspects of a culture to the learner. For example, racism and sexism are often integral aspects of culture, written directly into the language itself, and towards which no one should have to show infinite tolerance or unproblematic acceptance.

Aside from these problems of a more general nature and putting the best possible construction upon the likely effects of the culture-through-language propositions, there is a serious logistical difficulty. Making this rationale a prominent or even dominant basis for language teaching and language mainte-nance often means that a smattering of a language (a few lessons a week or for a short time) appears adequate. A few words of a language, it would seem, give you a feel for the language group's 'culture' or, for native non-English-speakers, a sense of the institutional respect being given to their first language. But in terms of genuine respect, serious cultural understanding and basic cognitive and linguistic goals, such programmes might be, and in many circumstances have proved to be, completely inadequate.

The third suggested purpose of language study is that language learning is a means to the 'maintenance of ethnic languages and cultures'. This purpose expresses a threefold intention. First, there is a genuine need to preserve Aboriginal languages, particularly as a number of them are seriously threatened. But this concern does not apply to the immigrant languages of the past two centuries, all of which have ongoing organic histories elsewhere. Second, there is an implicit assumption that cultural conservation is an inherent good. While not wishing to dispute that for many people it is a desire and a good, it is not necessarily a general and universal good for all people, in all circumstances. This was one of the central propositions we put forward in Chapter 1. Third, cultures are not simply and unproblematically open to maintenance in the Australian context. Another crucial proposition in Chapter 1 was that in the Australian setting (in which levels two and three of our scheme integrally relate to each other) cultures take new forms. If the proposition about cultural maintenance is tendentious, the proposition that it will necessarily be maintained through language is even more so. Of course, language maintenance facilitates communication across generations, for example. But it does not ensure there will be no generation gap, either in terms of broader Australian structural and peer pressure, or in the development of new linguistic genres.

The *Report on a National Language Policy* deliberately emphasizes its fourth stated purpose for language study: 'the development of the general cognitive and linguistic abilities of students'. We would argue that this should be the central rationale for formal first language learning for students of non-English-speaking background and second language acquisition for students of English-speaking background. Programmes consistent with this rationale and adequate to social participation as an ultimate goal would include transitional bilingual programmes, maintenance bilingual programmes, and generally the teaching of languages other than English to a standard and degree of intellectual seriousness similar to that traditionally expected in foreign language teaching (without necessarily being traditional in terms of pedagogy), beginning as early as possible and sustained over a number of years. For students of non-English-speaking background, teaching to these ends will help ensure that there is not a linguistic break on entry to school that interrupts lines of cognition in the process of development. For all students, language learning that provides a genuine intellectual challenge can not only aid linguistic development in all languages being learnt, but also aid students' cognitive development and further their ability to abstract. As we argued from the literature survey in Chapter 2, this is not an inevitable part of all forms and degrees of bilingualism. Rather, it is a possible result of language teaching oriented to these ends.

The report, however, is cautious in its conclusion about the practicality and likely effectiveness of bilingual programmes (Senate Standing Committee, 1984: 57–8, 141–4). For all language teaching, it calls for 'a research programme designed to establish the nature and extent of the cognitive and linguistic benefits arising from a range of language learning programmes in Australian schools' (1984: 138). Given varying pedagogical and social consequences that, we have argued, emerge from differences of emphasis in the rationales for language teaching or language maintenance, this call seems to be extremely important.

The fifth and final purpose stated in the report is 'general development of personality'. The central contention supporting this is that 'language study contributes significantly to the development of individual self-esteem, since the introduction of the language into the school encourages children of that background to value it and appreciate it as an asset' (1984: 138). As with the culture-through-language arguments, making this a primary rationale can allow for language teaching programmes that are only really effective as tokens. There are also larger arguments to the effect that general success in school and the possibility of access to social goods are conducive to self-esteem in a more profound way. Language teaching can contribute to the formation of this more convincing self-esteem, through achieving or by manifestly trying to achieve, the linguistic-cognitive goals in the report's fourth stated purpose for language study.

Our aim in the above presentation has not been to be critical of the stated purposes of language study or language maintenance presented in the *Report on a National Language Policy*. Viewed in the context of the list, none is exceptionable. Rather, we have tried to point to various possible effects of emphasizing different purposes, or ordering the purposes in different ways.

There remains, however, the critical question of which languages other than English? The report's answer is to suggest:

> purely on an indicative basis . . . that for the majority of the school population the priorities of the present time might be: two or three languages of ethnic groups within the Australian community — not necessarily the largest groups and not necessarily all of European origin; Japanese, Indonesian and Chinese, as Asian languages of major importance to Australia; French, German, Spanish, Arabic and perhaps Russian, as major world languages and two or three Aboriginal languages determined after consultation with Aboriginal groups.

This formulation is interesting for its acceptance of a conventional categorization of 'community', 'Asian' ('our Asian neighbours'), 'world' and 'Aboriginal' languages which has little analytical or descriptive usefulness. Moreover, it ducks the issue of which two or three 'ethnic languages' might be chosen or even the criteria that might be used for their selection. This reflects a general and fairly inevitable aspect of the language question in Australia, simply about the logistics of servicing such a large number of relatively scattered linguistic communities. A difficulty throughout the report itself is that general statements of goodwill do not seem to be considered in terms of practical and fiscal possibilities.

One problem for languages in Australia and inherent in pluralist multiculturalism is that, in the face of real practical difficulties of implementation, policy-makers can easily advocate self-help on the part of communities and individuals. So a language policy, according to the report, need not require an open-ended and 'huge commitment of public funds' (1984: 2). Yet, since the publication of the report, the Federation of Ethnic Communities' Councils, consistent with the goodwill of the report, has called for considerable increase in funding language programmes. Failing this, in the name of pluralism and community autonomy, after-hours 'ethnic schools' might well have to take on a large number of the responsibilities (often without adequately trained teachers or satisfactory materials) which are properly those of mainstream education systems.

Against this policy situation we have to place the actual experience of language teaching in the name of multiculturalism. The Cahill *et al. Review of the Commonwealth Multicultural Education Program*, under which particular support has been given to 'community languages', reports no 'substantial and lasting change in the Australian schooling system' resulting from the programme (1984: xii). In particular, the review team pointed out that there were few high quality programmes in languages other than English in the primary school (1984: xiv). Even in aggregate terms only 1.6 per cent of primary students in New South Wales were undertaking such courses, of whom 55 per cent were native speakers of those languages. At the secondary level French and German added up to three-quarters of language teaching (1984: 112–14). The team concluded that the Commonwealth's Multicultural Education Program had had little impact on the general pattern of studying languages other than English in the secondary school, although there was some excellent individual programming (1984: 345). In terms of rationale and approach the team underlined some of the concerns we have expressed above in pointing out that they found 'much naivete about the level of proficiency that can be achieved in programs of one hour per week' (1984: 285).

With respect to language maintenance, and despite its obvious positive disposition towards teaching languages other than English, the review team found that students were more keen to learn these languages in primary school than they were in the secondary school (1984: 298). They also found that there was not much evidence of teachers or schools wanting to go beyond minor language sensitization courses (1984: 324). Apart from the area of language maintenance for which there was some (although not overwhelming) support, there was either ambivalence or hostility towards teaching languages that appeared to have a low status in the Australian or international situation (1984: 347). On the issue of practicability the Review concluded that if the goal is that all children in all Australian schools are to have the opportunity to study a language other than English, it would require a massive infusion of funds, leaving aside the issues of whether 'teachers and students want this and whether there are sufficient numbers of teachers to achieve this in the short term' (1984: 336). Another serious area of concern was that of methodology and materials development.

The Multicultural Education Program was abolished in the Federal budget cuts of 1986. State governments were left to pick up some language programmes, but many simply ceased or were suspended, to be revived in some form or other under new National Language Policy funding from 1988. There is still a considerable degree of uncertainty as even the National Language Policy funding is only for three years. As a subject area and in staffing terms there is a strong feeling of vulnerability and marginality.

The most significant recent event in the development of language policy in Australia has been the publication and implementation of the 1987 *National Policy on Languages*. Written by Joe Lo Bianco, and building upon the 1984 *National Language Policy* from the Senate Standing Committee on Education and the Arts, this represents an important development in multiculturalism and language policy, albeit hamstrung by the logistics of political considerations and funding constraints (Lo Bianco, 1987).

In the *National Policy on Languages* we see the development of multi-culturalism away from cultural pluralism towards social equity. The Policy is, of course, very much a compromised document, having had to cover everything from the situation of English, to the place of Aboriginal languages, to the questions of community language maintenance, to learning 'foreign' languages used in Australia, to learning languages of 'economic importance'; to the needs of the communication disabled. It reflects a range of interests such as government pressure to use language as a means of extending economic links with Asia, and the pressure of ethnic community organizations for funding for language maintenance.

Reflecting this comprehensive approach, the broad social goals of language policy are stated by the report to be 'enrichment, economic opportunities, external relations and equality'. Establishing the status of languages in the Australian context, English/Australian English is proclaimed the national language. Aboriginal and immigrant 'community' languages other than English (including the languages of the deaf) are explicitly recognized, their use in education and service delivery advocated, and the right to their maintenance recommended. Specifically, in the teaching and learning of languages, three guiding principles are set out: English for all, support for Aboriginal and Torres Strait Islander languages; and, perhaps most dramatically, a language other than English for all. In the more general area of service delivery the report also notes the importance and roles of interpreting and translating; public libraries; languages in relation to the media and communication technology; and the need to improve language testing procedures.

On 5 June 1987 Federal Cabinet approved $15 million for the implementation of the policy in the remainder of 1987–88 and $28 million in 1988–89. Of this $13 million will go in a full year to an expanded ESL programme; $7.5 million to 'community' languages and 'languages of economic importance'; $1 million towards a National Aboriginal Languages Policy; $2 million to Asian languages; $1.8 million to the formulation of the National Agenda for Multicultural Australia to be produced by the new office for Multicultural Affairs; and $2 million to adult literacy.

Despite the apparent progress, however, this area is still fraught with difficulties. When relatively small amounts of money are translated into concrete programmes, they can easily slip into tokensim. Ethnic communities have already complained bitterly about the funding levels for their languages. There is also an assumption that the states will come to the party and match Federal funding, in education programmes for example. This is not necessarily going to be the case. Moreover, multiculturalism, particularly at the level of practical education programmes, is now seen almost solely to be an element of language policy, rather than vice versa. This has meant the neglect of critical socio-cultural programmes, such as those under the Multicultural Education Program (axed in the 1986 budget cuts) aiming to reduce levels of racism in schools.

The Lo Bianco report, despite the variety and complexity of political pressures that have come to bear on it, represents an important and positive development in policy. The main problems will arise in the exigencies of implementation. A truly equitable multicultural language policy, however, would require a government commitment which, in this political context, we would be naive to expect.

New Attacks on Multiculturalism

Meanwhile, multiculturalism has come under increasing attack in Australia, first in 1984 with the so-called 'Blainey' debate in which well known Melbourne University Professor or History, Geoffrey Blainey, received prominent media exposure for many months over his claim that Australia was accepting too many Asian immigrants (Cope and Morrissey, 1986). In 1988 the debate resurfaced, this time in the Federal Opposition Liberal-National Party Coalition. For the first time since World War II bipartisan support for Australia's immigration and ethnic affairs programmes has ceased. The opposition now advocates reduction in the numbers of Asian immigrants and an end to multiculturalism in favour of a new 'One Australia' policy.

Perhaps of more immediate and direct seriousness for education and language policy, however, a number of prominent academics and educational researchers have come out publicly and argued against the value of specialist multicultural education programmes. Their intervention comes at a time when a vacuum of policy and practice is developing as progressivist education is being wound down. The basis of this winding down is principally fiscal. We have witnessed the end of the Federal Multicultural Education Program, cuts to the Participation and Equity Program, reductions in in-service training programmes, to cite just a few notable examples. But at an official level much of the rhetoric of progressivism continues, except that its basic support structures are being removed, one by one.

Into this vacuum the new critics of multicultural education are somewhat opportunistically moving. One of their emblematic themes is that the conventional wisdom and the theory about educational disadvantage, upon which much educational policy and funding have been based, are mythical. As Trevor Williams argues in his ACER Research Monograph, *Participation in Education*, $429 million or 9 per cent of the Commonwealth's Education Budget was spent in 1984–85 in support of programmes such as the Disadvantaged Schools Program, the Participation and Equity Program and the Rural Schooling Development Program. Yet 'among these eligible to enter higher education . . . there is no socio-economic imbalance to speak of' and 'there is little evidence . . . that gender, geography and ethnicity restrict access to education' (1987: 13–14; 115). Others, notably Birrell, Bullivant and Mistilis, have aimed specifically to show that being of non-English-speaking background is not a factor which produces educational disadvantage. In fact, they argue that this might even be an advantage.

It could be argued that these critics of multicultural education are creating a new myth which is potentially very dangerous. Immigration continues at very high, indeed increasing, levels. Currently the figure is over 100,000 per annum, and the sources for immigrants are more diverse than ever. Not only has Labor shed its traditional misgivings and increased immigration significantly in recent years, but reports indicate that the conservative parties, given the chance, would increase Labor's intake significantly and, despite the professed 'One Australia' policy, this will necessarily come from a wide variety of cultural and linguistic backgrounds. This produces a situation of cultural diversity which needs to be serviced in all core social institutions. It is probably more critical in education than in any other arena, given its socializing role and its role in opening doors to social participation. A society in which immigrants are de facto excluded, or in which existing residents feel bitterly the competition of immigrants in education and on the labour market, could become extremely volatile, unpleasant and unproductive. Education has a crucial role in fostering social cohesion in a multi-ethnic context, ensuring that equitable access is available to all groups. The new critics of progressivist education might well be right to challenge the effectiveness of some of the programmes that have attempted to right educational disadvantage. But the issues those programmes have attempted to address, with some success at least, are still real and pressing. In the rest of this section we will examine in some detail the major arguments of each of these cirtics.

Williams' main argument is that preference produces participation. From the beginning of his report he is mindful of the relationship of research, policy and funding. He sets out to re-examine the cluster of presuppositions upon which special purpose funding has been based. His major finding, in a nutshell, is that although inequality cannot be denied, it cannot be explained in terms of educational disadvantage. Thus the barely hidden implication for access and equity policy is that specialist funding is at best an inefficient use of resources and at worst a waste.

How does Williams reach these conclusions? Success in the early years of schooling is shown to be a key factor contributing to future participation in the post-compulsory phase of education. This reflects poorly on an elementary education system when, as Williams points out, only 37 per cent finish year 12 and only 31 per cent move on the tertiary education in a TAFE college, 9 per cent in a university and 10 per cent in a CAE.

> By age 19 one in every five persons has enrolled in higher education either at a university or a CAE. Three-quarters of these are in degree programs. In each instance the social mix of student populations fails to reflect the social composition of the population as a whole. Seventy five per cent of students in higher education come from white collar backgrounds. Those from wealthy families outweigh those from poorer families by three to one, relatively speaking. Disproportionate [i.e. relatively larger] numbers of persons from non-English-speaking immigrant backgrounds attend. Marginally smaller proportions of rural students are represented. The participation rate of students from non-government, non-Catholic schools is more than three times that of students from government schools. Gender differences are minor overall but smaller proportions of female year 12 graduates enrol in higher education. Level of achievement in school has a marked effect on participation with 10 per cent or more of higher achieving students attending, relative to less than 10 per cent of those in the lowest achievement quartile. And few persons completing less than 12 years of schooling ever enter higher education by age 19. Of those who complete year 12 about 50 per cent enrol in University or CAE. (1987: 113–14)

Setting aside for a moment the alleged disproportionate representation of immigrant groups of non-English-speaking background, the conclusions

Williams draws from what would seem to be damning evidence about the importance, yet relative ineffectiveness, of the education system are peculiar indeed. '. . . While social status restricts participation, it does not restrict access. Social status differences are mostly differences in the preference for education' (1987: 115–16).

This sounds very much like the old story of equality of opportunity and unevenness of individual motivation (which happens to correlate with socio-economic background). What, then, according to Williams, should be done in education to improve retention rates? The implications of Williams' 'findings' are not explicitly spelt out other than to suggest diversification of assessment procedures, curriculum and teaching methods. This suggestion is rather contra-dictory, however, when Williams' own evidence shows that non-government schools which maintain traditional academic curricula and orient themselves to traditional assessment and credentialling produce much higher retention rates. The conclusion, in this context, is extremely curious.

> More generally the best hope for increasing retention at least and both learning and retention at best, are the so-called alternative year 12 programs being mounted in several states. While their success remains to be demonstrated, they seem to be doing all the things one would expect to have an influence on the educational preferences [sic] of young people.

Retention to what end? The 'alternative' subjects in the diversified curriculum practically preclude movement into education in universities and colleges. Williams' conclusions might well be consistent with a thrust that minimizes financial commitment to education. This approach does not require state schools to be resourced in the same way that non-government schools are, with their higher retention rates and credentialling for college and university. Even less does it demand affirmative special resourcing of some schools so that retention rates for post-secondary education are equalized. The report seems to be saying that no amount of funding will change the fact that some groups just do not want to participate. The school's job is to make schooling attractive in relation to what are perceived to be existing 'preferences'.

> Since a policy of multiculturalism prevails, low participation rates by ethnic groups need not be interpreted as being inequitable. They may be, but empirically one cannot separate choice from equity, or the lack of it. If one were to interpret lower participation rates as evidence of inequities when in fact they may be reflections of ethnic group values, then programs of compensation would *de facto* erode the distinctive values of the group in question and, by definition, be discriminatory. (1987: 16)

At this point the education system abdicates any social project other than to maintain differences of inequity and label them ex post facto 'preferences'. In another twist, Williams points to overrepresentation of immigrant groups of non-English-speaking background in post-compulsory education. Consistent with his overall argument, this seems merely to indicate a stronger 'cultural' preference (1987: 70–1).

This generalization falters, however, at a number of key points. First, the sample consists mainly of children whose families are of Greek or Italian origin, and not recent groups such as of Vietnamese, Lebanese or Turkish origin. As we will show in the next section of this chapter, aggregation of specific ethnic groups and generalizing about the 'ethnics' can mask, on the one hand, an uneven distribution between ethnic groups in which some groups achieve academically less well than others and, on the other hand, patterns of differentiation within ethnic groups resulting from factors of socio-economic positioning. Indeed, it seems that certain strata of some longer established groups of non-English-speaking background are performing well at school, while other, particularly more recent, immigrant groups display a distinct pattern of underachievement. Second, among longer established NESB groups there is a greater proportion of Australian-born English mother tongue and bilingual students than among more recent immigrant groups. Third, the statistics on students finishing school in the early 1980s need not tell us anything about the present school situation, in which 'diversified' curriculum reduces students' options in terms of formal academic credentialling (with curriculum forms and expectations polarizing between schools in different socio-economic contexts) and in which the economic situation and prospects of social mobility of newly arrived families are much bleaker than they were for the immigrants of the 1950s and 1960s. Fourth, the report itself contains some evidence contrary to its own generalization, namely, that language difficulties of non-English-speaking background students are only compensated for by the great value placed on education, and that girls of non-English-speaking background seem to be participating less. But this latter factor is claimed to be 'a reduction of advantage rather than an increase in disadvantage' [!] (1987: 70–2).

Another particularly influential commentator on multicultural education has been Melbourne academic, Robert Birrell. His paper, 'The Educational Achievement of Non-English-Speaking Background Students and the Politics of the Community Languages Movement', begins, in much the same vein as Williams, by linking the supposedly misguided assumption of educational disadvantage for groups of non-English-speaking background with a misallocation of resources into specialist programmes, such as community language programmes. The disadvantage argument, Birrell claims, was used by ethnic political lobby groups, but it is not based on any empirical reality. If there had been any initial problems associated with coming from a non-English-speaking background, the crisis is now over for the majority of immigrants because not only are most NESB students now born in Australia, but they are doing better in aggregate than Australians (Birrell, 1987).

Birrell, in fact, wants to make a case for another group — working-class students of English-speaking background. This is now the most consistently disadvantaged group, and education policy and funding aiming at equity should target this group in preference to promoting community languages (1987: 19–20, 28). Birrell oversimplifies this division. In fact, working-class/ethnics is not an either/or opposition. Class and ethnicity intersect, often in such a way that factors of ethnicity compound educational difficulties relating to class.

How does Birrell locate the rise of specialist educational servicing? In general terms he aligns the special educational arrangements for NESB students with ALP policy, anxious to placate the 'ethnic' lobby group and based on a misguided theory of disadvantage. It needs to be pointed out in order to moderate his persistent attacks on the ALP, however, and to set the historical record straight, that much of the current direction of multicultural policy was shaped during the period of the Fraser government and that 85 per cent of 'multicultural' funding goes into English language teaching. Ironically, some of Labor's instinctive political reactions in attempting to dismantle multicultural education are the same as Birrell's: that the working-class are those really in need and that 'ethnics' need no special treatment.

Birrell goes on to argue with the cultural deficit model of disadvantage which has not only been used (appropriately, in Birrell's view) as a basis for ESL teaching, but also in programmes, such as community languages, aimed at bolstering self-esteem and identity through respect for aspects of cultural background such as language and cultural maintenance. He points out that identity and self-esteem are not necessarily enhanced by such strategies. Indeed he provides evidence which suggests that identity and self-esteem increase with success in the school system (1987: 4). For Birrell, the implication emerging from this is the positive value of assimilation. Although assimilation involves hardships, he does not think the process can or should be made easier.

Birrell accepts unequivocally neither the liberal democratic rights arguments about maintaining culture and language nor the arguments about cognitive advantage associated with bilingualism. He suggests that the possible strengths of each argument are not sufficient to take away from resources that would otherwise go towards the enhancement of the core culture in Australia.

Viewing the statistics, Birrell admits that length of residence affects school performance and that there are temporarily lower levels of achievement. But 'the experience of coming from a migrant background does not seem to cripple a student's educational progress', he concludes. There are problems associated with migration, but they fade with time. This, he claims, is underscored by the statistics on post-compulsory education. The groups that performed badly in the 1970s data, particularly the Greeks and Italians, are now overrepresented in the 1980s in HSC participation. 'This achievement occurred despite the lower measured IQs and the lower socio-economic status of students of NES orgin', he claims (1987: 4, 10).

It seems that NESB students ignore the 'reality' of their low IQ levels and stay on at school to the bitter end. None of this leads Birrell to question IQ testing, which in reality measures school experience more than it measures the elusive phenomenon of natural 'ability', nor to problematize the sort of daily school experience these students suffer. Nor does he ask what makes NESB students less 'realistic'. Moreover, Birrell's arguments rest upon a minority of the school population — those who make their way through the higher levels of post-compulsory education. A significant piece of evidence in his arguments is ESB/NESB entry to Monash University in which NESB students are doing better proportionately to their numbers in the population at large. What about the majority of NESB (and ESB) students who do not? This is an issue we will return to in the next section of this chapter.

Birrell recognizes the reality of hardship and discrimination. But because their retention rates to HSC are high, he infers that NESB students are not seriously disadvantaged by this experience. So, it seems, we should live with racism, so long as HSC participation appears equal. Indeed, 'if IQ is taken as a proxy for intelligence, and if the ideal is that students should be encouraged to perform to the best of their ability, then it is the low achieving but relatively "bright" Australians who deserve the extra funds and attention.' Yes, says Birrell, NESB students suffer and there are traumas of transition. But, 'whatever the problems of cultural adjustment, it is possible that migrant children have more resilience and better modes of dealing with these challanges than identity theory postulates' (1987: 12, 14). By extension, this same view of the world could be used to reduce the welfare state further, by removing state assistance to disabled people or scientists so they too could develop greater resilience and modes of dealing with the daily challenges they face.

Real advantage, Birrell concludes, comes from being of NESB. This is evidenced not only in HSC participation but by qualifications and occupation. Of the small proportion of the Australian population now gaining university degrees, people of Greek and Italian backgrounds are marginally over-represented. He does not refer, however, to unemployment figures where NESB youth are also overrepresented (AIMA, 1985).

Family support and 'ethnic' valuing of education and upward mobility have meant that the challenges of migration have often been overcome. 'They have been competing with Australians who have generally lacked the same intensity of parental support or protection from distracting influences, notably peer youth culture.' The schizophrenia involved in living in two worlds is also no problem because 'the private ethnic world of family, community and religion seems to be readily compartmentalized from that of the Australian school without the trauma some have feared' (Birrell, 1987: 20–1). It is almost as if such compartmentalization is a virtue. Apart from ignoring the personal tensions for NESB people which cannot be entirely positive, there is a more general social issue. The supposedly impoverished culture of many Australian homes and schools, exhibiting alienation, individualism and cultural decentredness, might well have been enriched by a society moving towards multiculturalism, rather than arguments like Birrell's that simply pit the interest of one group against another.

Brian Bullivant, a Monash University academic widely published in the area of multicultural education, has also seriously challenged the 'conventional wisdom' about the educational disadvantage of NESB children. In his detailed ethnographic survey of six Melbourne schools, Bullivant claims to have found evidence of overachievement by NESB students, attributable to the 'migrant drive' and the 'ethnic work ethic' (Bullivant, 1986, 1987). His research purportedly found little evidence of discrimination, despite there only being a limited emphasis on multicultural education. In terms of educational achievement, 'ethnic' students showed a preference for staying at school for the HSC, despite the fact that their teachers often did not think they would make it (Bullivant, 1986: 11–13). In contrast, Anglo-Australians seemed to emerge as the 'new self-deprived'.

Stereotyping did appear to be going on and there were complaints of racism and sexism. Although Bullivant claimed that his research was not fine-grained enough to assess the significance of this, he concluded that it was not a deterrent or a handicap. In fact, it might even be an element towards an explanation of NESB educational achievement. He also concluded, however, that Anglo-Australians are prejudiced against Asians and NESB students for their work ethic, and notes prejudice in the other direction as a corollary (1986: 16–17, 24).

The quality of this experience surely does not disprove the validity of special-purpose education programmes. Bullivant's evidence, despite his finding that NESB students suffer no relative disadvantage measured in academic performance, simply underlines the importance of a rejuvenated and redirected socio-cultural dimension of multicultural education. School experience cannot only be measured in terms of academic results. What happens if social tensions emerge, including even a problem of poorly motivated, 'self-deprived Anglos' and intercultural tensions centred on the motivation to succeed? Rather ironically, Bullivant's last word is that the more 'ethnics' assimilate to Australian values/culture, the more they start to approach the norm in terms of work values and academic performance! Does this mean that they, too, can learn to be self-deprived?

The key features of the arguments of the new educational critics are becoming predictable. The last one we will consider here, Nina Mistilis, begins by discussing the supposed myth of ethnic disadvantage which she will subsequently attempt to demystify. The 'left', she claims, has traditionally argued that the migration experience produces 'stunting', 'linguistic deficiencies' and 'low educational attainment' for NESB students. Even the second generation's performance is supposed to be determined by their parents' context. On the contrary, her evidence from the 1981 census shows that 'in respect of tertiary education qualifications, all second-generation origin sub-groups had a rate similar to or higher than [third and subsequent generation Australian-born], and that the second generation is not disadvantaged.' Differentiation by gender also shows that 'most women of NES origins are not disadvantaged'. She concludes:

> The notion that structural and institutional factors in society, the migration experience and personal characteristics of the second generation pre-determine their (low) occupational class position or militate against reasonable educational progress for those of NES origins is not supported in the light of the findings of this paper. (1986: 23, 27)

Mistilis does not go so far as to ascribe a cause to the statistical phenomenon she describes. But the other three writers we have discussed here make a definite causal presumption. The presumption, for all three, is that school achievement is not a product of social structure and the institution of schooling, but 'cultural' factors principally to be located in the dynamics of the family.

Williams, for example, argues that 'social status' is the only factor that seriously restricts participation, but that it does not restrict access. Given equality of opportunity, the problem lies in working-class preferences. These preferences 'reside in both families and students' (1987: 116). Responsibility here is shifted onto the victim, in a variant of the cultural pathology model of social disadvantage (analogous to Moynihan's 'pathological black family' line of reasoning). The most the school can do is diversify curriculum to make schooling more attractive to disadvantaged students. In fact, this cultural mode of argumentation, in which curriculum is diversified to increase retention rates, is a distorted perspective on a social-structural reality in which retention rates are increasingly the result of youth unemployment. Curriculum, in response to this, is diversifying as a logistical necessity. It is not being diversified to increase retention rates for any profound educational reasons but as a reactive holding-job in difficult economic circumstances.

On the question of ethnicity and education, Williams, Bullivant and Birrell all use a cultural pathology model to explain educational success or lack of success, even if their results are the reverse of what one would expect. For example, Bullivant speaks of the 'migrant drive' and the 'ethnic work ethic' on the one hand, and 'self-deprivation' on the other, clearly ascribing school achievement to familial-cultural factors rather than institutional educational factors (1986: 1, 22–3). Similarly, Birrell views the problem in terms of a lack or a surfeit of 'family discipline', 'ethnic pride' and 'social values' (1987: 18, 20). Aside from the problem of the simplistic reversal of NESB/ESB, educational disadvantage/advantage equations which we will analyze in the next section of this chapter, our point here is that the mode of analysis is narrowly cultural rather than social-structural. In other words, these analyses are based on a theory which locates the roots of social access in the familial-cultural rather than the school system and structural socio-economic relations. The victims and the successes of the education system have their own cultural pathology to blame or thank. In other words, the school system has a limited role or no role to play in bringing about social equity. This theoretical consequence is entirely consistent with the explicit political thrust of these analyses: that educational programmes aiming to right supposed disadvantage are inappropriate and ineffective.

The Sociology of Cultural and Linguistic Diversity in Australian Education

There is nothing unexpected or original in what the new educational critics are saying: that there is considerable intergenerational mobility for NESB children through education. This is predictable in the context of the migration process and the long post-war boom. Moreover, many progressivist educational programmes centring on cultural identity and language maintenance are indeed often problematic. But there is a sophisticated debate on this subject going on within the ranks of those who support multicultural education. Socio-economic positioning is a very important determinant of educational success. This, we know, is a truism. The message, however, of the new critics that there is no longer a role for multicultural education is very dangerous, even if it is a handy rationale for funding cutbacks. We will now discuss contrary evidence. This clearly shows that forty years of mass immigration have produced an educational situation in Australia fraught with problems and complexity.

First, educational advantage and disadvantage are distributed unequally between groups of different cultural and linguistic background. This uneven distribution of performance is considered by Williams, Bullivant and Birrell to indicate that 'ethnicity' is a general factor which predicates educational success.

This oversimplifies and distorts a complex situation. While some NESB groups appear to be doing well in terms of educational performance and intergenerational mobility, and on average NESB students on some measures can be shown to be doing as well as or better than their ESB counterparts, other groups are doing very poorly. A sample based on some major well established ethnic groups (such as Williams') can seriously misrepresent the situation. His results do not at all mean that generalizations about 'ethnicity' can be made. An interesting example of this problem of uneven distribution is Barbara Horvarth's disaggregation of NSW Department of Education statistics which, purportedly, showed no average NESB disadvantage measured in class placement in streamed schools. In fact, reworking the same statistics, she showed that, although some NESB groups (such as those of Greek background) seemed to be performing better than average, others were performing significantly worse (for example, those of Aboriginal, Maltese and Lebanese background) (1986). Similarly, Hugo's recent analysis of census statistics shows overall intergenerational upward mobility for migrants, comparing first and second generation educational qualifications. Nevertheless, although second generation immigrants of Asian (14.0 per cent) and Polish (13.3 per cent) background have almost twice the probability of second generation Australian born (7.8 per cent) of having educational qualification of diploma or better, the figures are only 2.3 per cent for those of Maltese background and 5.3 per cent for those of Italian background (Hugo, 1987: 253). Recent research by the Inner London Education Authority shows a similar uneven distribution in which, to varying degrees, African, Asian, Indian, Greek, Pakistani and South-East Asian background groups perform better than average in end-of-school examinations than their ESB peers. On the other hand, Turkish, Caribbean and particularly Bangladeshi pupils perform worse (ILEA, 1987). It is critical, however, that this phenomenon of uneven distribution is not put down to cultural pathology, but to the complex overlay of class (homeland and immigrant) and ethnicity, in which, in all probability, class is the more critical variable, albeit frequently expressed through cultural-ethnic identity and aspirations.

Second, we simply do not have adequate statistics to generalize about NESB as a general enabling/disabling factor in Australian education. There is considerable evidence, however, that in many circumstances it is definitely disabling. Notwithstanding the serious difficulty of uneven distribution, for every statistic and every claim that NESB students in aggregate are doing well, and that there is therefore no special 'ethnic' problem in education, there are counter-claims and counter-statistics. Even some aggregated NESB figures often show the opposite to what the new educational critics claim to be the case. For example, the NSW Department of Education class placement study shows that far fewer NESB students make it into selective high schools. To take just two examples of a phenomenon which this survey showed to be true of all Sydney selective schools, the selective Fort Street High School has 40.5 per cent of its students of NESB, while the contiguous general high schools average 63.8 per cent. The selective Sydney Boys High has 22.8 per cent and Sydney Girls High 16.9 per cent, while contiguous general high schools have a staggering 64.3 per cent of NESB (*Sydney Morning Herald*, 8 May 1987). Not only does this say a lot about the effects of the school system on NESB students; it also throws into serious question the impact on NESB students of the 'aptitude' tests which determine placement in selective schools. Our problem is not to pit statistics against statistics. The truth is that we do not have adequate statistics on school achievement (not retention rates, which are very problematic, as we will argue below) to be able to make valid generalizations. Until researchers have access to results comparable across the educational system (such as School Certificate moderator spreads correlated with census data or HSC results disaggregated by ethnicity), we can only conclude from some fragmentary evidence that a few NESB students are doing well and a lot are doing badly.

Third, intergenerational mobility assisted by education, such that it is, does not compensate for the undeniable relative immobility of the first generation of immigrants. Even if there is some intergenerational mobility through education in some cases, the picture for the first generation is almost universally bleak. Birrell, for example, is willing to admit this, but argues that second generation success compensates for first generation disadvantage. Despite Birrell's resignation, the education system could make an impact on all these groups to bring them towards the figures for second generation Australian-born, even adult migrants for whom English learning and higher education are no less important needs than they are for the rest of the population. The first generation, it should also be remembered, includes those who migrated as babies and those who entered the Australian school system mid-stream, as well as adults. Against the Australian-born figure of 7.9 per cent, 2.8 per cent of first generation people from the Middle East have an educational qualification of diploma or better, 1.4 per cent of Greeks, 1.6 per cent of Yugoslavs and 1.5 per cent of Maltese, to give just a few examples (Hugo, 1987: 253). The situation is even worse when we consider that many of these would be overseas qualifications which are not adequately recognized in Australia or not updated to meet the requirements of Australian conditions. No amount of second generation mobility can compensate for this first generation experience. Added to this, first generation immigrants are the group with the fastest growing unemployment as the traditional areas of unskilled work in secondary industry are those most seriously affected by the current economic restructuring. With inadequate English, first generation immigrants have inadequate access to meagre training resources.

Fourth, NESB students' mobility patterns in education are in part the long-term result of the post-war boom. This pattern has not necessarily carried though in the economically less steady years from the mid-1970s. In the 1970s and 1980s evidence shows that the trend to NESB upward mobility is being reversed. The immigrant families of the 1950s and 1960s did achieve considerable economic and social mobility, principally through the secondary labour market. The relative success of some of their children at school attests to this. But in the economic circumstances of the late 1970s and 1980s there is no certainty that the same mobility will occur for more recent immigrants, even in the long term. Not only are there economic indicators which point to this (DIEA, 1985), but this might well be a factor which could go some of the way to explain the uneven distribution of levels of educational achievement among NESB groups. Recent curriculum changes seem only to be compounding this situation. The demise of comprehensive curriculum, to be replace by diversified, 'relevant' curriculum, means that a new streaming is emerging which now condemns even the few who might have succeeded in schools in poor socio-economic circumstances to the 'Veggie English' and macrame curriculum. The educational mobility of the 1950s, 1960s and early 1970s was in part made possible by comprehensive curriculum. Diversified curriculum, on the other hand, reflects the 'holding job' schools now have in economic circumstances which, for those at the bottom of the ladder, are unlikely to improve in the foreseeable future. Parents' intuitive reaction to the social function of progressivist curriculum is surely based on some element of truth. A national poll conducted for the Australian Teachers' Federation showed that:

— private schools rated better than public schools;
— most people would send their children to private schools if they could afford to;
— two-thirds of those polled said government primary schools were not meeting their needs because there was not enough teaching of fundamental skills. (*Sydney Morning Herald*, 29 April 1987)

It is particularly clear that NESB parents in high NESB low socio-economic circumstances perceive curriculum diversification to be a handicap to their children. They frequently go to extraordinary lengths to finance their children through a private school education.

Fifth, high rates of NESB school retention do not necessarily imply commensurate academic performance. All the evidence points to the fact that NESB parents have high aspirations for their children (Burke and Davis, 1985; Martin and Meade, 1979, Sturman, 1986). This is a phenomenon integral to the migration process itself. But the subsequent high retention rates in post-compulsory education do not necessarily imply school success. So 7.8 per cent of the second generation Australian-born have achieved an educational qualification of diploma or better, and 3.4 per cent of those over 15 years of age are still at school. But for second generation people of Greek background a comparable 7.2 per cent hold these qualifications, even though 24.3 per cent are still at school. For Italians, the figures are 5.3 per cent and 15.4 per cent respectively (Hugo, 1987: 253). Even taking demographic spread into account, we are simply not seeing final results which in any way correspond to the school retention rates for these particular groups. To take one particular example, a newspaper report on Marrickville High School, a very high NESB density, low socio-economic context school in Sydney's inner west, tells how 74 per cent of senior students go on to senior school against a national average of 49 per cent. The principal explained that 'migrant families generally want a lot of their children, and they see education as a key to these things' (*Sydney Morning Herald*, 29 April 1987). Yet this school has one of the poorest results in New South Wales measured by HSC scores and university entrance. Retention, moreover, is not simply a function either of school success or of aspirations. As we argued earlier, retention is more a function of levels of youth unemployment than any new success on the part of the education system. Furthermore, despite the distortions produced by using school retention rates as evidence of NESB success, these rates are dramatically variable in ways that happen to coincide with the class and ethnic context of a school. The 'survival ratio' of year 9 to year 12 entry is 13 per cent at Francis Greenway High, 14 per cent at Mount Druitt High and 15 per cent at Shavery High. On the other hand, the ratio is 97 per cent at Randwick Boys High and 93 per cent at Mosman High (*Sydney Morning Herald*, 20 February 1987). None of these is a selective school. For the schools with poor survival ratios it happens that NESB and working-class demographic context substantially overlap.

Sixth, those students of NESB who succeed do so against longer odds. Even apart from the question of racism, which we will discuss next, success for NESB students often reflects parental pressure and a high degree of motivation, against longer odds than ESB students. The Campbell Review of ESL paints a depressing picture, especially for NESB students, even those Australian-born, as they enter the senior school (Campbell *et al.*, 1984). They have to fight against their supposed IQs, and those who 'self-select' academic success through dogged determination more often than not do so across the maths/science nexus, being somewhat less hampered in these subjects by their language difficulties. Of course, commentators like Birrell and Bullivant recognize this, but simply consider success against longer odds to be a virtue. Not only is this rather callous, but it ignores those who, unjustly, do not manage to succeed.

Seventh, racism is still a serious problem in Australian schools. NESB students face racism in their school experience, both structural racism in the 'coincidence' of high NESB population density, socio-economic context and alternative school curriculum, and high levels of attitudinal racism, albeit frequently in subtle forms which produce ghettoization. One student sums it all up, in a report by Henry and Edwards: 'A lot of people are going through hell because of their background' (1986). On the other hand, the perceived motivation and relative success of few NESB students, against long odds, produces an apartheid of sentiment in schools, with longer established ESB students expressing bitter resentment and NESB students expressing a degree of cultural contempt for their ESB peers. The seriousness of this situation in a society that has relied so heavily on mass immigration, cannot be overestimated. Racism is not simply a problem of 'migrant disadvantage'. Moreover, a spaghetti and polka multiculturalism, aiming to produce 'intercultural understanding', is not only counter-productive in constructing cultural stereotypes, but mis-represents students' fundamental concerns with bread and butter issues of education and employment (Kalantzis and Cope, 1981). Racism is not a gratuitous slandering of cultural phenomena. It is a bitter misapprehension of deeper lines of social division.

Eighth, generalization about the performance of ethnic groups ignores the fact that they themselves are deeply divided both socio-economically and by school performance. Even if we accept the statistics that some NESB groups are doing well in education relative to the ESB population, this generalization refers only to a very small minority of each group. So what if 7.2 per cent of second generation people of Greek background with a qualification of diploma of better compares favourably with the 7.8 per cent of their ESB counterparts, or the 5.3 per cent of second generation people of Italian background? What about the remaining 90 + per cent? Parity of performance does not mean there is no project for multicultural education. Indeed, the dismal non-performance, either in absolute terms or relative to aspirations, is a cause for great concern. As a preface to our elaboration of this point, we should note that by Western world standards, Australia's educational performance is very poor. It ranks lowest among OECD countries in public expenditure on education: 5.8 per cent of GDP compared to Sweden's 9.1 per cent, for example (Commonwealth Schools Commission, 1985: 189). This is even significantly lower than the USA's public expenditure with its extensive private university and school system. When we put together the facts that Australia is simply being left behind in the high-tech stakes and that Australia has had the largest immigration programme of any country (bar the peculiar case of Israel) in the post-war period relative to its population base point, the situation is nothing short of disastrous. The old reserve army of unskilled immigrant labour is no longer needed. We could have an economic and social calamity on our hands within a few years. To concretize the situation for the 70 per cent of ESB and second generation NESB people with no post-school educational qualifications, the reasons for this in each case are very different. Certain aspects of ESB working-class culture, education and structural context portend limited education. The reasons for limited education for NESB students are very different from ESB working-class groups: language learning context, racism, the particular non-commensurability of family culture and the culture of educational success and so on. This is not to deny that the powerful common factor of social class is at play for both ESB and NESB groups. But, critically, for NESB groups, issues of ethnicity and class compound in complex and specific ways. Generalizations based on university entrance, which make conclusions about 'Greek' educational success, for example, aggregate a group which is significantly class-divided. Nor can such 'findings' be taken to imply that we can forget about the special needs of the vast majority of school students of Greek background. No simple generalizations can be made from comparative, aggregated results. A complex variety of factors compounds educational disadvantage.

Ninth, gender further complicates the ethnicity-class relationship. There is a great deal of evidence of sexism in education. This is an especially acute problem both for many NESB girls and for their male peers, particularly given the ambiguity of non-sexist education policy and the ethnic cultural maintenance strategies that have been an aspect of multiculturalism (Kalantzis, 1988a). Many cultures, including the dominant culture, integrally include sexism. In terms of academic performance there is also considerable evidence that the aspiration-performance gap for NESB girls is particularly great (Burgess, Parker and Rickert, 1985).

Tenth, in the middle range of post-compulsory education — technical and trades qualifications — NESB students are underrepresented. At the same time, NESB youth unemployment is unusually high. TAFE participation of NESB students has been shown to be poor (Burke and Davis, 1985). On the other hand, in what is surely a corollary to this, for some NESB groups, very high rates of unemployment are in evidence. Even though a larger than average minority of Asians are gaining higher educational qualifications, 16.9 per cent are unemployed (twice the national average), including 40.6 per cent of Vietnamese. As well as uneven distribution among ethnic groups, we are clearly seeing here an uneven distribution within groups. This situation is probably even worse than the unemployment statistics reveal, given the particular problem of hidden unemployment in some NESB groups (AIMA, 1986). This unemployment situation also explains, to a significant degree, high NESB school retention rates.

We feel this evidence all adds up to a case for the need for a rejuvenated multicultural education, contrary to the partial evidence (in both senses) of its new critics. We have also alluded to some of the problems of progressivist and multicultural curriculum. It is to this question — of analyzing multicultural education practice to date and forging concrete ways forward — that we will turn in the next section of this chapter.

But returning for a moment to the new critics of multicultural education, both Birrell and Bullivant include critical commentary on multicultural education. Birrell questions the psychological assumption that fostering ethnic identity and cultural maintenance through education produces increased school achievement. He points, on the contrary, to the success of Chinese, Japanese and Jewish students in American education, despite the explicit assimilationist of 'Americanizing' values that have dominated the US school system (1987: 4). The link of cultural identity and self-esteem to educational achievement is, indeed, unproved. In fact, self-esteem might well be more a consequence of achievement in mainstream social and educational terms. Moreover, Birrell's fundamental concern with social access, rather than cultural maintenance as a priority of the school system, is not altogether misplaced. But his explicit advocation of assimilation necessarily would involve a revival of racist assumptions about superiority/inferiority and the alienation of culturally 'different' students, which excludes in reality while assimilating in appearance. Multiculturalism and social equity are not mutually exclusive goals, as Birrell implies.

Similarly, Bullivant notes the ineffectiveness of multicultural education in some of the schools he surveyed, despite evidence of racism. He comments:

> a curriculum that is unduly weighted with a selection of the expressive aspects from the cultural stock, and stresses life styles may not provide young people with sufficient instrumental survival knowledge to compete for life chances when they leave school.... Equipping children with a surfeit, say, of ethnic community languages, history and music in an attempt to improve their cultural awareness, may be of far less survival value in the final analysis than mathematics, skills in using computers and accountancy. (1987: 49)

Be this as it may, we strongly oppose Birrell's and Bullivant's implication that no multicultural education is needed. Rather, multicultural education needs to be strengthened to include a more powerful equity component. As their 'no programme' perspective fits well with their 'no problem' analysis of the situation of NESB students, so our perspective of equitable multiculturalism is founded on an analysis of the serious, complex and ongoing educational needs of both NESB and ESB students.

The old, pluralist multiculturalism, resting heavily on the presentation of different cultural identities and the maintenance of community languages, does not necessarily solve the problem. Indeed, it often creates many more problems than it solves. Our concern is that a two-pronged multiculturalism emerges from the failure of progressivist, 'diversified, culturally relevant' curriculum, weakened further, beyond its own inherent limitations, by fiscal cutbacks. This multiculturalism should:

1. aim at social equity through multicultural curriculum strategies; and
2. tackle the pressing problem of racism directly.

We would contend that multicultural education needs to move beyond a simple pluralist model which is very vulnerable to attack in the current political and economic context. While appreciating a great deal of validity in many of the propositions of pluralist multiculturalism and respecting its historic contribution in the general development of multiculturalism in education in Australia, we want to argue for an equitable multiculturalism. Educators have a duty to build upon the positive achievements of pluralist multiculturalism in order to make multiculturalism a stronger and more demonstrably effective and efficient process in schools. It is time to move on. Indeed, we would like to suggest there are positive indications that we are moving on, the Lo Bianco *National Policy on Languages* being important evidence of this.

The late 1980s represent a watershed in this field. Official policy statements have in part resulted in an atmosphere of acceptance of multiculturalism in schools. In practical terms the only funding now available in the area of multicultural education is for ESL and LOTEs. The squeeze on these funds, however, means that they are directed to the most urgent areas of need. The practical inability to secure a mandatory second language for all students continues to limit the status and delivery of LOTEs. The concept of 'language of economic importance' has also shifted emphases and favoured languages. Materials development has been slow and not coordinated to support the programmes that have already been begun. In view of these difficulties and in response to the critics of specialist multicultural education programmes, the next part of this chapter examines alternative approaches to language in multicultural education.

Pluralism and Equity: Multicultural Education and Linguistic Diversity

As is clear the above historical introduction, central to the rise of multiculturalism in Australia have been increasing demands that languages other than English be taught in schools. Whereas all language teaching in the past had been 'foreign' language teaching to formal academic ends, there are now persistent demands that 'community' languages and 'languages of economic importance' be taught. Multilingualism is an aspect of multiculturalism. Variety of linguistic background should be serviced and supported in a number of social areas, including education.

There is nothing exceptionable about these claims. One can critically distinguish from the debates outlined above, however, that there are orientations to pluralistic and equitable multiculturalism. Different rationales in teaching languages in schools produce different processes and different outcomes. Curriculum process in language teaching should be based on the premise that linguistic life histories are not simply to be celebrated and reproduced. An equitable approach to the language question should be interventionary.

In the teaching of English, curriculum should not be diversified on the presupposition that different students are inevitably destined to different educational and social outcomes, as practically occurs in the distinction of traditional academic English teaching from 'communication skills' (how to fill out Social Security forms or apply for a job). This is to advocate neither a return to the traditional academic curriculum nor the universal teaching of 'standard' English. But there are some communicative-cognitive forms essential to effective and genuinely open social participation. This does not necessarily have to involve middle-class accent, style or the high culture of traditionally empowering usages of English, but certain more fundamental tools of sociolinguistic access that the traditional academic curriculum differentially dispensed to some groups but not others.

To achieve these fundamentally common educational ends, different pedagogies will need to be employed. English as a Second Language teaching is an excellent example of this. Its ultimate end should be, in basic linguistic-cognitive terms, no less than any other English teaching. ESL is a specialist servicing to cater to real plurality and to intervene in order to make education more equitable.

For effective teaching of native languages other than English and the non-interruption of lines of cognitive-linguistic and social development, various forms of maintenance or transitional bilingualism need to be experimented with. Furthermore, all languages other than English should be taught to a standard and degree of intellectual seriousness equivalent to that traditionally expected in foreign language teaching. The ultimate goal of such teaching should not necessarily be 'community' forms of the language, but 'standard' forms not defined traditionally or by status but by linguistic-cognitive generality. In this context, different 'community' genres and usages can be analyzed and adapted. None of this necessarily means traditionalism in terms of pedagogy. Differential servicing is necessary to achieve these ends, depending on the forms of language used by the students. But the end of the process need not simply be to reproduce these forms.

In practical terms, the following measures are also required in the move to a more equitable approach to teaching languages other than English: the development of evaluative devices to assess the nature and form of first language usage; pedagogical processes which introduce students to a variety of genres and forms of the language; the availability of languages other than English to all students for the intellectual reasons conventionally ascribed to 'foreign' language teaching and thus, for practical reasons, not necessarily one's native language; careful evaluation of educational outcomes; parallel socio-cultural programmes that assist students to investigate, among other things, the nature of language in culture and society, racism and intergenerational cultural maintenance or conflict. For the sake of efficiency and effectiveness, this last quest cannot be an isolated objective of language teaching or even one that language teaching itself can achieve.

Given the centrality of English in Australia and the large number of students needing specialist programmes, some serious attention needs to be given to developing models which link and exemplify different methodologies and content. To date English as a Second Language has had marginal status in terms of research, training and professional accreditation and reward. With the paucity of research and materials development in this area, the mainstreaming movement again could further inadvertently reduce the impact of positive movements already underway. Curriculum development in English as a foreign language would also be enhanced by a coordinated cross-fertilization of other than English curriculum programmes, particularly with regard to the process of language acquisition in general. The debate between traditional and more recent variants of communicative methodologies has yet to be resolved in a fruitful way.

While variant pedagogies and specialist educational techniques are necessary to service adequately the linguistic plurality that exists in Australia, the aim of all language learning should be towards forms of language that provide broadest and most potent cognitive and communicative usefulness together with initiation to a range of linguistic genres, idioms and types of discourse. Given the logistical impossibility of meeting pluralistic rationales about servicing of native languages, the educational benefits of learning any other language in a systematic and sustained way should be open to all students throughout schooling. For certain categories of students, transitional or maintenance bilingual programmes might also be important to prevent disruption of lines of cognitive development on entry to school.

Conclusions

One of the principal purposes of Chapters 1, 2 and 3 has been to present alternative approaches to multiculturalism and multilingualism, and suggest possible consequences of each approach. Chapter 1 contrasted simple pluralist and holistic views of the concept of culture for multiculturalism. Chapter 2 examined the practical ways in which various approaches along the lines outlined in Chapter 1 have manifested themselves in Sweden, Canada and the United States, and highlighted specific features of the debate. This chapter has discussed some of the perceptions and the alternatives available for Australian language policy-makers and practitioners.

In the language question there seems to be extremes of argumentation, which we will represent here by two quotes about the English language. The first is from Chipman, about the 1984 *Report on a National Language Policy*.

> By and large the Committee rejected, albeit cautiously, the pernicious doctrine of dialectical and sociolectical egalitarianism, according to which each sub-group's particular variety of English (e.g. 'western suburbs English', 'working class urban English') is just as 'valid', and therefore worthy of institutional preservation and reinforcement through the school system, as any other, and in particular as the 'prestigious' Standard Australian English. The Commonwealth Schools Commission advised the Senate Commission (para 4.18) that 'the tendency in the past has been to consider the dialect as a defective form of English which required correction'. The Commission criticised (ibid.) the approach whereby the school 'attempted to eradicate what was considered to be (sic) incorrect pronunciation, grammar, and use of vocabulary'. That a major educational bureaucracy such as the Commonwealth Schools Commission should actually criticise schools for attempting to correct what they 'consider' (might they not be right?) incorrect grammar etc. is indicative of the extent to which educational rot is contributing to the wilful destruction of standards in Australian schools . . . .

> The Committee urged that Aboriginal languages, or some of them, should be available for matriculation level examinations in the way other 'community languages' are available. Perhaps they should, but I would have hoped (perhaps naively) that an absurd assumption of linguistic and cultural egalitarianism would not be the major premise on which to base a case for including a particular language study in the most senior school examination. (1985: 16–17)

At another extreme, we have wild proponents of simple pluralism, as exampified by Rigg and Kazemek:

> We are angry. We are angry at the circularity of reasoning which makes assumptions about people based on their socio-economic status, and

then uses these assumptions to construct a hierarchy of functional competency. As academics, we are angry that correlations are being passed off and accepted as causes. We are angry at the unquestioning . . . materialistic   definition   of   success; . . . unexamined assumptions about what sorts of functions characterize adult life; . . . assumptions that there is and should be one national standard for all people, one way of doing things . . . .

In 1975 Northcutt wrote, 'It is surprising, perhaps even shocking, to suggest that approximately one of five Americans is incompetent or functions with difficulty.' One in five. That's 23 million . . . . When U.S. Secretary of Education Bell announced the Literacy Initiative in the fall of 1983, he said, 'You have heard before this shocking statistic and I repeat it simply for emphasis: 23 million Americans are functionally illiterate.' . . .

There probably are a great many Americans who need help, some needing help with literacy skills, but before any of us repeat that figure, let's check it out. Before we label people as 'illiterate' or 'functionally incompetent,' let's look at how individuals function in a wide variety of specific situations with a wide variety of specific purposes. We don't have 23 million 'functionally illiterate' adults, as Bell would have us believe. We have an uncounted number of real people, each one using literacy in different ways. To lump any number of people together as illiterate or incompetent denies them the respect that they deserve, that each of us deserves. (Rigg and Kazemek; 1985: 5–7)

It takes little imagination to transfer the general socio-linguistic stance of each quote into a view of the place of minority languages in a Western industrial society.

Neither extreme is a workable or equitable base for language policy and practice. Chipman's obsessive denial of multiculturalism, based on an openly avowed dislike of egalitarianism, involves denying people services relevant to their specific needs and a pedagogical stance which, in effect, militates against access to social goods for significant proportions of people from minority language backgrounds. Ironically, however, the other extreme also denies access to social goods by condoning structural and cultural relations (communities are never isolated) which reproduce inequity. Between these extremes, there is, however a middle course. Multiculturalism can be a policy for social participation and equity. Just as the modern world has simultaneously unified humankind structurally and made a level of cultural diversity an integral feature of everyday life, so policy-makers should ensure that the unification is equitable and that diversity, while being a right, is without prejudice to equity.

We can follow through three sets of consequences of each of the above approaches. A Chipmanesque approach to the diversity of cultural and linguistic backgrounds in the Australian population, for example, would include a programme of teaching 'Standard Australian English', and more generally, a cultural policy of what some members of his Australian neo-conservative school of thought call 'anglomorphism'. This is almost precisely a theoretical repetition of the policy and practice previously called 'assimilation'. Possibly, perhaps probably, such a policy would not consider specialist ESL teaching to have educational validity. Rather, it could postulate that working towards 'standards' in English, and teaching all students through a 'traditional academic' curriculum, might well stop the supposed educational rot. In this scenario language teaching other than English would be 'foreign' language teaching of a traditional academic variety. Such a traditional education would presumably allow the process of 'anglomorphism' to take its 'natural' course, and give those of non-English-speaking background with genuine talent equal opportunity to win the prizes in the lottery of life.

Chipman's view in 1985 is far from being the conventional wisdom, in a way that it might have been in 1965. But, if multiculturalism fails to establish itself as a rigorous area of research and an effective concept for social policy, there is no reason to think that views of this kind might not become conventional wisdom again in the next few decades. It is the relative weaknesses and lack of clarity in the field that he and his colleagues so sharply focus upon. We should look carefully at the United States, where the educational reforms of the 1960s and 1970s are now giving way to a 'back to basics' and 'English Only' movements.

At the other extreme, radical pluralism is based on a populist democratic assumption that speech communities are made by their members rather than social circumstances, and we are to respect the autonomy and validity of the elected languages of individuals or groups. Of course, against Chipman's arguments there is much to be said for this view. Attempts to impose 'standard' middle-class professional forms of English upon working-class groups through traditional curricula and upon people of non-English-speaking background have not, by and large, produced significant linguistic or cultural shifts. This is not just for structural reasons, but also because such attempts are simply bad pedagogy. It is important to build upon and develop existing traditions and cultures, rather than to work from hidden agendas of prejudice and condemnation.

On the other hand, speech communities are not isolated. They often reflect and reproduce structural relations and patterns of inequity. In the field of teaching first languages other than English, a teaching programme might attempt little more than to reproduce the particular form of language used in the domestic situation. But this language might not be adequate for technical, academic or formal use, in either Australia or the place of language origin. It might not extend socio-linguistic range and cognition. At the same time, simply reproducing non-standard English, might similarly deny students eventual access to further education and to halls of power, where there are not only unfortunately prejudicial markers of status (such as accent) but also forms of thought and social manipulation embodied in language that have a more universal usefulness in an industrial socio-linguistic setting and that should not be the preserve of any particular social group.

Striking a middle course, however, both the *Report on a National Language Policy* (Senate Standing Committee, 1984) and the more recent Lo Bianco report (1987) point out that a notion of equity underpins the policy of multicultural-ism. If this is the course to be taken by policy-makers and practitioners, a number of consequences follow, some of which are already in train or in embryo in Australia. First, specialist ESL teacher training, in-servicing and materials development are essential. One can only point to the results of the Campbell *et al.* report to support such a proposition (1984). Second, if this middle course is taken, languages other than English should be taught more on long-term peda-gogical and social grounds than on short-term political grounds. Consequently, all such teaching should be on the scale conventionally expected in foreign language teaching. There should be no hierarchy of prestige or of ultimate intellectual rigour and seriousness. This is not to say that various pedagogies and starting points might be required according to needs. Such programmes should not, in the long term, simply reproduce existing usages and genres. They should extend language usage both for cognitive reasons and to extend the realm of possible social applicability and thus social access. This will require full-time and itinerant teachers, and coordination which ensures that the size of a language population is not the dominant basis for the selection of language. It requires that criteria for selecting a language be established, that teacher training be extended, and that materials be developed at both centralized and decentra-lized bases.

In terms of teaching second languages other than English, it is arguable that using small-scale language teaching as a token to multiculturalism eventually might well prove to be counter-productive. It might seem to be unnecessary special treatment or awaken people to more serious needs through the experience of poorly satisfying previously inarticulate needs. Moreover, there is no certainty that cultural appreciation and tolerance come through language teaching alone, least of all through a superficial or tokenistic variety. Serious language policy needs to be closely linked into a programme of social literacy across the curriculum, such that issues of non-racism and multiculturalism are explicit and integral parts of the content of all language teaching, as well as other subject areas.

Having traced the nature and consequences of these three scenarios, we should sound a note of caution. It is all too easy to condemn the practices of language models that have emerged in the past decade. But, as a substantially new area of social policy in Australia, we have to give credit to those who have made space for experimentation, those who have fostered the emergence of multilingualism and multiculturalism as viable policies and practices. There is still a long way to go.

It is inevitable that as a new practice struggles to establish itself it will suffer mistakes and celebrate successes. This book aims to contribute by highlighting some of the vexing issues, and by an examination of the relationship of the theory with the practice. It has concentrated on the educational issues around the language question, particularly with regard to schools, but also around the question of the maintenance of minority languages in general.

4
Evaluating Language Proficiency

Mainstream social institutions have ignored until recently the reality of cultural and linguistic diversity brought about by post-war mass migration. In the arena of education, for example, standardized forms of curriculum and assessment, in a single national language, reflected the dominant ideology of an era in which the homogenizing process of the 'melting pot' was supposed to be at work. However, since the cultural and linguistic impact of immigration has grown more and more significant, there has been an increasing recognition of the reality and lasting nature of diversity. Changes in curriculum and language assessment have reflected this recognition. In Australia and the United States, for example, there has been a 'progressivist' movement which has diversified curriculum with a move away from centralized, core curriculum to locally produced, 'relevant' forms of curriculum and assessment. Standardized, objective assessment should be, it is argued, replaced by ongoing, informal procedures that provide subjective accounts of individual progress.

Yet the growing recognition and servicing of cultural and linguistic diversity have their own limits. To test or assess in ways which are culturally and linguistically relative, can also be at the expense of measuring those areas of linguistic skill necessary for educational success, those skills required for social access and social equity. The traditional, standardized, linguistically and culturally biased assessment procedures excluded large social groups from success in the education system, and we are certainly not arguing for a return to these measures. However, new mechanisms of language learning and assessment, which recognize the reality of pluralism and reward students in terms relative to cultural linguistic background, equally can exclude certain groups from access to mainstream social and educational institutions, but this time under the veil of democratic rhetoric.

This chapter will discuss the difficulties of pluralized, differentiated forms of language pedagogy and assessment. It will suggest that if testing is to have educational legitimacy, either as a way of setting curriculum goals and diagnosing language difficulties, or by introducing the possibility of improving standards, then it can only succeed on the basis of a well articulated curriculum. More specifically, it will report on the content and results of language tests that we designed as part of the research project undertaken by us for the Australian Department of Immigration and Ethnic Affairs to investigate the relation of community languages and mainstream culture.

Background to the Research

As part of its responsibility for immigrant settlement policy and its interest in language and multicultural policy, the Department of Immigration and Ethnic Affairs resolved to undertake a national survey of five linguistic groups in Sydney and Melbourne, focusing on attitudes towards language maintenance. Funding limitations, however, reduced this intention to a survey of two languages in one region. The languages chosen were Macedonian and German, taken to be representative of extremes in the range of languages other than English present in the Australian context: Macedonian being the language of generally more recently arrived immigrants, complicated by dialect divisions and only recently standardized in its place of origin; German, on the other hand, representing an older, more established language, for a long time part of mainstream foreign language learning. The area decided upon for the survey was the Wollongong-Shellharbour region of New South Wales.

The narrowing down of the research project to this point, despite the best of intentions on the part of the officers of the Department of Immigration and Ethnic Affairs, is instructive. It forces one to ask what is possible and what will be funded in this area? We know that good strategy always has to demand what exceeds the immediately possible, and in the area of 'community languages' this is very much the case. It is not at all unusual, particularly in this area, for the desirable to be drastically reduced to what is claimed to be possible or reasonable under the circumstances. Even though we might lament this, we must also be aware of what is practicable, and of how to facilitate, carefully and successfully, the implementation of practical initiatives.

Initially, our brief was principally to survey attitudes to community languages in order to make some contribution of a scientific nature. Scientific, unfortunately often only means 'expressed in numbers'. But we found, even in the way of quantitative work, relatively little Australian research to support many of the new emphases and directions in the drive for 'community languages'.

The emphasis on 'attitudes' is, of course, in keeping with the fashionable notions of 'needs', 'relevance' and 'community involvement'. But that attitudes were conceived to be the central question in the language debate indicates a critical dilemma which is the central question of this book: whether 'community languages' are a political palliative or a pedagogical imperative. Insofar as the maintenance of 'community languages' is regarded as worthwhile, this should not just be an accommodation to public opinion. Rather, it should be seen to be critical in the servicing of educational needs.

Against this background the study took two directions. One was to investigate the attitudes of people of German and Macedonian background in the Wollongong-Shellharbour region, both informally in discussion groups and formally through questionnaires. This process is summarized in Chapter 5. Because we felt that studying attitudes alone would be an insufficient scientific basis to inform policy decisions, we pressed for an extension of the brief to examine language proficiency in English, Macedonian and German. As it was not feasible to do this for all age levels and social circumstances, and given the time and funding limitations, we decided to conduct this part of the study in years 5 and 10 in seven Wollongong schools.

In this chapter we will be looking at that part of the research which was an attempt to balance the attitudinal aspect of the language question with information relating to the function of language as an educational tool, in the specific case of children and schooling. We assessed 111 children across seven schools. Forty-two of these were a control group of native English-speakers, and the rest were children of Macedonian or German background. We decided to assess students in year 5 because they were at a stage in their schooling which was critical in terms of language development and extension, and year 10 as at this stage they were preparing for work or further study in tertiary institutions. We originally intended to draw our sample from year 11 but had to change this to year 10 when it was discovered that very few children of Macedonian background made it into their senior years (years 11 and 12) in the sample schools.

We had three major aims in conducting the language assessments. Our first goal was to evaluate the children's English language performance in educational contexts on academic and non-academic language tasks. There is an obvious need for such information on children from non-English-speaking backgrounds (NESB), as there are serious indications of educational underachievement of some groups of these children in Australia. The fact that we had to change our sample from year 11 to year 10 was, in itself, an indicator of this. Second, if language programmes are to be considered as part of everyday, mainstream schooling, it is necessary to have information on proficiency in the mother tongue of different children who might be targeted for 'community language' programmes. Third, we wanted to establish whether there was any correlation between proficiency levels in English and proficiency levels in the mother tongue.

The theoretical framework we worked with in the development of the tests was the dominant paradigm in language teaching in the late 1970s and early 1980s: that of attempting to define, teach and test 'communicative competence'. We will outline the theoretical background to this paradigm, discussing both the advantages and the problems of adopting such an approach. Tests that we designed attempted to incorporate the essential features of this paradigm, and for our particular purposes they were successful. They gave us useful indicators of the students' proficiency levels, showing a marked underachievement of the majority of the children who had English as a second language (ESL) and indicating areas of education that needed urgent attention, areas that the education system has a responsibility to address. Of course, evaluating students' language proficiency levels by itself is not enough as there are other factors such as socio-economic environment, family situation, teachers' attitudes, school curriculum and gender differentials, to name but a few, which influence school outcomes. Assessment results often reflect not what a child can or cannot do, but what the school (or other factors) have or have not done in preparing them for life. In the break-up of the results we have tried to take some of these factors into account.

The process of attempting to develop a 'communicative' test also shed light on the need for further research in this area: the inherent problem of working within the notion of what constitutes communicative competence, the confusion at the level of practice that is created by the distinction between competence and performance, and the plethora of confusing terminology that is often loosely defined and used interchangeably. For example, in what way can 'competence' be assessed as distinct from 'performance'? How is 'performance' defined? What is the difference between teaching and testing 'communicative competence' or 'communicative performance?' Until these questions can be adequately answered, the major issue for the 'communicative language testing' movement will be defining and describing more rigorously the theoretical construct on which language tests are based. Applied linguists have listed criterial features of 'performance' and 'competence' tests (see Carroll, B.J., 1961, 1980; Morrow, 1979; Clark, 1978); these give useful guidelines but they do not provide a model of language within which to work. In the last section of this chapter we will reflect on these problems and will suggest future directions for research and test design for the school context. We will suggest that a more coherent model of language can be gained from insights from systemic functional linguistics, and this can provide a useful framework for designing tests in the future.

Our particular intention in the research project was to design tests to fulfil a very particular purpose. We do not, therefore, claim that our tests would be suitable for other educational purposes, although components of them certainly could be. It is the test results and the discussion arising out of the process of designing the tests that we hope are useful. In particular, the process of enquiry into language testing in schools made us aware of the degree of confusion and change in educational testing both in terms of theory and classroom practice. So in the next three sections we will first set the educational context by looking at the present state of language testing in schools, giving reasons for this state of confusion. This will be followed by a brief discussion on the theoretical background to language testing, in particular discussing the principles of communicative language testing. We will then give a description of the tests and a summary of the results.

Setting the Context: Language Testing in Schools

The task we set ourselves was extremely ambitious, but we felt it was necessary to contribute to the language debate in Australia by presenting a model of research which asked questions which had pedagogical implications and made the language question more than just one of sentiment or politics. Due to time and funding limitations we had decided to modify existing tests, assuming that there would be a battery of tests to choose from.

We discovered, however, that there was a scarcity of available materials for the purposes of evaluation. We did not wish to use a standardized test (for reasons we outline below), so we were forced to design our own evaluation instruments. Problems of comparability between English, Macedonian and German dogged the whole exercise, but what follows, we hope, is a contribution to what we see as a pressing need. The exercise is not so much a statement on English, German or Macedonian languages themselves. Rather, it is an examination of what might be required in terms of research for the successful implementation of any language programme in a multicultural context. Our research made it clear that there is a vacuum in this area, both in terms of knowledge about language, the needs and experiences of students from non-English-speaking backgrounds and in terms of there being no instrument to evaluate this experience adequately.

It appeared that teachers either used traditional, standardized tests (the minority) or they had rejected 'objective' testing procedures completely. The majority of the teachers we interviewed advocated informal and subjective language testing procedures and objected to systematic language assessment for two main reasons. First, they believed all existing language tests are culturally specific and therefore inappropriate; and that most traditional, standardized tests only give an account of the student's ability to manipulate abstract grammatical rules and not of their ability to use language in real contexts. We do not dismiss these objections. It is extremely harmful to slot children into selffulfiling categories, or to draw assumptions about the child's intellectual abilities from their performance in a language test (Cummins, 1980b, argues this point extremely well). However, it is essential to be able to diagnose children's language difficulties so that appropriate teaching and learning strategies can be formulated. For the students' needs to be adequately catered for the teacher must know, as precisely as possible, what stage of linguistic development has been reached. This is particularly the case for children with language difficulties. In practice, however, because of the lack of adequate and recently developed materials, the choice for teachers has been either not to test systematically at all, or to use conventional standardized tests. This disjunction, we believe, is a result of two parallel developments: one stemming from applied linguistics, one from educational theory. We discuss both of these in turn.

Language Testing and Applied Linguistics

Language teaching is directly influenced by developments in applied linguistics. In both these areas a parallel movement has taken place, a movement away from the structuralist view of language towards a view of language as communication. In this view discourse and the uses to which language is put play a central part. In language teaching this development is generally referred to as the 'communicative approach' and it has resulted in a plenitude of classroom materials that claim to be 'communicative'.

However, developments in language testing have been at odds with these wider shifts and it has been suggested that assessment procedures still remain outside the mainstream of applied linguistics. The view of language incorporated in many tests has increasingly become at odds with both the theories of language use and language teaching materials. Many of the available tests embody outdated theories, and, as Morrow (1979) argues, if the theory is not accurate, then the validity of the tests is called into question.

It could be argued that testing cannot be expected to follow the ever-changing whims of language teaching fashion, but when the tools no longer reflect the practice with which they are connected then something needs to change. This is not to say that there have been no significant developments in language testing over the last ten years. Researchers and applied linguists have made progress in the field, especially in research into the structure of language proficiency, attempts to describe and test the components of language proficiency (Oller, 1979; Palmer and Bachman, 1981; Canale and Swain, 1980, just to mention a few), and developments in ESL testing. However, this has still not had a major impact at the level of practice. This is particularly the case in primary and secondary schools where traditional language tests, based on grammatical structures, are still used. In both these and in adult contexts, we agree with Rea (1985) who argues: 'Evaluation is universally accepted as one of the basic tenets of any curriculum design, yet an examination of commercially available language teaching texts reveals, sadly, that language testing is infrequently attributed any useful function within the teaching and learning process' (1985: 15). She continues: 'In particular, I feel a definite lack of guidance on (i) the relationship between types of tests and the different purposes for testing; (ii) the design of item types suitable for inclusion in communicative language teaching programmes; and (iii) the appropriate selection of specific test formats and item types at different stages in the (communicative) teaching and learning process' (1985: 20).

The practice of language testing is confused precisely because these questions cannot be answered by the paradigm that operates around the notion of 'communicative competence'. They cannot be answered until there is an accessible and descriptive model of language in use that can be modified and adapted for language teaching purposes. This is why many teachers still resort to 'structural' teaching and testing: structural linguistics does provide a model of language from which to work. This is certainly not to say we should go backwards; developments in the last twenty years since the era of structural linguistics have been enormous. In the last section of this chapter we present a possible way forward. We are not arguing that it is the only way to proceed but it is one direction worth investigating. We will now look at developments in educational theory, and in particular curriculum design, to account in part for the current confusion in language testing in schools.

Language Testing and Educational Theory

The dominant paradigm in education in Australia at the moment could be called 'progressivist'. This is not the term that many mainstream educators would apply to themselves, but is one that we are going to use for the purposes of this chapter in order to outline, in very broad brush-strokes, the main lines of curriculum debate in the last few decades. Importantly, 'progressivist' educators define themselves in critical reference to 'traditional' educators, again a term that we will use as a matter of schematic convenience to describe an amalgam of theories and practices. In this section we will briefly characterize the opposition between traditional and progressivist curriculum theory in an attempt to explain the position language testing has in schools today.

We are at present witnessing a turning point in Australian education; there is a 'back to basics' movement that does not think progressive education has brought any significant or valuable social change. This movement includes not only people who might be seen to have a vested interest in traditional curriculum, but also ordinary members of the 'community' who strongly believe their children need conventional academic skills and accreditation to succeed. There has been a growing concern about educational standards and what are perceived to be falling standards of literacy and academic achievement. Calls for standardized assessment are again surfacing. At national and state levels there are increasing pressures on schools and education systems to produce indications of their performance — ones that will satisfy community demands to know what students are achieving throughout their school years. At the same time there is a growing recognition among teachers that lack of explicitness in curriculum documents is causing problems in producing satisfactory assessment procedures that would be accurate in terms of state standards and yet give a true picture of students' achievements. Current, informal 'progressivist' assessment procedures are unable to demonstrate student achievement clearly in terms which are explicit and which relate to state or national standards. This vacuum could allow for the imposition of standardized tests which are incompatible with educational curriculum objectives. In New South Wales this is more than just a possibility. The new Liberal-National Party Education Minister has introduced compulsory, standardized testing in years 3, 6 and 10. The concern is if we do not take heed of the 'back to basics' movement, the traditional rejoinder to progressivism, we will not be able to preserve what has been gained in curriculum development over the last ten to fifteen years.

It is important to act and to recognize writings on the wall. In the United States progressivist education has increasingly come under attack in recent years. 'Back to basics' is the educational slogan of the 1980s. 'Standards' in traditional academic skills areas and a nationalistic American history and citizenship (with major textbooks having titles like *Our Great Nation*) are the order of the day. The reasons for this development are complex, but economic recession and a 'realistic' assessment of how children might 'succeed' socially and economically in hard times seem to be central factors.

In the United Kingdom, as early as 1975, the Bullock report expressed concerns about falling educational standards and, in particular, was concerned about the standards of language development:

> Further and higher education institutions often remark on the inability of their entrants to write correct and coherent English. The committee was furnished with examples of essays [which] contained numerous errors of spelling, punctuation, and construction, and were a disturbing indication that the students who wrote them were ill-equipped to cope with the language demands they would meet in schools . . . . We underline our conviction that standards of writing, speaking, and reading can and should be raised. (1975: 4)

More than ten years later the Kingman report on the teaching of English in the United Kingdom expressed similar concerns: 'There is a widespread concern that pressures on time and energy, together with inadequacies in the professional education and training of teachers and a misunderstanding of the nature of children's learning, are causing important areas of English language teaching to be neglected, to the detriment of children's facility with words' (1988: 1). The report attributes this, in part, to development in educational practice that we label as progressivist. They continue:

> The distraction today is in part the belief that this capacity [to use language effectively] can and should be fostered only by exposure to varieties of English language; that conscious knowledge of the structure and working of the language is unnecessary for effective use of it; that attempting to teach such knowledge induces boredom, damages creativity and may yet be unsuccessful; and that the enterprise entails imposing an authoritarian view of a standard language which will be unacceptable to many communities in our society. (1988: 1)

It is in the light of these and other observations, articulated as a concern about educational standards, that the conflicting 'ideals' of progressivism and traditionalism need to be examined.

Progressivism / traditionalism

The ideals of liberal, progressivist education were ideals of the 1960s and 1970s. A.S. Neill's *Summerhill*, Postman and Weingartner's *Teaching as a Subversive Activity*, Illich's *Deschooling Society* and the books of John Holt were all indicators that people were trying to think imaginatively about a different sort of education and perhaps a different sort of society. They were creative actors with a confidence that they were doing something new. They critically defined their progressivism against what they regarded as traditionalism. Old-style curricula handed down official learning content from on high in the form of prescribed texts or courses to be followed. Students were to learn and accept (by rote, if necessary) the One True Interpretation of the world. It might be irrelevant to students' own needs, boring and even a set of downright lies, but it was at least socially useful knowledge in the sense of creating well behaved citizens.

The new, progressive education would change this. It would move beyond the mere acquisition and manipulation of a set of ideas that other people deem to be most relevant. It would not be formal and factual, but open and flexible, encouraging students to develop skills to make up their own minds, to form their own world-views. Instead of becoming passive, non-creative social cogs, they would become critical and creative social agents. They would not become used to accepting received knowledge from above, passively submitting to the intellectual and moral judgment of social 'superiors'. Rather, they would read the world critically to form their own opinions and participate confidently. Education would not be someone else's relevance. Education would instead be truly relevant, working from questions relating to students' own needs and desires. Imposed curricula are tantamount to cynical manipulation by the powerful. Standardized, objective testing which negatively labelled children would be replaced by the more relevant, informal and subjective procedures involving observation and anecdotal evidence.

The distinctions of curriculum content as opposed to curriculum process, and of core curriculum as opposed to relevant curriculum characterize the fundamental differences between traditionalism and progressivism, and clearly highlight the paradigm shift in attitudes to language testing.

Process/content

One of the key tenets of liberalism is that Western industrialism is ideally an 'open' society. Karl Popper is the most noteworthy of recent exponents of this common idea; we live in a society open to questioning, open to piecemeal change, and open for each of us to participate in some small way. Instead of there being compulsory social dogma, there are fluid institutions open to our questioning and gradual transformation.

It is along the lines of this logic of openness that progressivist education defines 'curriculum'. Curriculum is a process (and is thus open) and not content (which would indicate social dogmatism). Educators are not there to hand down the only true interpretation of the world (a fixed content), but to help their students develop processes for questioning their world, making up their own minds and acting according to their own freely formed consciousness. Particular importance is attached to such things as 'capacity to reason', 'to solve problems' and 'to think critically' etc. These are seen as socially useful skills, not only important in schools but for successful participation in the community. Educational institutions, then, have a responsibility to develop these kinds of mental abilities and capacities in the students. Munby (1978) places a similar emphasis on the teaching of 'mental' skills and abilities to adult ESL learners and provides an inventory of micro-skills to teach from. This inventory includes such skills as 'expressing the communicative value of sentences and utterances', 'identifying the main point or important information in a piece of discourse' and 'extracting salient points to summarise' (1978: 127–9).

Apart from the difficulty of clearly defining and then isolating such skills for teaching and testing, the major issue is that content or knowledge is seen as something that may be divorced from considerations of the language processes in which content comes into being. Furthermore, there is a general view that these skills are more important than the content or information, because, it is argued, these are generalizable skills and cut across 'contents' and so are much more useful to teach. Knowledge is thought of as a kind of product, and the skills and abilities are thought of in process terms. Once mental processes are developed, students can master different products.

However, we argue that the major misconception here is with the relationship between language and knowledge; and between language and mental skills. It is the misconception that prevails in twentieth century educational psychology, that language has no more than a neutral role in relation to thought and to content, and that language is there to serve ideas, and that the ideas are an independent entity. However, both language process (skills) and language product (knowledge) are two aspects of the same phenomenon. Language is both a process and a product, and to view it meaningfully as text, one needs to take both perspectives. Furthermore, as Christie (1986) argues:

> Neither knowledge nor reasoning may be usefully thought of apart from the discourse patterns within which both are created. 'Content' does not reside somewhere (normally unspecified) to be picked up and explained in language, any more than thinking processes exist in the head, to be given expression in relevant language processes. Neither content nor thinking process exists till it is realised or created in appropriate discourse patterns. (1986: 6)

In other words, to learn content is to learn language; it is to learn how to recognize and manipulate the discourse of different disciplines, and to learn how to address issues and solve problems in a way which is characteristic of a particular subject. In fact, success or failure at school is closely tied to the student's ability to construct discourses appropriate to different disciplines.

The process/product dichotomy finds expression in the assessment area in two related ways. The progressivists argue that it is far more important to assess the process, and not be as concerned with the 'end' product. This way of observing the process is to identify the 'mental skills' and abilities the student brings to bear in the performance of the task. No longer, then, is it appropriate to evaluate just the 'end' product in objective terms; but criteria need to be designed against which the learner's process can be judged.

The first problem is that assessment of this kind, criterion-referenced assessment, is frequently evaluated in terms of poorly specified and vague criteria and is therefore open to subjective appraisal and affected by immediate classroom context and teacher opinion. As long as these 'skills' are considered to be separate from the language in which they are encoded, they will continue to be vague. How can you test 'ability to reason', or 'ability to scan a text' without clearly describing the way these processes are encoded in various linguistic patterns characteristic of different disciplines? It is the learner's ability to construct discourse relevant to different disciplines that we need to assess; the ability to recognize, interpret and manipulate the various 'content' areas. The problem is seeing these 'mental' skills and abilities as more important than 'content'; that is, seeing language process as a separate identity to language 'product'. This content/form opposition is a false dichotomy that has plagued linguistics, and now is wreaking havoc upon educational practice. We discuss this in more detail in the last section of this chapter.

Relevant curriculum/core curriculum

Against the alleged social authoritarianism of core curriculum, progressivist educators have argued for relevant curriculum. The key words of such an approach are 'needs', 'diversity', 'choice' and 'community relevance'. For example, in the name of relevance and with a growing awareness of class, ethnic and gender divisions, it is now argued that curriculum has to be diversified appropriately. The only valid and successful teaching is relevant teaching. Students will learn best what they feel they need to learn, and these felt needs are variable according to class, gender, ethnic and local community circumstances. The core curriculum of comprehensive schooling has been a conventional academic curriculum which, while succeeding in middle-class schools on its own terms, has failed huge numbers of working-class children and children of non-English-speaking background. Moreover, the core curriculum has not been value-free. While teaching towards power, ascendancy and conventional social success, it has in fact been trying to impose middle-class values on society as a whole, ignoring other cultural traditions and needs and, predictably, failing children in all but middle-class circumstances.

There is considerable force to this argument for curriculum diversification, but it has serious dangers too. Cultural diversity is not a diversity of equals. The job is not merely to respect the divisions for what they are, but to right the injustices of everyday lack of power. How will diversification of curriculum, in order to meet a diversity of needs, avoid reproducing social stratification at the same time? Working-class or immigrant children may appear to need or want trade skills, or leisure or unemployment skills. Do we teach just these? Some cultural groupings appear to need or want a strict sexism reproduced. The curriculum might be differentiated in the name of a democratic populism. But this equally might end up doing nothing to change educational outcomes. Who is to gauge what different groups want or need? How do curriculum policy-makers know that they are not projecting an academic misconception about what groups want?

In practical classroom terms, diversified 'relevant' curriculum can have three counter-productive consequences. First, it does not prevent teachers teaching from within their own particular value system. This is not to say that teachers should deny their own values. It is merely to point out that diversified curriculum, despite its claims, can be effectively just as prescriptive as centralized curriculum. Second, diversified 'teaching' curriculum does not preclude unjust projection about what a social group 'needs'. Finally, diversified 'relevant' curriculum is based on an assumption that expressed needs are real needs. A student's expressed needs might be to destroy a telephone box or to indulge in pornography. But students might be unaware of real needs, for which satisfaction of their expressed needs provides only a temporary and unsatisfactory solution. As Michael Ignatieff argues in *The Needs of Strangers*: 'By definition, a person must know that he desires something. It is quite possible, on the other hand, to be in need of something and not know what that one is. Just as we often desire what we do not need, so we often need what we do not consciously desire' (1984: 11). The extension of this philosophical shift, for language testing in schools, is that assessment needs to be relevant to the learner's needs, and that it must be sensitive to the diversity of the students' linguistic and cultural backgrounds. If students are to be assessed at all, it is to be on the basis of criteria which are self-referenced against the students' own past performance.

The problem, however, is that these results do not always usefully describe current educational trajectories nor do they predict long-term educational outcomes in relation to all other students at the same year level. More importantly, though, this kind of assessment can be at the expense of measuring the linguistic knowledge and abilities necessary for educational success. Simplistic pluralist assessment procedures and pedagogy with limited objectives of esteem and cultural maintenance do not necessarily help students acquire those educational skills necessary for social access and perhaps action in a late industrial society.

So the need that has to be addressed is for the development of systematic assessment procedures that are not culturally inappropriate, that can assess the students' communicative abilities and that are sensitive to the diversity of the students' linguistic and cultural backgrounds. Moreover, as English is the language of instruction in schools, success in English therefore being essential for cognitive and intellectual development, these tests need also to be able to measure the students' ability to use the language for educational purposes. The problem, therefore, is to try to devise a test that is capable of measuring individual differences but not to the point where all forms of language are seen as purely relative. The test needs also to be relevant to the linguistic and cognitive demands placed on children at school, and as such be able to provide measures of knowledge and abilities necessary for educational success.

For many years now teachers have been encouraged to pursue language across the curriculum policies, and the importance of language as a principal resource for learning has been argued for a long time. However, while endorsing the notion that language varies according to subject area, most curriculum and assessment procedures have failed to point to the linguistic implications of this, and consequently teachers have often felt at a loss in deciding how to teach or test according to the different language demands of each discipline. In particular, they have lacked tools both for explicit teaching about language, and more importantly, for assessing the students' linguistic development and language needs in each subject area. The Bullock report in 1975 asserted that: 'In general, a curriculum subject, philosophically speaking, is a distinctive mode of analysis. While many teachers recognise that their aim is to initiate a student in a particular mode of analysis, they rarely recognise the linguistic implication of doing so' (1975: 189). In 1988 the Kingman report reiterated this while acknowledging that 'most teachers agree that many of the recommendations [of the Bullock report] have not been implemented and that their implications have not been followed through with sufficient rigour and in detail' (1988: 2).

What is needed is for curriculum documents to be developed that deal explicitly with different genres or text-types of each subject area. For example, learning science or maths involves learning how to construct discources relevant to these disciplines, that is, it involves 'learning how to mean' in different ways. To learn a subject involves defining and addressing questions in ways particular to that subject. These ways of reasoning and of enquiring are realized or created in appropriate discourse patterns. For example, certain genres are more critical for effective learning in science than they are in history or English. The genres for learning to write in science are reports, explanations, experimental procedures and argumentative writing (see Macken, 1989), whereas for history there is a greater focus on such genres as expository writing which requires interpretation of historical events. These discourses of different disciplines need to be explicitly dealt with; it is a very difficult task for children to learn these just by immersion, and many children will fail to do so.

The fundamental question about testing in schools is 'what do we test?' One of the problems, as argued earlier, is that language testing has been divorced from the curriculum; the major issue is the development of a well articulated curriculum that explicitly deals with the language demands of each discipline. In other words, for assessment criteria to be systematic and educationally relevant they need to be linked to curriculum objectives, and to be seen as an integral part of the curriculum.

The first step is the development of rigorous and systematic curriculum procedures that focus explicitly on how different subjects structure knowledge, and how this knowledge is realized through language. Teachers can focus on the text-types or genres that their students will need in order to master the contents and processes of particular disciplines. Such an approach sees process and content as two complementary aspects of the same phenomenon. It is only now that testing, an essential part of the curriculum process, can be efficiently and systematically administered.

The most valuable assessment system would involve teachers in monitoring student achievement over a significant period of time and would include the use of an assessment profile. It would include techniques such as careful observation and recording (reinforced by in-service training) but coupled with rigorous and meaningful instruments that can be selectively used when detailed and specific information is required. It is important that the information revealed from the assessment procedures is elucidated for all who are affected by it — teachers, students and parents. Such information can then feed into other programmes, for example, specialized ESL instruction. In addition careful language assessment is important for the construction and design of community language programmes.

We have attempted to outline the reasons for the state of confusion and change with language testing in schools. The most significant effect of this confusion is that, in practice, language testing has been largely neglected over the last decade or so. We are by no means suggesting a return to traditional assessment procedures. We do argue that as there is strong evidence of linguistic underachievement in many children whose first language is not the language of mainstream educational institutions, so language tests need to be designed that diagnose their particular areas of difficulty. These tests need to give the students and teachers an indication of what stage of language development the child has reached in the different subject areas needed in the school context.

We will now turn to a more specific discussion, outlining the 'communicative' tests that we designed, first discussing the particular theoretical paradigm that we were working from. Due to the vacuum in language testing practice we needed to design our own, and it was the process of doing so that made us acutely aware of the problems and issues concerned with language testing in schools. We will look at the specific issues to do with language testing: the purposes and requirements of tests, and the rationale for communicative language testing. It is a movement of such significance that it needs to be dealt with in detail. The specific tests we designed attempted to assess 'communicative' as well as 'academic' skills. Although we highlight the problem of working within a 'communicative competence' framework, the tests fulfilled the very particular need we were addressing, and the results were significant. We will end with a section containing a more general discussion with suggestions for a comprehensive and rigorous framework for guiding language assessment in schools.

Theoretical Overview: Current Issues and Approaches to Language Testing

In this section the purposes and requirements of language tests will be considered, as the content and format are directly affected by the test purpose. Because the content of the tests we devised is derived from a theory of language use, this too will be briefly considered.

The purposes of tests

Traditional language tests concerned with assessing aspects of the lexical, structural and phonological system of language were similar in content and method although the purposes of the different tests may have been quite varied. More recently, with the move towards communicative and relevant testing, there has been an emphasis on test purpose where the content and method of a test are related to a particular and clearly specified purpose. The following list broadly summarizes the main uses of language testing. While the categories are not mutually exclusive, they indicate different emphases in measuring student ability or potential.

1. Proficiency Tests
   to assign students to appropriate language classes;
   to assess readiness for a course of instruction;
   to diagnose specific strengths and weaknesses.

Diagnostic tests generally consist of sections which measure different language skills or components of a single broad skill. On the basis of the individual's performance on each section, a performance profile can be plotted which will show their relative strength in the areas listed.

2. Achievement Tests
   to measure student achievement of instructional goals; achievement tests are used to indicate individual or group progress towards the instructional objectives of a specific study or training programme;
   to evaluate the effectiveness of instruction.

3. Aptitude Tests to measure aptitude for learning.

In general terms the instruments we devised were proficiency tests for the purposes of diagnosis. The specific purposes of the tests were to measure reading, writing, listening and speaking skills among students of German, Macedonian and (control) English-only speaking backgrounds in years 5 and 10. Our aim was to assess both proficiency in the mother tongue and proficiency in English. For this purpose comparable instruments were designed in English, Macedonian and German. We needed instruments that would give us indications of the students' language ability in carrying out a series of tasks in educational contexts. We were interested in looking at the processes involved in the performing of the task, as well as the actual outcome. Because of the particular nature of the research, however, a qualitative profile was not enough. We also needed a quantitative measure for statistical reasons. Although the tasks performed in the different languages were similar in nature, they were not, of course, identical. The practical problems of comparability will be discussed later.

The requirements of tests

Any test must meet several requirements. The requirements traditionally identified as important are:

1. *Discrimination*:   Tests must have discriminatory powers. That is, a test must differentiate people who can perform aspects of a test from those who cannot and/or it must differentiate different degrees of ability.
2. *Reliability*:   A test should consistently give the same result for similar performances. It should give the same results every time it is used (within a short period) on the same subject, regardless of who is giving and marking it. In general, the more samples of students' performance taken, the more reliable the assessment of their knowledge and ability will be (hence the widespread preference for objective tests in which a large number of items may be included). Other factors include variable test conditions, student motivation and scorer reliability; the last is nearly perfect in multiple-choice tests, but tends to be low in the case of free-response tests, such as oral interviews where the scorer must make a series of individual judgments. There are different ways of measuring reliability. For objective testing, reliability is usually measured by split-half correlations, parallel forms, or retesting using the same test within a short time on the same candidates. More recent tests which use direct methods are more subjective and thus have lowered reliability, although it could be argued that face and construct validity are increased. To make subjective assessment procedures as reliable as possible, ratings criteria have to be clearly specified, and carefully described. This is one

of the most challenging tasks for communicative language testing, as the existing rating schemes contain general, impressionistic and imprecise descriptions of language behaviour. Unless these are based on a model of language that is concerned with describing actual language behaviour, this lack of precision is impossible to avoid. We have argued in the last section of this chapter that if the ratings criteria are linguistic and explicitly and comprehensively described then they are not so open to individual judgment and therefore more reliable.

3. *Validity:* The validity of any test, its most important characteristic, may be broadly defined as the extent to which the text measures what it is intended to measure. In the selection or preparation of any test, two questions must always be considered. What exactly does the test measure? How well does it measure it? Several types of validation can be applied to tests in an attempt to answer these questions (see Davies, 1968).

Face Validity: The test appears to be sound. This might seem trivial, but as Davies (1986) says, 'in education it is often important to show as well as know that what is being done is relevant.' To the extent that our tests contained realistic, communicative operations we can argue that they had face validity.

Content: Generally applied to achievement tests, this assesses the degree to which the test reflects the content of a syllabus. As argued earlier, language testing has tended to be developed separately from issues of the curriculum, and therefore content validity has been low. Although this is not relevant to our tests described in this chapter, in general it is essential that the tests are a component of the curriculum — if the tests and curriculum are based on sound educational practice, then the tests themselves will have a positive effect in the classroom (see 'washback' validity). More recently Palmer and Bachman (1981) have defined content validity as 'the extent to which the selection of tasks one observes in a test-taking situation is representative of the larger set (universe) of tasks of which the test is assumed to be a sample' (1981: 135). In our tests we attempted to design tasks that are similar to those the students would perform at school. However, content validity is an issue still unresolved with communicative language testing. The difficulty of extrapolating from the learner's ability to perform one task to his/her ability to perform another needs to be further investigated before a test of this kind can claim to have content validity.

Predictive Validity: This is the correspondence between the test results (where the test is used to predict future performance) and some criterion of later success (a further test, for example). That is, the test accurately predicts performance in some subsequent situation.

Concurrent Validity: The test gives similar results to existing tests which have already been validated. Predictive and concurrent validity are external criteria and as such are empirical measures. However, Morrow (1986) argues that concurrent validity is an 'irrelevant issue', as there is little point in measuring a communicative test against a more traditional one. Davies (1983), however, argues that predictive and concurrent validity are the only criteria that are not eventually circular and so are the 'best evidence of a test's validity'. (1983: 141)

Construct: The test accurately reflects the principles of a valid theory of the nature and description of language and of language learning.

Washback Validity: Morrow (1986) adds *'washback validity'*, and we agree with him when he argues that 'this is one of the principal responsibilities of testing. This is the degree to which the test has an effect on classroom practice.'

4. *Objectivity:* The other requirement which has traditionally been put forward is that of objectivity. The unreliability of traditional examinations with essay types such as 'Discuss...', 'Outline...', 'Compare and contrast...', which are subjective in the sense that they require the examiner to make a personal judgment about the answers, is a matter of concern. In reaction, 'discrete' point tests were set up to eliminate any differences in results due to variations among different markers, or due to variations in the judgment of one marker at different times. Marking ceases to rely on opinion and becomes mechanical. As proponents of communicative language testing point out, the difference between 'objective' and so-called 'subjective' tests lies basically in the marking. The compiling of a multiple-choice test is as subjective (in that it involves judgment and selection) as the setting of essay titles. The answering of such a test, too, involves choice and is therefore subjective.

5. *Practicality.* The other requirement traditionally identified as important is practicality, which is to do with:

> how economical the test is (short and to the point is considered better);
> how easy the test is to interpret;
> how easy the test is to score.

With language testing, weighting is given in favour of one requirement or another, depending on the writer's pedagogical viewpoints, and the particular aims and objectives of the test. In fact, the history of language testing can be seen in terms of the different priorities given to these varying components.

With our tests the major concern was to try to guarantee face, construct, concurrent, and to a lesser degree, content validity. Predictive and 'washback' validity were not relevant criteria for our puposes. The test results largely correlated with the teacher assessment and 'report' cards on the students and to this degree we can claim our tests had concurrent reliability. As our tests were significantly different from other available tests, more formal measures of concurrent validity would not have been relevant. We attempted to make our tests as reliable as possible by clearly specifying the criteria, trialling the rating scales, and by having explicit guidelines and detailed briefing sessions for the markers. However, language tests derived from a 'communicative' paradigm do not, and will not, have high reliability until the model of language on which they are based is more sophisticated.

Communicative Language Tests

In this section we will be looking at the characteristic features of communicative language tests, the associated problems and their practical implementation. Morrow (1979, 1986) could be considered to be the principal advocate of communicative language testing. He argues that both 'discrete point' and 'integrative' tests (for example, cloze and dictation, see Oller, 1971; 1979) were tests of linguistic competences: 'neither give any convincing proof of the candidate's ability to actually use the language, to translate the competence (or lack of it) which he is demonstrating into actual performance in ordinary situations i.e. actually using the language to read, write, speak or listen in ways and contexts which correspond to real life' (1979: 149). Morrow then argues for a performance-based test. To get an indication of the student's ability to use language, one needs to look at performance in actual communicative situations. This leads to the question: what constitutes effective communication and what is involved in performance? Morrow lists features of language use that need to be built into the design of a communicative test.

> Language use is *interaction-based*. Even letter-writing involves interaction in that the addressee is taken into account by the writer.
> Language use is *unpredictable*.
> Language use is always *contextualized*. Language always functions in a situation. Language is not decided upon first and then made appropriate to the situation. It is structured by the demands of its context of

use. The elements of the situation — the participants involved, the code, the message form and the topic — determine our use of language and our interpretations of what people say.

It is *purposeful*.

It is *authentic* and *behaviour-based*. (1979: 149)

These are some of the general characteristics of language in use that most existing tests fail to take account of, and we agree they are important features to take into account in test design. However, these generalizations do not supply a theoretical framework. The model of communicative competence that has had the most influence on language testing is perhaps that proposed by Canale and Swain (1980), and updated by Canale (1983a). It follows on from the two-dimensional Hymesian model which argued that the Chomskian notion of competence excluded any consideration of competency for language use, and had omitted 'by far the most important linguistic ability — to produce or understand utterances which are not so much grammatical but, more important, appropriate to the context in which they are made' (Campbell and Wales, 1970). Canale and Swain proposed a four-dimensional model which consisted of grammatical, socio-linguistic, discoursal and strategic competences. By strategic competence they are referring to the mastery of verbal and non-verbal communicative strategies. In practice, however, there are inherent problems of maintaining the theoretical distinction between competence and performance, even with the extended notion of competence. For example, it is certainly not clear how each of these competences interact with the others, nor what criteria should be used to identify a language problem as socio-linguistic or grammatical or discoursal. The notion of strategic competence is particularly problematic, not only because these have not been clearly identified, but also it is unclear what role they play in cross-cultural communication. Swain (1985) argues that it is crucial to have a theoretical framework to start from, and so the components of communicative competence they proposed are a useful starting point. When we designed these tests in 1984, in the absence of a more adequate model, we found the Canale and Swain parameters the most useful framework. First, we will outline some of the problems we faced in the attempt to design a communicative test.

Problems with Communicative Language Testing

The main problems of communicative language testing are to do with extrapolation, assessment and reliability. In other words, how do you extrapolate from the candidate's performance on one task to his/her ability to perform other language tasks? How do you deal with the conflicting requirements of reliability and validity and how do you assess these communicative tasks? We will discuss these three issues in turn.

One of the major problems is that of extrapolation, that is, to what degree can you extrapolate from the learner's ability to perform one task to his/her ability to perform others? A test can only measure students' abilities on a selected sample of tasks/exercises. The reliability of the test, though, is determined by the extent to which conclusions can be drawn about students' ability to handle similar tasks. It could be argued, then, that it is necessary to sample as large a number of tasks as possible, which conflicts with test efficiency and practicality. With tests of grammatical structure, extrapolation is not such a problem. It is often argued that a grammatical description is generative, and therefore economical and systematic (see, for example, Littlewood, 1981; Widdowson and Brumfit, 1981) and additionally, because of the generativity of the grammatical system, grammatically-based tests have strong claims to predictive validity. On this, Davies argues: 'what remains a convincing argument in favour of linguistic competence tests (both discrete point and integrative) is that grammar is at the core of language learning . . . grammar is far more powerful in terms of generalisability than any other language feature. Therefore grammar may still be the most salient feature to teach, and to test' (1978: 226). However, people do not communicate in words and sentences, but in texts which are both purposefully and functionally related to the context of situation. Grammatical knowledge is one aspect of the ability to communicate, it is therefore important to test. Grammar is, though, only meaningful within text, and needs to be seen and tested as one aspect of the learner's ability to construct meaningful discourse. It is not only a mistake to neglect testing grammatical knowledge, as some communicative tests have done, it is also a mistake to focus solely on grammar, at the expense of other aspects of language. Discrete item tests do not indicate proficiency in language ability (oral or written), they merely indicate the ability to handle educationally decontextualized testing situations.

To summarize, then, it is not that the assessment of grammatical skills is unimportant, rather that they should be assessed in realistic communicative contexts. Therefore, it is in the assessment stage that grammatical skills are focused on. In the final section we will argue that if you are working within a model of language that incorporates genre, discourse, grammar, lexis and phonology, then all of these are seen as interrelating components of language proficiency and as such all need to be looked at in the language assessment process. We are not claiming that such components have not been foregrounded in the communicative language testing literature, but, as argued above, listing these components does not provide us with a theoretical framework from within which to teach or test. What is needed here is more than this: a descriptive model of language that provides us with the tools for describing each level of language where such tools also indicate the relationship between each level.

The importance of authentic language in interactive contexts is one central principle of communicative language testing. As a result of this many language tests, or as they are often referred to, performance tests, consist of the students carrying out authentic tasks or activities. Apart from the difficulty of achieving authenticity in the classroom, an even more important issue is the criteria that is used for the selection and design of the tasks and activities. There has been a tendency to design activities that assess 'fluency' (see Brumfit, 1984) with little consideration of 'accuracy', and to concentrate on informal conversational skills and in the written mode on less technical text-types such a narratives. In school contexts, in particular, it is important not to neglect academic tasks and activities, for example, the teaching and testing of text-types such as reports, experimental procedures and 'expository' genres. Cummins (1984) argues very strongly that the conversational aspects of language proficiency need to be seen as distinct from the 'academic', 'cognitive' language skills:

> The considerable evidence that Oller and his colleagues have assembled to show that academic and cognitive variables are strongly related to at least some measure of all four general language skills (listening, speaking, reading and writing) raises an important issue for conceptualising the nature of language proficiency in academic contexts. Specifically this evidence suggests that there is a dimension of 'language proficiency' that relates strongly to literacy and other 'cognitive/academic skills; however, it seems apparent that not all aspects of language proficiency are cognitive/academic in nature. For example, in a first language context, 'conversational' aspects of proficiency (e.g. phonology, fluency) are clearly unrelated to academic and cognitive performance. There is also considerable evidence from second language acquisition research that conversational L2 skills are not strongly related to academic L2 skills. (1984: 132)

Let us return to the problem of extrapolation. Morrow (1979) argues that the enabling skills proposed by Munby (1978) and Carroll (1980) provide a possible solution to the problem of extrapolation. Enabling skills include, for example, distinguishing main point from supporting details, understanding relations within sentences and deducing meaning of unfamiliar lexis. Morrow claims that these can be identified in operational terms and they are performance-based but that their 'application extends far beyond any one particular instance of performance' (1979). His argument is that these enabling skills can be identified by an analysis of 'performance' and they yield data which are not just relevant for a single instance of 'performance' but for a large number of tasks.

This sounds appealing, however the problem with this is that of vague, inadequately described terminology. It is very difficult to devise 'reading' or 'listening' questions or tasks that will clearly indicate which particular enabling skill the learner is having problems with. Additionally, Alderson (1981) and Weir (1981) have raised the problem that no one yet knows what the relationship is between such skills or what the relative weighting of separate skills is.

Despite these problems, the argument that we need to be able to get an indication of the processes that the students are going through in the performance of the task, as well as an indication of the outcome, is a very important one. Enabling skills provide a possible way of looking at the process. However, we need to be aware of the restrictions of operating within this framework and we need to express caution in generalizing about a person's performance in one task to his/her ability to perform other tasks.

This brings us to the problem of reliability. Direct testing methods, such as 'authentic' communicative tasks, do have lowered reliability, and this is an unresolved problem of communicative language testing. Specifying the ratings criteria very closely is an important way of avoiding unstable results. One possible solution is to strike a compromise between the two approaches of direct and indirect assessment of language. When we designed these tests, we advocated a two-stage approach as a way of overcoming the extrapolation dilemma, as well as a possible compromise between the conflicting demands of validity, reliability and efficiency. The first stage involved the development of a direct test that is valid but with decreased reliability. The second stage involved the development of efficient, practical and objective tests of high reliability and decreased validity. The indirect tests then are a 'reliability' check on the more direct, subjective procedures. Davies (1978) and Weir (1981) argue for a similar combination of communicative, integrative tests with discrete point tests. As a test needs to have a framework to ensure consistency and reliability, we decided to have a combination of the two approaches, with the emphasis on the communicative aspect. The compromise appeared in the rating procedures rather than the content or form of the test itself.

We decided that for the productive skills of speaking and writing we would attempt to devise a 'global' communicative test that focused attention on language use. We chose realistic situations that involved genuine interaction. In relation to these tasks we attempted to measure both the student's overall performance as well as the strategies and skills which had been used in the process of performing that task. With listening and reading tests it is more difficult to see how the global task has been completed. With the tests of listening and reading comprehension, the questions were predominantly concerned with enabling skills, and attempted to identify the student's ability to manipulate such skills. These provided general indicators sufficient for our purposes, but for more general diagnostic purposes the problems identified above need to be kept in mind.

To conclude, we needed to develop a test that measured both overall performance in relation to a specified task and the strategies and skills which have been used in the process of performing that task. It had to be concerned with establishing its own validity as a measure of those skills and abilities it claimed to measure. We decided that rather than opting for traditional methods that have greater reliability and objectivity, but have suspect validity, it was better to investigate ways of obtaining more reliable measures of communicative abilities.

It remains to discuss the problem of assessment for communicative language testing. When the concern of the test is to make some sort of judgment about actual language use, the conventional rating procedures are no longer appropriate. As a reaction to the assessment procedures of traditional tests, multiple-choice and discrete point tests were systematic, efficient and objective. However, the results of task-based tests cannot be so easily expressed by objective, quantitative scoring. With these tests the concern is not whether candidates have passed or failed. The point of the test is to assess what they can do.

The problem that immediately arises is whether it is possible to assess production in ways which are not so subjective as to render the test completely unreliable. An interim solution proposed by Carroll (1980) and Ingram (1984) is to design an operational scale of attainment in which different levels of proficiency are defined in terms of a set of performance criteria. There are quite a few criteria that have now been developed, including the ratings procedure adopted for the Royal Society of Arts Examination and the Australian Second Language Proficiency Ratings (ASLPR) designed for adult ESL learners in Australia. The emphasis of the RSA rating scale is on providing a profile of the learner, while the emphasis of the ASLPR is on providing a rating scale.

Carroll (1980) distinguishes levels of performance by matching the student's performance with operational specifications which take account of the following parameters:

Size.

Complexity: of text which can be handled.

Range: The variety of enabling skills, structures and functions presented in a test.

Speed: The speed at which the task is performed.

Flexibility: Shown in dealing with changes, of, for example, topic.

Accuracy: The extent to which the candidate has mastered correct formal usage, and the correctness of the information he/she draws from or presents in a text.

Appropriacy: The degree to which the style of performance corresponds to the legitimate expectations of other users.

Interdependence: From reference sources and interlocuter.
Repetition.
Hesitation: in processing text.

These specifications are related both to receptive and productive performance. Carroll argues that there are two ways of approaching this: 'We may either present a number of tasks of varying difficulty, producing performance at corresponding levels, or present a single task and rate the testee according to the level at which they perform it' (1980: 31). As an interim measure, Carroll defined three levels of task difficulty: target level, which represents completely satisfactory performance; basic level, which is the lowest level of performance which it is appropriate to test at all; and between these two there is the intermediate level. These criteria and those levels of difficulty have been adopted as the rating procedure for the Royal Society of Arts Examinations in the Communicative Use of English as a Foreign Language (1981).

The ASLPR scale also involves a direct approach to the assessment of second language proficiency. The scale describes language performance at nine points from zero to native-like proficiency in each of the four macro skills. The candidates are then rated by observing their language behaviour and relating this to the most nearly matching performance description. It is important to emphasize that the ASLPR is not a test but rather an instrument designed to assess the performance level of adult ESL learners.

The ASLPR and Carroll's parameters (the rating procedures adopted for the RSA examinations) were designed for adult second language learners. The target group in our research, however, was year 5 and year 10 students from non-English-speaking backgrounds. As the major component of our tests were tasks, it would not have been desirable to rate these by conventional objective means, and as we did not have other more rigorous measures available to us, we modified the ASLPR and Carroll's parameters to suit our purposes.

The criteria and scales we devised are rather crude interim scales and need much more time and research spent on them. We strongly recommend that such research take place as there are no such assessment procedures that have been developed for children (see last section of this chapter for a discussion on work that has just been started in this area). As stressed, language testing still has an essential function as long as the instruments do not reflect outdated theories, are not loaded with cultural bias and are used for diagnostic rather than labelling purposes. We believe our tests are one step further in this direction, and with more time and research many of the problems we discuss in this chapter could have been alleviated.

We decided we would adopt a system whereby the student's performance was marked in terms of each of the criteria (between 0 and 2) and so individual differences can be seen on each dimension. In this way a profile of the student's performance can be plotted out. These marks were then totalled to give a score for listening, for writing, etc. So there were two scores for each of the macro skills (except writing); one being the results of the 'objective', discrete point sections of the test, the other being the results from the criterion-referenced rating scales we developed for each macro skill. It has been argued that it is undesirable to add the scores on the separate dimensions of the scales as this can hide individual differences. However, we felt, for practicality and systematicity, that it was necessary to have the totalled scores for each macro skill.

The Format and Design of the Evaluative Instruments

Following is a brief description of the assessment procedures that we designed in English, Macedonian and German. Before discussing the results, we will discuss the problems of designing comparable tests in two languages. The details of the assessment tasks, rating procedures and reliability indices are discussed in Kalantzis, Slade and Cope (1986). Here we will give a brief description of the assessment tasks and the main features of the rating procedures that were used.

When we designed the assessment procedures, our first concern was that the tasks to be undertaken should be realistic, communicative operations and should include both academic and non-academic language activities. The tasks should resemble, as closely as possible, the type of linguistic demands made of children of the target ages. When designing the tasks, we first considered the following questions:

1. What are the general areas in which the target students actually *use* English, Macedonian or German?
2. What are the general areas in which the students *need* English, Macedonian or German?
3. How well, and with what degree of skill, do they need to perform in these areas?

We restricted the study to looking at only classroom interaction and we did this in all four skills of speaking, listening, reading and writing. For most of the students we assessed, a major setting for communicating in English is the school. This is not the case with Macedonian or German, where, despite the fact that in some instances those languages were taught in school, they were essentially languages used at home and in other contexts outside the school. Our intent, however, was not to measure just the domestic and community use of the first language, but to devise comparable, bilingual tests that are essentially measuring those skills necessary for educational success. As we discuss below, this presented a number of problems in the designing of the German and Macedonian tests, in particular finding relevant material for the reading and listening sections of the test.

We wanted to get an indication of the students' ability in all four skills, so the assessment procedures had four major sections. The listening and speaking assessment tasks are related, as are the reading and writing.

For the purposes of objectivity and reliability, we designed a listening and reading test that had marker objectivity. We tried to ensure that the content represented the kind of tasks that confronted the language users at school. These assessments has a multiple-choice format, which focused on lexico-grammatical features (such as the ability to deduce the meaning of unfamiliar lexical items), discourse features (for example, cohesive devices) as well as generic features (the ability to identify the particular text-type and its characteristic schematic structure; see Martin and Rothery, 1986). The multiple-choice questions were designed to assess the students' ability to interpret and understand these features.

We trialled these assessment tasks with ten ESL and ten native English speakers. In the listening and reading evaluations we tried to identify how the students processed the text and what they found most difficult. We did this by trying a variety of questions/approaches and by discussing the process and outcome with the students. On the basis of the trialling, the final content and format of multiple-choice questions evolved.

In the trialling of the task with native speakers we identified what linguistic skills and strategies are likely to be needed to carry out the task effectively, and we designed a matrix which included these elements as a checklist to guide the markers. The matrix was used for the markers to write down detailed comments, and the ratings scale we designed was used to allocate a mark. We will now briefly describe each segment of the assessment tasks, the examples being from the English version. We will first discuss the section of the tests on the evaluation of oral interaction.

As we were restricted to the kinds of interaction that the students at school are engaged in, we had two issues to consider: teacher–student interaction, and student–student interaction. We decided to have an oral interview (involving teacher–student interaction) and a student–student task. As we needed to administer the questionnaire about attitudes to language maintenance, we decided to include it as part of the oral interview and by doing so it provided us with a purposeful communication task where a genuine transfer of information was taking place. Having an authentic task to complete overcame many of the problems associated with oral interviews. In the trialling of this element of the evaluations we tried a variety of approaches, for example, interviewing two or three students together, but we decided it was both more efficient and more likely to elicit extended responses if we interviewed the students individually (for a detailed discussion see Kalantzis, Cope and Slade, 1986).

The student–student task was by far the most successful component, both in terms of the students' involvement as well as the linguistic skills it demonstrated. This was designed to evaluate a student's communicative effectiveness when interacting with another student. We chose a barrier task which involved giving and interpreting instructions or descriptions. The students faced each other, but were separated by a physical barrier, so neither could see what the other was doing. The barrier was low enough for them to have eye contact. By using such a task, we could assess the students' effectiveness in communicating precise instructions and the ability to clarify and repair where necessary. It was also possible to assess the recipients' ability to interpret information, to seek clarification and to respond appropriately. There are problems with making definitive statements about recipients' listening ability based on this type of task, as this is affected by the clarity of the information given and so on. This, therefore, was only one of the aspects of the listening assessment.

The aim of the task was for 'B' to build (year 5) or draw (year 10) a replica of the model 'A' had constructed. Thus 'B' had to ask as many questions as possible. As students often perform this sort of task at school, they found the demands familiar. After completing the task, A and B compared drawings/model, B reported to A on her/his version, and if it were not the same, A corrected, re-explained and so on. They then described what had happened to the teacher/evaluator. The task involved the manipulation of abstract, analytical concepts and as such was close to the cognitively demanding, content reduced end of the continuum outlined by Cummins (1984). In this way the two sections of the assessment of oral interaction gave us an indicator of the student's basic interpersonal communicative skills, and also his or her ability to perform in educational/academic language tasks.

For the Macedonian and German assessment procedures the same framework was used as the English language evaluations, although different topics were suggested for the interview to stimulate discussion. Similar tasks were used for the student–student interaction. They were slightly modified to make them more appropriate. For example, the diagram for the year 10 students was altered to exclude objects and symbols that they would not be able to identify in Macedonian and German.

The assessment tasks for listening skills had three aspects: the oral interview, the barrier task and the listening activity on tape. The students' listening ability could be partly gauged through the oral interview and the barrier task. As it was difficult to judge by these alone, we also included a separate and specific listening task. Furthermore, as argued earlier, for the purpose of objectivity and reliability, we designed a listening and reading test that had marker objectivity and hence reliability. We tried to ensure that the context was realistic, and for year 5 we chose a principal's school announcement, and for year 10 an authentic extract of taped casual conversation. These were followed by multiple-choice questions. We were aware of the limitations of using multiple-choice format (see, for example, Alderson *et al.*, 1986), but we decided for the purposes of practicality and objectivity that it was the most effective form we could use for our particular purposes.

The evaluation of reading skills had two aspects: a reading passage with multiple-choice questions and the students were also asked to read aloud the first paragraph of this passage. It could be argued that reading aloud is not an authentic task, as native speakers very rarely perform this activity. However, it is not unusual for children to read aloud at school (even at the secondary level). In fact, it is often seen as an essential part of the development of literacy skills. There are technical skills of reading aloud which can provide useful indices of reading ability. It is thus an important diagnostic technique enabling the identification of particular problems students may have. As we asked the children to read the first paragraph of the reading passage they had previously been tested on, the overall context was familiar.

It is important to stress again that the design and format of the German and Macedonian assessments followed the same theoretical framework as those for English. The German and Macedonian listening and reading evaluations were also passages followed by multiple-choice questions. Despite trialling and extensive modifications, the content of these passages remained unsatisfactory, and reflects the lack of locally produced material in Macedonian and German relevant to Australian students.

The evaluation of writing consisted only of one task: a free writing activity that was directly related to the theme of the reading passage. This free writing technique was one that the students were familiar with and as such was seen to be a relevant task.

There were three major problems in designing the German and Macedonian tests. The first problem was finding fluent Macedonian and German speakers who were aware of the theoretical and practical developments in language assessment. We believed this pedagogical understanding was important as the design of the assessment tasks involved much more than the translation of those we had already produced in English. For example, it would have been culturally inappropriate simply to translate the listening and reading passages. However, for any comparisons to be made, it was also necessary to design comparable tasks that had the same framework and that were based on the same theoretical principles.

The first stage of the design of the Macedonian evaluation instruments involved a Macedonian exchange teacher in consultation with us. We explained our framework in detail, and discussed the importance of ensuring cultural relevance in the design of the instruments. A university lecturer in Macedonian and a Macedonian school teacher were consulted for the second stage of the design. The reading and listening passages that were first constructed, they felt, were not relevant or appropriate for children brought up in the Macedonian–Australian community. The inappropriateness was seen both in terms of the topic of the material chosen and the lexico–grammatical items it contained. In cooperation with us and the exchange teacher, the material was amended to be more relevant to the Australian/Macedonian context, while still attempting to balance this relevance with the requirements as 'standard' or literate forms of the languages.

The German assessment tasks were devised by a German teacher from Sydney in consultation with us. She worked within the framework used for the English evaluations, and chose listening and reading passages that she felt would be suitable. In a second stage the tasks were modified by two German teachers from Wollongong, as these were seen as inappropriate vehicles for evaluating the German with which the children in the Wollongong area were familiar.

In both cases it was clear that much needs to be done at the materials development level and on assessment procedures for languages other than English, so that there is a pool of experience and material to draw upon for research and for teachers. In many ways we had to construct our assessment procedures from scratch. We hope the experience will provide a basis for further necessary action research in this area.

The second major problem concerns comparability for languages which are put to quite different uses in the Australian context. Bearing this in mind, we aimed the procedures at two general major uses to which both English and the mother tongue might be put: everyday communication and formal schooling situations.

The third problem was the impossibility of standardizing the German and Macedonian assessment procedures against a control group of native speakers. This involved more than the impossibility of administering these to control groups in Germany and Macedonia. The languages spoken there display differences in form, content and purpose compared to the German and Macedonian spoken in Australia.

The results will only be discussed briefly here, and in more detail in the following chapter. Although several first language maintenance programmes were being run which involved the sample groups in some of the day schools we surveyed and a number of the sample group attended community run 'ethnic schools' outside normal school hours (and despite the fact that most of the sample were born in Australia), our battery of evaluations showed that English language proficiency was lower for the Macedonian and German groups than for an English L1 control sample from the same schools. In the L2 evaluations students scored considerably better in oral than they did in literate forms of the language. This pattern of results showed no sign of improvement between the primary and secondary school components of the sample. In other words, ESL programmes had not brought even Australian-born NESB students up to the average standard of their ESB peers. The L1 experience had not been used constructively to this end, and the practical requirements of L1 learning (such as employment in translation/interpreter services, or the possibility of working overseas) had not been realized through significantly improved literacy proficiency. Perhaps limited language maintenance goals (relevant to existing domestic usage, for example) had been met, but not broader objectives relating to social access and participation.

In conclusion, despite these methodological difficulties, we succeeded in creating assessment procedures which we consider successfully measured comparative L1 and L2 ability. Standardized language tests in a national language, although they might crudely forecast success in a monolingual education system, tell us nothing of the complex relation of L1 and L2 language abilities which unfairly disadvantages many NESB students. A radical and simplistic move to a pluralist paradigm, however, measuring language abilities relative to background and 'community' context also can disadvantage NESB students. Simplistic pluralist assessment procedures and pedagogy with limited objectives of esteem and cultural maintenance do not necessarily help students acquire those linguistic capacities necessary for social access and participation in a late industrial society. L1 and language teaching and assessment for NESB students could work towards those literate and abstracting forms of language necessary to read the broader social structures; 'standard' forms of language necessary for Australian trade interaction with the country of origin or socially mobile return migration; and language ability necessary for employment in translation/interpreting/teaching service in Australia. In the relation of L1 with L2, transitional bilingualism can maintain lines of cognitive development in mainstream subject areas as students' language abilities develop. Finally, 'community' languages should be taught and discussed with the same degree of intellectual seriousness as traditional foreign languages.

With these objectives in mind, language assessment in a multilingual society needs to be able to measure the complexity of the L1–L2 relation through assessment in both languages. This needs to be comparable and to evaluate those general forms of language which will be the most effective educational/communicative tools to social equity. Evaluation and pedagogy which are simply relative to the multiplicity of 'community' contexts, aiming no more than to preserve and maintain these cultural–linguistic differences, are an inadequate response to the undoubted limitations of the old, standardized testing procedures.

Given the situation of linguistic diversity in Australia, it is essential to devise bilingual assessment procedures that are able to give indications of the student's linguistic development in both his/her first language as well as in English. In this research we wanted to devise comparable assessment tasks which would be sensitive to students' linguistic and cultural backgrounds, as well as in selecting forms of language which are necessary for educational success and mobility. Our tests are very much an interim measure but we hope will provide the first step in a necessary process of developing systematic assessment procedures for children of non-English-speaking backgrounds.

This discussion has not focused specifically on assessment for community language programmes; rather, it is intended as a more general discussion on language testing in schools. We will now outline briefly some suggestions for future directions for language testing, in particular arguing for the need to adopt a systematic and comprehensive linguistic framework that can guide the assessment process.

Future Directions for Language Testing

Many applied linguists writing in the area of communicative language teaching and testing acknowledge the inherent problems of attempting to work within a 'communicative competence' framework. For example, Swain (1985) states: 'Competing claims about the efficacy of communicative language programs, for example, cannot be verified unless one can agree upon what is meant by competence and performance' (1985: 38). It is generally agreed that it is only through the development of a more adequate theory that this current confusion will disappear. Furthermore, because it is considered to be unrealistic 'to expect such theories to eventuate in the near future' (Brindley, 1986: 12), it is argued that in the meantime it is important to build from this notion of communicative competence: 'test development should *build from* existing knowledge and examples [otherwise] what I consider to be at stake is the gradual and systematic growth in our understanding of the nature of communicative competence' (Swain, 1985: 36–7). This is precisely the position we took when we were designing the tests, although we realized the importance of including analytical, grammatical components, particularly for the assessment of academic skills. It has only been since then that we became aware of the work on systemic-functional linguistics, and realized the applicability of that paradigm for language teaching and language testing. The model rejects the distinction between competence and performance, and the high degree of idealization that the analysis of competence entails, and perhaps it is only by doing so that it has been able to arrive at a functional description of language in its social context of use.

The high degree of idealization that is built into Chomsky's model is inherent in the distinction he draws between competence and performance. He insisted that a linguistic theory to be systematic could only deal with underlying rules of competence and not with 'grammatically irrelevant conditions or memory limitations, distractions, shifts of attention and interest, and errors' (1965: 3) which affect performance. Chomsky's purpose in drawing such a distinction was to bring natural language within the scope of explicit formalization, which was one of the goals of generative grammar. This was incurred at a certain price: mainly a high degree of idealization. In this paradigm, language was abstracted away from all contextual factors which shape our use of language. Those aspects of language use which are of concern to linguists with a sociological or applied interest were, by necessity, ignored. The high degree of idealization and abstraction of their framework is of little interest to the linguist or educationalist whose concerns are with linguistic interaction, whose interests are sociological rather than strictly psychological.

There are two ways of dealing with this problem: one way is to extend the notion of competence to take into account aspects of performance, such as the speaker's ability to produce to understand utterances which are contextually appropriate, the position adopted by Hymes in his reformulation of competence, as communicative competence; the other way is to reject the distinction altogether, the position that Halliday (1978) and other systemic–functional linguists have taken.

There are inherent problems in adopting this first position. First, there is a limited sense in which we can talk about what a speaker 'knows' and what a speaker does separately; they are merely two aspects of the same phenomenon, they have no actual identity apart from each other, and for descriptive or applied purposes it is clearly not possible to isolate one from the other. The distinction is not only impossible to maintain in practice (for example, finding ways of assessing underlying competence, when competence can only be inferred through performance) (see Rea, 1985), but it also causes confusion at the level of theory. For example, what will a theory of communicative competence look like? What will a theory of performance look like? How will these two differ, and what will connect the two? The other related problem is that attempts to provide theoretical models of communicative competence, the most influential being Hymes (1972) and Canale and Swain (1980), are not descriptive, and only outline general components or parameters; they do not account in a linguistically motivated way for systematicity of the co-variation between language and context. The very division of competence from performance, with its concomitant idealization of language, prohibits from showing in a systematic way the relationship between language and context.

Halliday with his rejection of the competence and performance dichotomy argues that a descriptive framework is needed whereby language and context are systematically and functionally related to one another. He accepts a much lower level of idealization, and states: 'instead of rejecting what is messy, we accept the mess and built it into the theory . . . . There is no need to bring in the question of what the speaker knows; the background to what he does is what he could do — a potential, which is objective, not a competence, which is subjective' (1978: 38). Halliday's functional grammar has as its goal accounting in a principled fashion for the uses of language, where use is merely an instantiation of the meaning potential of the speaker. For Halliday, the question is not what the speaker knows, but what the speaker can do and in the linguistic context specifically in what the speaker can mean. Therefore, the contrast is between potential and the actualization of that potential, where the relationship between potential (linguistic system) and actualization of potential (text) is that of realization: where every instance of language (text) is related back to the linguistic system as a realization of particular options. The key concept is that of realization, where the linguistic system is conceived of as a potential to mean, which is instantiated or realized through text.

The important question here is how does Halliday show the systemic correlation between language and context? He suggests that social situations, or contexts of use of language, correlate with semantic choices, that are in turn realized by the grammatical resources. For instance, variation in the social relationship between speaker and addressee will correlate with different speech functional choices in the semantics (for example, straight command versus polite request), and those speech functional choices are then realized by the particular

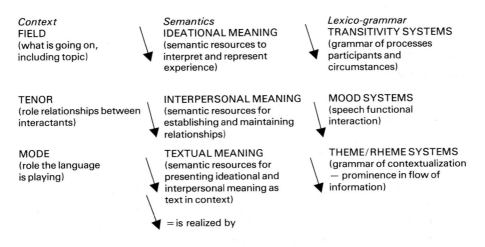

Figure 4.1 The Relationship between Context and Language

grammatical choices, specifically in the grammar of mood (see Halliday, 1985a). This systematic correlation is represented in Figure 4.1.

Semantics represents the interface between the grammar of the text, and the social environment of the text. The three metafunctional components — ideational, textual and interpersonal — provide the hook-up between the register variables and the lexico-grammatical system. These components are essentially semantic, but they are manifested in the language itself, and enable us to make the bridge between the grammar and the context of situation. The tripartite description of register relates to the tripartite organization of the grammar, into the systems of transitivity, mood and theme (see Halliday, 1985a).

The implications for language testing should be clear: it provides a model of language that shows *systematically* the relationship between language and context; and, second, as it is a functional grammar concerned with the ways people construct discourses to achieve certain purposes, it is concerned not with the analysis of isolated sentences, but with texts.

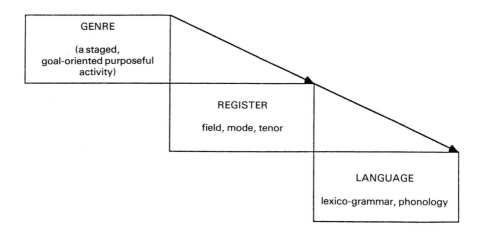

Figure 4.2 Semiotic Planes: Genre — Register — Language

Martin (1983), working within the systemic–functional framework, has developed the notion of realization, arguing that register realizes a higher-level semiotic plane, which he labels 'genre'. He argues that both register and genre are semiotic systems that are realized by language; and that 'language' functions as the phonology of register, and both register and language function as the phonology of genre' (1983: 21). This relationship is presented in Figure 4.2 (modified from Martin, 1983). Martin defines genre as 'staged, goal oriented puposeful activity in which speakers engage as members of our culture' (1983: 25). It is referred to as staged as we make these meanings in steps; it usually takes more than one step for participants to achieve their goals. There are as many genres as there are recognizable social activity types in our culture. There are popular written genres such as instructional texts, newspaper articles, magazine reports and recipes. There are educational genres such as expository writing, reports, experimental procedures, etc. and there is an enormous range of everyday genres that we take part in in our daily lives, such as buying and selling, telling narratives, gossiping and exchanging opinions. All of these genres are ways of exchanging meanings to achieve some purpose.

Martin refers to the overall patterning of texts as the schematic structures, and they are a realization of the overall purpose of the text. For example, Slade (1988) has found that gossip texts in casual conversation among acquaintances at work have this generic structure:

Third Person Focus ^ [Substantiating behaviour ^ Pejorative Evaluation ^ (Probe) ^ (Wrap-up)] where ^ means that the element on the right follows that on the left and ( ) indicates that the element is optional. [ ] indicates domain of recursion or sequencing.

These patterns represent the overall text structure, and it is because of these obligatory stages that we recognize a stretch of text as gossip. In the case of education the two written genres of report and narrative have the following generic structure (see Martin and Rothery, 1986):

Report: General Classification ^ Description
Narrative: (Abstract) ^ [Orientation ^ Complication ^ Evaluation ^ Resolution.]^ (Coda or Reorientation).

Martin and Rothery's work on 'genre' has had such a significant impact on education in Australia that is now widely known as 'genre theory'. It is, in essence, a theory of language use, a theory of what we do with language and how we do it.

In second language teaching, learners need to be guided in how to predict from generalized contexts what kind of social process or genre they can expect, and then on a greater scale of delicacy what kind of text, and in turn, what communicative skills, strategies, lexico-grammar will be appropriate for the realization of that text. That is, they need to be able to predict what kind of language will be appropriate and successful for the particular situations they will be involved in. For school contexts, in particular, genre theory provides a comprehensive and systematic framework for showing explicitly how language structures knowledge in different subject areas. Some of the key written genres of schooling include reports, narratives, explanations, procedures and argumentative genres like exposition and discussion.

Different subject areas utilize specific oral and written genres. The linguistic realizations of each are quite different, and recent research has shown (Martin and Rothery, 1981, 1986) that children at school do not necessarily master the conventions of these genres purely by being 'immersed' in language. These genres can be analyzed in linguistic terms, and therefore genre theory provides not only a framework for the analysis and description of language across the curriculum, but also a basis for curriculum design and assessment.

To demonstrate briefly how systemic–functional linguistics can provide a *comprehensive* and *linguistic* framework for assessment, we include two figures on the linguistic criteria relevant to assessing students' ability to handle reports 'in science', an important genre for learning in primary school (see Figures 4.3 and 4.4). These are from Macken (1989), who is a member of the Language in Education Research Network (LERN), a group of academics and teachers (including Kalantzis, Slade, Cope, Martin, Rothery and Kress) who are concerned with the state of language education in schools.

PURPOSE:
telling how the world 'is' in social science and in science

STAGING:
general classification and description of phenomena
taxonomizing of information in terms of class/sub-class or part/whole relations

TENOR:		
(growth of objectivity in writing) relations of expert/expert or expert/novice;	–	generic (non-human) participants as 'theme'
	–	grading and measurement of phenomena

FIELD:		
(progression from common sense to technical knowledge)	–	taxonomic organization of technical vocabulary
	–	simple present tense (universal)
	–	relational, material and behavioural processes
	–	exemplification e.g., addition, purpose and comparison
	–	nominalization
	–	logical relations realized within sentence as conjuctions as well as nouns and verbs

MODE:		
(creating a context within the text for the reader)	–	phenomena as 'theme'
	–	clause combining (paratactically, hypotactically or via grammatical metaphor)
	–	generic participants presented and tracked consistently throughout text

Figure 4.3 Reports: What Is Possible in the Genre

Genre/ Register	'C' range texts	'B' range texts	'A' range texts
Purpose/staging . . . learning to describe how the world 'is' in science ⟶			
	simple list of generic statements	General Classification ˆ Description	taxonomizing according to class/sub-class or part/whole; use of headings and paragraphs
Tenor:........... .... growth of objectivity in report writing ⟶			
interpersonal meanings	'I' as theme; expressions of attitude	generic participants as theme; grading of phenomena	generic participants as theme; grading and measurement of phenomena
Field............ .... moving from common sense to technical knowledge ⟶			
experiential meanings	common sense, 'speech-like' descriptions of field	some technical language to name new insights; some exemplification	taxonomic organization of technical language (part/whole or class/sub-class relations); exemplification and nominalization
Mode........... .... creating a context for the reader (via text) ⟶			
textual meanings	loosely coordinated single-clause sentences	integrating clauses within the sentence	parataxis, hypotaxis and embedding of different clause types within sentence
	conjunctions at sentence boundaries	conjunctions within the sentence	reasoning expressed as nouns and verbs as well as conjunctions
	inconsistency of generic reference	consistency of generic reference	control of an extended set of generic referents

Figure 4.4 Indexing Linguistic Markers of Achievement within Report Genre Using Sample Texts from Years 2 and 5

Figure 4.3 identifies the generic structure of the genre and lists some of the typical language patterns which are determined by the register (field, mode and tenor). This figure has been designed for teachers, and technical terminology that is included is adequately described in the introduction. Figure 4.4 is a matrix showing linguistic features which are typical of written texts of this genre. The linguistic features are used to help to distinguish between bottom range (C), middle range (B) and top range texts (A). Criteria, as in Figure 4.4, which are comprehensive and linguistic, can help overcome the problem inherent in communicative language testing, that of rating scales that are subjective and hence unreliable. As argued earlier, to make subjective assessment procedures as reliable as possible, ratings criteria need to be clearly specified and carefully described. Because of the lack of an adequate linguistic framework, the ASLPR and the RSA rating scales have vague and ill-defined terminology, so the problems of subjectivity and lowered reliability remain. However, criteria, as in Figure 4.3, which are *explicit* and *linguistically*-based are not so open to individual judgment, are more systematic and therefore more reliable.

In conclusion, we will list five principles that Macken (1989) argues should guide the process for evaluating students' writing. We would argue that these are relevant for the assessment of students' language abilities across curriculum areas and for assessment in community language programmes. These are:

1. The evidence of student achievement ... needs to be criterion-referenced and these criteria should be comprehensive and linguistic.
2. The assessment criteria should be linked to curriculum objectives.
3. Those criteria should be explicit.
4. These criteria should be ... expressed in a language that teachers can use and share with others.
5. These same criteria should be available to students and be used to help them improve ... in all subject areas and contexts. (1989: 3.2)

Systemic-functional linguistics provides a model of language that, because of its functional orientation, has particular applicability for education. Because of the practical concerns of applied linguists, the competence and performance distinction drops us into no-man's land, whereas in Halliday's functional approach language as use is mapped onto language as system. We are not, therefore, left trying to bridge the gap between competence and performance; his model of language through the central concept of realization relates actual language use to the underlying linguistic system.

5
An Empirical Case Study:
German and Macedonian Language Maintenance in Wollongong

Purposes

In shaping our research programme, we attempted to be mindful not only of the information required by the Department of Immigration and Ethnic Affairs, but also of the reasons why this information might be required. Our brief was as follows:

> The Department of Immigration and Ethnic Affairs has primary carriage for developing policies designed to ensure the successful settlement of immigrants to Australia. An essential element of this has been the development of policies of multiculturalism encompassing the right to cultural maintenance while acknowledging the government's responsibility to provide English-language learning opportunities and the obligation incumbent upon settlers to become proficient in the national language, English. In addition, this Department has a significant role in consultations of an ongoing and ad hoc nature with other Commonwealth and State bodies and non-government organisations which have functions and activities in which the language skills of clients, and consequently of the personnel employed, are important considerations.
>
> The principal objective of this study is to obtain authoritative data on the differing attitudes to maintenance of the mother tongue held by Macedonian and German communities within Wollongong and Shellharbour LGAs and to assess how this is linked to proficiency in English, attitudes to languages other than English and to views of personal identity.
>
> In particular the study should ascertain the attitudes of respondents towards:
> * Major problems they are facing as an ethnolinguistic group (such as possible loss of language by children),

* the desirability of ethnic language retention across the generations,
* the allocation of reponsibility for ensuring retention of language,
* the value of second language skills in Australian society.

The study should also assess the degree of

* existing Macedonian and German language skills in the respective communities for the four macro skills of understanding, speaking, reading and writing,
* proficiency in English in both communities in these four macro skills.

This brief, even when narrowed down to two linguistic groups in one region, covers an enormous area and raises many extremely difficult questions. If we had viewed the Department's requirements and purposes as purely informational, a practical narrowing-down could only have been quite arbitrary. We could, for example, have considered some segments of information more accessible and more readily or more thoroughly quantifiable, and concentrated on them.

We decided, however, to examine closely the Department's purposes in commissioning research into the maintenance of languages other than English in Australia. In some ways, reading the brief carefully, the Department's purposes were somewhat similar to those of an opinion poll. It is important to have a record of what people want in order to 'ensure the successful settlement of immigrants to Australia'. Multiculturalism is to ensure the 'right to cultural maintenance'. But to implement policy with precision or effectiveness, the reasons and means by which people might wish to exercise this right need to be ascertained.

It is worth, at this point, considering the concept of 'right'. Rights are not necessities or duties. It is not a universal necessity that languages other than English be maintained in contemporary Australia. A policy of thorough adult and child English teaching, with all the best and specialized techniques of second language learning could be argued to be enough in terms of practical, material universal necessity. A thorough, expert, well-funded and sensitively executed monolingualism could be a viable approach in a society which has had mass immigration. Nor does the concept of right connote any duty of immigrant groups to maintain languages other than English. A right to non-English language maintenance merely means that people may wish to, desire to, or feel it important that they maintain their mother tongue. Failing universal material necessity and enforceable individual duty, the concept of right takes us into the realm of opinions, desires and attitudes. This was precisely one of the principal aspects of our research brief — and quite rightly. In liberal democracy, social policy should accommodate and incorporate many desires and beliefs, even if they do not seem to be universally necessary.

On the basis of rights, a welfare state makes structural spaces of the expression of wants and desires. This might not be possible or might not find its fullest expression unless institutionalized. The desire to maintain languages other than English in Australia, for example, though not a necessity for the government or a duty on the part of immigrants from non-English-speaking backgrounds, might not find adequate expression without the provision of government-funded, formal teaching situations. This institutional support, rationalized as a right, is to a large degree a matter of demographic deference, after massive and continuous post-war immigration to Australia. Opinions and attitudes are important in terms of the management of consensus. New opinions and attitudes have emerged because a significant proportion of the population is now of non-English-speaking background.

This, however, is by no means the whole picture. Alongside a now acknowledged right to maintain languages other than English, there has been a 'government responsibility to provide English-language learning opportunities and the obligation incumbent upon settlers to become proficient in the national language, English'. This proposition is put much more sternly; English language learning is not simply an accommodation of needs and desires, but a matter of necessity and duty. Hence our decision for the second major part of the research brief: to assess actual language proficiency in English and the mother tongue, and the relationship between the two.

In other words, the picture emerging of the underlying purposes of the brief is, on the one hand, to assess desires, opinions and attitudes which might lead groups of non-English-speaking background to exercise a right, and, on the other, to assess the world of necessity and duty in terms of effective, necessary communication. There can be a crucial relation or disjunction between these two purposes. When there is a disjunction in practical policy terms, 'community' language courses and services might be offered in such a way that at least an official gesture to 'cultural maintenance' is registered. In this case the pedagogical implications tend to take on a secondary emphasis. On the other hand, we believe there can be an important relation between the two purposes. Some forms of non-English language maintenance (indeed, a general commitment to language teaching in Australian education) may well be critical in terms of the development of effective communication, not just within groups of non-English-speaking background, but in terms of the development of communicative competence in English, access to the tools of education and effective social action and (in the case of the young) unimpaired cognitive development. Matters considered simply as rights (in terms of making space for the exercise of desire) might well be of equal importance to the same social ends which make the teaching and learning of English a necessity and duty.

Accordingly, we took the research brief rather more seriously than simply to reflect attitudes. Casting desire for the maintenance of languages other than English only into the realm of attitudes, might well have neglected certain necessities involving strategies directed towards the acquisition of effective communication, and the consequent access to social goods. These are matters of real, deep-seated needs. Insofar as the maintenance of so-called 'community languages' is regarded as worthy, it is not just a (preferably minimal) accommodation to public opinion. Rather, it should be seen as something more serious in terms of the servicing of real needs. Less than that will ultimately be of little more genuine usefulness. It could even become a simple expression of political pragmatism on the part of policy-makers; do as little as possible, as cheaply as possible, to please as many as possible, regardless of the pedagogical, cognitive and social consequences.

The most critical site of language maintenance or non-maintenance is intergenerational, and, in particular, in the socialization of children. One generation frequently desires to have its children maintain their mother tongue. In terms of people's attitudes (officially classified as 'cultural maintenance' in a 'multicultural society'), an institutional gesture will do the trick by making some space for the exercise of desire (now officially classified as a 'right'). Being in a rush to meet immediate desires (with a view that it is better to meet them minimally than not at all) will profoundly affect the style and content of policy. It does not take much to do a little bit towards 'maintaining culture' and show that the government is hearing and responding to wishes. So 'community languages' might have a very different style and emphasis than the conventional 'academic' teaching of 'foreign' languages. In contrast, a view to real needs might involve a quite different approach. For example, non-English languages might be maintained in order to continue unhindered lines of children's cognitive development, in tandem with the learning of English.

In our interpretation of the purposes of this research we thus made two major decisions. First, we felt it was important not merely to register opinions but also to assess needs. Opinions can be accommodated by gestures and tokens, but in the long term such political pragmatism often backfires, both for the people to whom the gestures are offered (the inadequate satisfaction of a need can be an impetus for making more articulate and effective demands) and for those who miss out on special (and seemingly unjustified) treatment. So, as well as registering opinions, we attempted to assess the social purpose of maintaining languages other than English. Social policy, in short, should be more sophisticated than, for example, making immigrants feel at home away from home by giving their languages a modicum of institutional respect. In methodological terms this is why we conducted both an attitude survey and language proficiency tests, and view the results as critically related for sophisticated policy formulation and social practice. Second, we have regarded education as a major site for the maintenance of languages other than English, not just because language maintenance or non-maintenance occurs most decisively in the socialization of a new generation, but because formal education is an area in which governments can intervene to establish and institutionalize rights or duties in a way which is more straightforward than, for example, might be the case for the household.

Methodology

One of the first suggestions in framing the research proposal was to examine a major Canadian survey as a possible model (O'Bryan *et al.* 1976). Some of its key questions (to give an indication of its purposes and methodology) were as follows:

17. What in your opinion is the most important part of the . . . (group) . . . way of life for . . . in Canada?

> Festivals and holidays.
> Religious beliefs.
> Language used.
> Food.
> Other (specify).

18. Do you think there will come a time when most . . . in Canada will have forgotten all about their ethnic past?

> Depends (on what)?
> No.

20. In your opinion, how many people of . . . origin in Canada do you think speak . . . ?

> All or almost all.
> More than half.
> About half.
> Less than half.
> Few or none.

26. On the whole then, how desirable do you think it is for . . . in Canada to speak . . . ?

> Very desirable.
> Somewhat desirable.
> Neither desirable nor undesirable.
> Somewhat undesirable.
> Very undesirable.

52.   How effective do you feel the school was in teaching or developing the use of . . . ? Was it

Very useful?
Somewhat useful?
Not very useful?
Not at all useful?

142.   What proportion of the time does your child use . . . when (he, she) speaks to you?

Always.
Most of the time.
Some of the time.
Never.

143.   How has (he, she) felt about learning or continuing to use . . . ? Has (he, she)

Strongly liked to?
Somewhat liked to?
Does not care?
Somewhat resisted it?
Strongly resisted it?

144.   Have you ever had disagreements with (him, her) about this?

Yes.
No.

229.   One final question, and then we're finished. Everything considered, how do you think your ethnic background had affected your chances of getting ahead in life as a Canadian? Has it

Interfered a lot?
Interfered a little?
Not affected?
Helped a little?
Helped a lot?

Two problems immediately arise for us from this style of research. First, from a practical point of view, the cost of administration (including interpreters) would be enormous, if we were to produce results that would in any way be methodologically sound. Accordingly, our original research proposal was shaped in critical reference to the Canadian survey:

On the basis of its research experience, the Centre considers the use of orthodox/standard sample survey techniques is not appropriate for this study.

The use of such orthodox sample survey techniques would require an enormous financial outlay. Given the large number of factors to be taken into consideration, and the necessity of having sufficient number of cases in each category/cell, such a survey assumes awesome dimensions. The inordinate length of the O'Bryan *et al.* Canadian survey gives some indication of this.

The general disadvantages of the sample survey approach include:

(a) the difficulties of statistical validity given uncertainties about the statistical universe from which the sample is drawn.

(b) increasing evidence that there is a growing resentment among migrant communities to long interviews by government and commercial agencies on intimate aspects of their lives, often with no immediate or even foreseeable return in terms of improvement to their lives. One can expect that refusal rates, often already high, may in fact be on the rise, particularly where ethnic organisations can no longer be satisfied that they wish to commend such surveys to their members.

(c) difficulties in recruiting sufficiently qualified bilingual Macedonian interviewers and the time and monetary cost of translating responses (especially qualitative data) into English for purposes of analysis.

(d) the need to carry out considerable research prior to the formulation of the questionnaire in order that appropriate questions might be asked; such research would add considerably to the cost of research. However, no matter how comprehensive such research is, there will remain the usual difficulties of sacrificing nuances and qualitative responses for answers that are amenable to statistical manipulation. This has particular difficulties where it involves people engaging in self-evaluation of language use in the often time-pressured setting of long interviews.

Some alleviation of the problems of surveying non-English speaking populations can be achieved by using the 'snow-balling' technique; but problems of representativeness remain, as do the general inadequacies of the survey schedule technique in terms of high cost for often suspect data with difficulties of analysis, particularly where programmatic implications (surely the object of such research) are desired.

As our overall research programme developed, a second major problem arose for us about work along the lines of the Canadian survey. Even if made practically viable and methodologically rigorous, it only elicits a very limited kind of information. Asking people what they immediately feel about the effectiveness of school in maintaining their mother tongue and how children feel about maintaining their family's language, for example, tells us nothing about actual effectiveness of schooling or real pressing needs or ultimate non-essential needs (left unestablished), of which people might not be fully aware. It simply registers often relatively uninformed opinion. Opinions are, without doubt, important. But they also embody information of greater use to the political pragmatist than to the social scientist. For example, social policy might, on the basis of an objective assessment of the social situation, view its role as interventionist or educative and not simply, and unproblematically, a mirror of opinion. The whole frame of the Canadian survey presupposes a politically pragmatic social policy.

As an alternative to opinion surveying, a key informant research strategy was proposed.

Such an approach would recognise that there are bilingual workers from both German and Macedonian communities who have over the years acquired expert information on language maintenance (in the areas of home, pre-school, school, workplace, welfare services, etc.) and that their knowledge can be drawn on through in-depth interviews. The validity of their observations can be established through small, specific surveys of targeted groups. For example, in the field of health, the knowledge of healthcare interpreters would be validated by surveying the universe of patients from that specific language group who are having medical treatment in a given hospital at a specified moment. Key informant interviews would also be supplemented and given a test of validity by the use of community consultations (held in community languages). The advantages of such an approach would be that seminars (drawn from church groups, women's groups, parental organisations, the elderly, youth groups, etc.) could be adequately briefed in advance as to the questions to be canvassed and that the often intimidatory setting of the doorknock interview can be replaced by the interaction that flows from discussions held in group settings. Key informant interviews could also be supplemented by interviews, both in depth and, where appropriate, through structured interviews with purposive sampling of targeted categories: employed/unemployed; old/young; recent arrival/long settled; low/high education level; male/female; etc.

Alongside this was to be an action research strategy which aimed not merely to register perceived needs, but to suggest, develop and even test strategies, of which the subjects of research might be (individually or as a group) unaware.

In the course of the research this programme had to be modified. It transpired (as we will discuss below) that there simply was not the range of key informants in the variety of social situations we had anticipated. This in itself was a significant research finding. Even the views of those involved in, for example, welfare provision, were often contradictory and difficult to interpret. Accordingly, we decided to present key informants with a questionnaire which not only elicited attitudes to language maintenance in general but presented concrete language policy alternatives (of which they might have been unaware) and asked questions about their desirability. More critically, we also issued questionnaires (along the same lines) to both children and their parents, with the former being evaluated objectively on language proficiency. In this way we could link attitudes and actual language proficiency.

Scope

Strictly speaking, our brief required us to consider language maintenance across the whole spectrum of pre-schoolers to the aged. Of course, quite different issues of language maintenance occur both for different age and socio-economic groups. Practically, the research programme was narrowed down to the following:

1. Language proficiency tests (in both English and German or Macedonian, with a control group tested in English only from each school), together with an attitudes survey for students in:

   School A: A year 5 group in a primary school in a lower socio-economic area, with a high density Macedonian population.

   School B: A year 10 group in a secondary school in a lower socio-economic area, with a high density Macedonian population.

   School C: A year 5 group in a primary school in a higher socio-economic area, with a low density Macedonian population.

   School D: A year 10 group in a high school in a higher socio-economic area with a low density Macedonian population.

   School E: A year 5 group in a primary school in a lower socio-economic area with a significant number of students of German language background.

School F: A year 10 group in a high school in a lower socio-economic area with a significant number of students of German language background.

School G: A year 10 group in a high school in a higher socio-economic area with a number of students of German language background.

Our original intention had been to establish the same pattern of school types we managed to find for the Macedonians, for the Germans as well. This was not possible for reasons we will elaborate upon.

2. An attitudes survey of all the students who took part in the language assessment, including those in the control group.
3. An attitudes survey of the parents of the students who were tested and questioned, including the parents of those in the control group.
4. Key informants' evenings and formal attitudes survey.

The Region: Socio-Cultural and Demographic Background

Our brief was to survey groups of people of Macedonian and German background in the Wollongong and Shellharbour local government areas. These areas, in a fashion almost unique in Australia, are dominated by a single industrial conglomerate. If only by virtue of the number of people they employ, companies owned by Broken Hill Pty (BHP) are central to the region's economy. Almost a quarter of the area's workforce works for Australian Iron and Steel (AIS) alone. Alongside this are directly related heavy manufacturing industries such as John Lysaghts (another BHP company) and other dependent metal industries.

Non-English-speaking immigrants make up 60 per cent of the non-salaried employees of AIS. Of a total staff of 14,137 in August 1983, 2521 were of Yugoslav origin and 222 of German origin. (BHP Public Affairs Department). Given that this is by far the largest place of employment in the region, the implications for the subjects of our survey are very important. Compared with other parts of Australia, a high percentage of the workforce is working-class or blue-collar and a lower than average percentage is white-collar or involved in service industries. Of the blue-collar working-class group, a much higher than average percentage is of non-English-speaking background (Morrissey and Palser, 1983). Although Yugoslav-born make up only 3.9 per cent of the population of the Wollongong region, they make up 17.8 per cent of the workforce of AIS, the majority of whom are classified as labourers. The picture is not so clearcut for those of German origin, whose representation in the workforce of AIS is roughly proportionate to their overall position in the population. This only means that those of German origin are just as strongly affected by the type and extent of employment at AIS as the regional population as a whole.

Compounding this situation is the significant increase in unemployment. AIS had reduced its workforce from nearly 22,000 in 1980 to about 13,000 when this survey was undertaken in 1984, with decreased demand for steel and technological changes. This had sent a multiplier effect not just through immediately dependent industries, but through the whole local economy.

Significant population growth in the post-World War II period, almost entirely the result of immigration, has tapered off since the mid-1970s. In terms of the two groups we were surveying this has meant that there has been less new settlement, and each group has aged in demographic terms and taken on a more 'established' character.

The Schools Surveyed: Socio-Cultural, Demographic and Language Teaching Background

This overall picture of the Wollongong-Shellharbour region belies considerable local socio-cultural variation. Our initial intention was to select primary and secondary schools to study children of German and Macedonian background which were in areas with high migrant population density / low socio-economic conditions and low migrant population density / high socio-economic conditions. This proved possible for the purpose of sampling students of Macedonian background (Schools A, B, C and D) but not possible for students of German background (Schools E, F, and G). In the case of the latter group we were not only hampered by the smaller size of the overall group and their demographic dispersion; an additional factor was that, even though the social class distribution of the German population appears the same as that of the general population in a predominantly working-class area, we were not able to find schools in which there was a surveyable number of students of German background and between which there was a clear differentiation in terms of the migrant population density and socio-economic status.

The following is a profile of each school and its catchment area. We have relied heavily for this on Keys and Wilson's survey of the region based on an intensive analysis of the results of the 1981 census (1984). The figures do not perfectly match the catchment areas of the schools we selected in two respects. First, the figures represent localities as defined by the census, and not strictly speaking the catchment areas of the schools. In each case, however, we have used the figures for the statistical locality or localities most closely approximating each school's catchment area. Second, the figures represent a period three years before our survey. We consider neither of these to prejudice the relevance of the figures as, in both instances, any differences are in the direction of the accentuation of the socio-economic variation we sought to ensure in our choice of schools. For example, the primary schools have smaller and socio-economically more homogeneous catchment areas than the statistical areas represent. On the second point, economic recession has in general most directly and immediately hit blue-collar workers, but those in higher socio-economic areas less severely and more gradually.

School A

Our focus in School A, officially classified as a disadvantaged school, was a year 5 group. In year 5 there were two streamed classes. Twenty out of thirty-five in the more advanced class and sixteen out of twenty-four in the less advanced class were Macedonian. This speaks not only for the demographic density of Macedonians in the area, but their relative lack of success at school. Moreover, this is in a school where almost all students were facing severe difficulties. Only forty out of the 385 students in the school speak English as a first language, but according to the teachers, this group is disadvantaged as well in terms of their socio-economic situation and the proportion of single-parent families.

Macedonian is taught four hours per week to all students in School A by a teacher employed only for that purpose. Remarks were made about conservative teaching style, but the school seemed well pleased with the increased involvement of Macedonian parents since the introduction of the programme.

According to the figures in the 1981 census, 88.9 per cent of the population in the catchment area for School A are overseas-born or of overseas-born parentage (of whom only 1.8 per cent are British- and Irish-born, which means that most of the immigrant population are of non-English-speaking background). Of the overseas-born, 33.7 per cent are Yugoslav. We should note here that the census category 'Yugoslav' is not well suited to our purposes, as it refers to an area defined geopolitically and not linguistically. The figures are of important indicative use, however, as the great majority of Yugoslavs in the Wollongong-Shellharbour region are of Macedonian language background and what we lose (statistically) in terms of other Yugoslav language groupings (such as Serbian and Croatian), we gain at least in part in numbers of Macedonians born in countries other than Yugoslavia (such as in northern Greece or Bulgaria).

In the catchment area for the school, 81.3 per cent of the workforce are classified as 'tradespersons, production-process workers and labourers', while only 3.1 per cent are classified as 'professional, technical and administrative workers'. This contrasts with overall Australian figures of 29.9 per cent for tradespeople, etc. and 20.2 per cent for professionals. There is a not unsurprising parallel with this in the statistics relating to levels of educational attainment: 8.3 per cent of the adult population hold a trade or other qualification as their highest qualification, against an Australian average of 18.4 per cent; 1.3 per cent have degrees or diplomas, against an Australian average of 8.7 per cent; and 50.2 per cent never attended school or left befc:: ¬he Australian minimal legal age of 15, against a national average of 26.8 per cent. It hardly needs pointing out that there is a strong relationship between levels of educational attainment and occupation. It will remain for us to show from our survey how this pattern is being reproduced in the next generation.

Other key socio-economic indicators are that median male income ($9979) is below the national figure ($10,906), and unemployment, at 8.8 per cent, is above the national average of 5.9 per cent. This is particularly accentuated in the 15–24 age bracket, where the figures show a rate of 17.2 per cent, against the national average of 11.5 per cent. This difference is likely to have been strongly accentuated as the period between the time when the statistics were taken and this research project (1981 to 1984) was one in which the AIS has shed nearly 30 per cent of its workforce. The impact of this change is underlined by the massive proportion of the workforce engaged in manufacturing (76.1 per cent compared with a 19.2 per cent national average) as opposed to infrastructure (electricity, water, construction, transport: 6.7 per cent compared with 16.9 per cent nationally) and services (shops, finance, community services, public administration, etc.: 16.3 per cent compared with 55.9 per cent nationally). While home ownership rests at about the national average, in the Australian context home ownership and socio-economic disadvantage often occur together. Public housing levels are below the national average, but this is a fortuitous circumstance of siting. More revealing figures are those for bedroom occupancy rates, which are above the national average, and multiple family households. This cannot be taken simply as a peculiarity of immigrant 'cultures', but as a register of socio-economic pressure. Similarly, 27.3 per cent of houses are car-less, against a national average of 14 per cent.

Women appear to be particularly burdened in this context. There is both a low labour force participation rate (which combines both the employed and those seeking employment: 50.3 per cent against 63.1 per cent nationally in the 15–24 age bracket, 36.3 per cent against 56.3 per cent nationally in the 25–49 age bracket and 25.6 per cent against 39.6 per cent in the 50–59 bracket) and also significant unemployment among those women classified as potential or actual labour-force participants (16.7 per cent against 6.8 per cent nationally). These figures indicate that the real female unemployment levels are probably much higher. Median female income is higher than the national average, which suggests that among those women in employment as much work is taken as is possible.

The statistics, therefore, show the catchment area of School A as one of high migrant population density (mainly of non-English-speaking background) in lower socio-economic conditions. Along with this are pertinent demographic trends which indicate a relatively younger than average population, but ageing towards the national average (as immigration tapers off), and high levels of masculinity.

School B

School B is a secondary school in an area which is much the same socio-economically as the locality of School A. Our original intention had been to survey year 11 students in the secondary school chosen, but there simply were not the numbers of Macedonian students staying on for years 11 and 12 for this to be feasible. While the overall school population for School B included about one-third students of Macedonian background, there were so few students staying on to year 11 that we could not muster a statistically useful group. After a significant dropout rate at the minimum school leaving age (50 per cent of the lower stream girls' class in year 9 were of Macedonian background), six out of twenty-seven were Macedonian in the higher stream year 10 boys' class and five out of twenty-eight of the higher stream girls, but ten out of twenty-nine of the lower stream boys were Macedonian and nine out of twenty-eight of the lower stream girls. This represents not only a significant dropout of Macedonian students by year 10, but also their higher numbers in the lower stream. Even after significant dropout before year 10, the year 10 to year 11 figures are further weighted against the Macedonian students. Compared with a total of thirty out of 112 students in year 10, the Macedonian representation dropped to five out of seventy-three in year 11.

No Macedonian is taught in School B.

The school situation is all the more dismal against general socio-economic and educational disadvantage. The Macedonians find themselves at the bottom of a social group which is itself depressed. On key statistical indicators, the pattern is similar (though not so severe) to the locale of School A: 66.3 per cent of the local workforce are tradespeople (29.9 per cent nationally) and 3.1 per cent professionals (20.2 per cent); 2.6 per cent are graduates (8.7 per cent); 40 per cent left school before age 15 (26.8 per cent). The median male income is below the national figure, and the median female income substantially so. Unemployment is high at 8.6 per cent (5.9 per cent), and 16.4 per cent for the 15–24 bracket (11.5 per cent). As with the area of School A, unemployment was much more severe by 1984 than it had been at the time of the 1981 census. Again, as 76 per cent of the workforce is engaged in manufacturing (19.2 per cent), compared with services at 24.6 per cent (55.9 per cent), employment cut-backs in the steel industry have hit hard. As an additional indication of the socio-economic situation, 24.2 per cent of households are car-less (14 per cent).

In this area 71.4 per cent of the population are born overseas or of overseas-born parentage (41.1 per cent) of whom 23.8 per cent were born in Yugoslavia (1 per cent). As in the area of School A, women have a lower than average labour-force participation rate. This means that the higher than average female un-employment figures (more than double the national rate) are probably conserva-tive. Patterns of demographic change (age, masculinity) are similar to area A also, and for much the same reasons.

School C

In the Wollongong-Shellharbour region, School C (a primary school) and its locality are almost the opposite to Schools A and B and their respective localities. Only 103 of 300 students are from non-English-speaking background, of whom thirty-seven are Macedonian. In year 5 there are five Macedonian children out of a total of forty-two.

No Macedonian is taught in School C.

The local area of School C, although one of the most prestigious and affluent of the Wollongong-Shellharbour region, in some respects only meets the national average in socio-economic terms: 29.0 per cent of those in the work-force are tradespeople, etc. (29.9 per cent), 28.1 per cent work in manufacturing industry (19.2 per cent), while 51.3 per cent work in service industries (55.9 per cent). This is in part a function of the particular industrial nature of the regional economy.

On other socio-economic indicators, however, the area is above the national average and remarkably different from the two other areas we have already described. Total unemployment stands at 3.2 per cent (5.9 per cent) and at 9.6 per cent among the young (11.5 per cent); 29.3 per cent of the population hold trade certificates (18.4 per cent) and 15.8 per cent degrees or diplomas (8.7 per cent). Only 14.2 per cent of the population is classified as having limited schooling (26.8 per cent). In this area 2.4 per cent of households are car-less (14 per cent). The median male income is $15,963 ($10,906) and only 10.2 per cent are classified as low income families (32.1 per cent).

Women enjoy average labour-force participation rates, below average female umemployment and above average median female income. The overseas-born or those of overseas-born parents in the area amount to 43 per cent (41.1 per cent), of whom 9.1 per cent are of English or Irish (that is, English-speaking) origin. Only 1.1 per cent of the local population were born in Yugoslavia.

School D

School D is a secondary school which was recently selective, and still maintains some of its previous academic orientation. Seven of the 152 students in year 10 are of Macedonian background, spread fairly evenly over six streamed classes, but with a slight weighting towards the lower streams.

No Macedonian is taught in School D.

The socio-economic situation in the major catchment area for School D is broadly similar to that of School C, though perhaps a little less affluent: 30.8 per cent of the workforce are tradespeople, etc. (29.9 per cent) and 27.5 per cent professionals (20.2 per cent); 23 per cent are trade certificate holders (18.4 per cent) and 11.4 per cent degree or diploma holders (8.7 per cent); 24 per cent have had limited schooling (26.8 per cent). The median male income is above the national median, though unemployment is slightly above the national rate. The area is, however, fairly uneven in socio-economic terms with significant public housing. Car-less households are at approximately the national average.

Women enjoy slightly less than average labour-force participation rates, higher than average unemployment and a median income less than the national figure. In this area 45 per cent of the population is overseas-born or of overseas-born parents (41.1 per cent) of whom 10 per cent are of British or Irish origin and 2 per cent Yugoslav.

Schools E and F

As Schools E (a primary school) and F are in close proximity, we have decided to discuss them here jointly. Notionally, they were supposed to represent a German language background group in a lower socio-economic area. While the area suffers somewhat for being a new suburb, the differentiation between the feeder area for this school and that of School G is not so clearcut as it is for the Macedonian students in Schools A and B compared with Schools C and D.

On many of the key socio-economic indicators, the catchment areas for Schools E and F are below average: 52.7 per cent of the workforce are tradespeople, etc. (29.9 per cent) and only 11.1 per cent professionals (20.2 per cent); 42.2 per cent work in manufacturing (19.2 per cent) compared with 34.2 per cent in service (55.9 per cent); 4 per cent are degree or diploma holders (8.7 per cent). The median male income is above the national figure, but unemployment is above average both for the workforce as a whole and for the 15–24 age group.

Female labour-force participation rates are below average, unemployment is considerably higher, and median female income well below the national figure. Although home ownership is high at 84.7 per cent (70.1 per cent), the car-less relatively few at 9 per cent (14 per cent) and multiple-family houses relatively few at 2.4 per cent (3 per cent), these are more indicators of the nature of the new outer-suburban development than of any substantial affluence. Here 52.7 per cent of the population are overseas-born or of overseas-born parents (41.1 per cent), of whom 11.2 per cent are British and Irish (7.8 per cent), 2.1 per cent Yugoslav (1 per cent) and 4 per cent German (0.8 per cent).

German has been taught at the School E for the past three years. It was introduced following community request. In kindergarten and year 1 students receive German tuition for two blocks of six weeks each year; this is the intention, although in practice it does not always occur for one reason or another. In years 2 to 6 students study German for two / two-and-a-half hours per week. This is an elective subject, so not all students participate. The year 5 class contains about twenty students, eight of whom have some sort of German background. It is a mixed class in that for some it is their third year of studying German at school, whereas for others it is their first year. The original idea of the teacher was that she would give entire lessons in German on topics that the students were studying in other lessons. She found, however, that this was not feasible and has since revised her ideas so that her emphasis is now on communication. Her stress is on the speaking and listening skills, followed by reading and lastly by writing.

Many other teachers are not generally in favour of German. They see it as an interruption to the normal course of study. There is a specialist German teacher at the school. There is also a specialist German room which is set up with posters, pictures, words, German children's books and dioramas (which the students help prepare). Unfortunately, not all German lessons are held here. On many occasions the German teacher is required to teach in 'normal' classrooms rather than the one she has created to stimulate the students in German.

One of the problems seen by the German teacher and the school principal is the transition of students from their school to School F, where German is not a particularly strong subject. On entering year 7, the students who have studied German at School E are split up over the various classes with perhaps two, three or four in each class. Here the problem is that while they have done an introductory course in German, the rest of the class has not, and so they start from scratch.

Students in year 7 in School F all study an introductory course in both French and German. At the end of the year 7 course students may elect to continue studying a language for years 8 to 10, and later for years 11 and 12 if it is possible. At present there is no year 10 German class. When the students were in year 9, there was a small class of students, however the German teacher left and it was several months before a replacement was found. By this stage the class had dwindled to four students and so the class was disbanded. Those four students then had to take up another elective.

School G

School G (a secondary school) is in an area without a numerically significant German population. In year 10, ten out of 150 students are of German language background. We had hoped to survey a primary school in the area as well, but there were too few students of German background.

In socio-economic terms the area contrasts, if not very strongly, with the area in which Schools E and F are situated. On the indicators of tradespeople, professionals, those involved in manufacturing and those in services, the area is closer to the national average. There is, however, a significant mining component to the workforce. Similarly, in terms of education, area G is closer to the national figures for degree and diploma holders and limited schooling than area E–F.

Similarly, the labour-force participation rate for women is closer to the national figures, as are female unemployment and median income. Here 52.7 per cent of the population are overseas-born or of overseas-born parentage, of whom 10.8 per cent are of British or Irish origin or parentage; 0.9 per cent are Yugoslav-born and 0.6 per cent born in Germany.

Every student in year 7 at School G must undertake an introductory language course (three periods of forty minutes each week). This includes a basic course in French, German and Italian and so enables the students to have a 'sampling' of each language to decide if they would like to do further study in it. At the end of year 7 students elect to continue the study of a language if they wish. Classes are formed in French, German and Italian provided there are sufficient numbers of students. Classes in years 8, 9 and 10 each receive five periods of forty minutes per week. If there are sufficient numbers, the subjects will continue in years 11 and 12, where they each receive six periods of forty minutes. If, for example, students have previously studied German in years 8, 9 and 10, but then find that there are not enough students to form a class in years 11 and 12, the following options are open to them:

1. they may change their minds and study another subject which fits into the school timetable;
2. they may stay at the school and study German via the NSW Department of Education's Correspondence School (usually a limit of two students per subject per school); or
3. they may transfer to another school where German is taught in the senior school.

French, German and Italian are offered as subjects at School G 'because that's the way it was' when the current language mistress came to the school, although she states that it was probably a school decision rather than community request that led to their introduction. There are currently twenty-six students in the year 10 German class, five of whom have parent/s born in a German-speaking country.

The Macedonian Language Background Group in the Wollongong-Shellharbour Region

It is difficult to pinpoint Macedonia as a geographical entity. It is a state within Yugoslavia, with an administrative centre in Skopje. Beyond this the situation is complicated by the existence of Aegean Macedonia (the northern part of modern-day Greece) and Pirin Macedonia (Western Bulgaria); and within the area of Yugoslavia named Macedonia there are significant numbers of Hungarians, Turks and Albanians.

The principal basis of Macedonian emigration is the familiar one of economic development. In Yugoslavia since the war there has been strong economic development, with the establishment of new industrial centres and the industrialization and collectivization of agriculture. The transformation of an essentially peasant-agrarian economy has tended to reduce labour needs faster than new industrial development could absorb those who had left the land. With resistance to immigration from Macedonia into the larger industrial centres of the (relatively more industrially advanced) north, and borders more open than any other East European country, this tended to constitute a push factor towards international labour migration from Macedonia. Alongside development, however, was a particular variety of underdevelopment conducive to substantial emigration. Modernization in some sectors did not preclude the continued existence of peasant agriculture, albeit progressively becoming more problematic as a permanent life-form, and more glaringly being seen as poverty rather than simple normal existence. It is this classic process of uneven development, in the transition from peasant-agrarian to industrial society, which was the principal background and impetus to Macedonian emigration to Australia.

The Macedonian language is Slavic, written in Cyrillic script (with relationships to Greek and Russian scripts). It shares some common features with Croatian and Serbian. The formation of post-war Yugoslavia has had two somewhat contradictory effects on the language: first, Macedonian has been formalized and institutionalized in a standard, written form, whereas previously for the vast majority of the population it had only been a spoken language. Macedonian was not taught or used in schools before World War II. Second, a romanized-script Serbo-Croatian is also taught in Macedonian schools today. (We found it necessary to test both in Cyrillic and a non-standard romanized version of Macedonian.) Considerable reform has occurred in the education system in Macedonia, particularly in the last decade. Most of the Macedonian parents in our survey experienced little and limited formal education, and then of a very rigid, pedagogically traditional variety.

In the 1981 census Yugoslavs in the Wollongong region generally compared unfavourably in socio-economic terms with other groupings. (In the following comparisons, figures for the Australian-born population in the Wollongong region are in brackets. The majority of Yugoslavs in the Wollongong region are Macedonian and relatively more disadvantaged than other Yugoslav sub-groups.) Correlations between Yugoslav birthplace and having a tradesperson's occupation stand at .74 (− .84), professional occupation at − .44 (.58), and employers − .38 (.57). The correlation of Yugoslav birthplace against employment in manufacturing industry is .77 (− .91) and in services − .63 (.73). Yugoslav birthplace against unemployment was only .29 (− .54) but this is likely to have changed as Yugoslav participation in manufacturing is very strong, and this has been hardest hit by the recession since 1981. The correlation of female unemployment against Yugoslav birthplace is stronger at .46 (− .70). Compared with the Australian-born, few Yugoslavs have high family income: − .41 (.50), many are car-less: .42 (− .52), bedroom occupancy figures are high: .54 (− .60) and multiple family households frequent: .84 (− .63). This last factor, as we pointed out before, cannot simply be viewed as a cultural attribute, but as a measure of socio-economic disadvantage in an urban environment where few houses are designed to be adequate for multiple-family occupancy.

Educationally, trades certificate-holding rates are low: − .39 (.54), as are those for degree and diploma holding: − .39 (.54) and those with post-school qualification in general: − .56 (.69). The correlation between Yugoslav background and limited schooling (less than to age 15) is strongly positive: .71 (− .66), as, hardly surprisingly, it is for those declaring their English to be limited: .89 (− .90).

The German Language Group in the Wollongong-Shellharbour Region

The background of the German group from which we took our sample could hardly have been more different from the Macedonians. There have been defined (if geographically changing) German states for more than a century, a German-speaking Austria, and clearly defined German-speaking groups in neighbouring states. The push factors in emigration have been fundamentally different for the German population, being, broadly speaking, massive crisis within European industrialism (fascism, war, the East-West split), rather than the trauma of development/underdevelopment. This background contrast is decisive for relative success in terms of the skills necessary to be able to use industrialism to one's socio-economic advantage.

The German language, again in sharp contrast to Macedonian, is a long-established official state language, with an extensive high-cultural and literary tradition. There are regional dialects as well as a standard, high-cultural form. The status and nature of the German language are very much reflected in the fact that it has long been taught as a foreign language in Australia in a trad-itional, academic sense. It is an international language of science and commerce with such a high cultural weight behind it that its study is frequently justified as an academic exercise in its own right.

In the 1981 census the German population in the Wollongong region sits in socio-economic terms roughly between Yugoslav-born and Australian-born extremes. From a study of the correlations it becomes evident that the Germans exhibit a socio-economic unevenness, rather than the relative uniformity of other groups. The relative position of those of German background is best repre-sented by comparing them with Yugoslav-born and Australian-born (see Table 5.1).

Table 5.1   Variables Associated with Place of Birth in the Wollongong Statistical District (expressed as correlation coefficients)

	Yugoslav-born	German-born	Australian-born
Tradespeople	.74	.16	− .84
Professionals	− .44	− .20	.58
Employers	− .38	− .30	.57
Manufacturing	.77	.13	− .91
Tertiary	− .70	− .23	.83
Infrastructure	− .59	− .04	.72
Services	− .63	− .25	.73
Total unemployment	.29	.26	− .54
Female unemployment	.46	.29	− .70
Youth unemployment	.17	.33	− .34
Trade certificates	− .61	.01	.69
Graduates and diplomats	− .39	− .20	.54
Qualifications generally	− .56	− .11	.69
Limited schooling	.71	− .10	− .66
Median male income	− .43	.18	.42
Median female income	− .33	.14	.36
High income	− .40	.01	.46
High family income	− .41	.01	.50
Limited English	.89	− .15	− .90
Multiple-family households	.84	− .14	− .63
High bedroom occupancy rate	.54	.30	− .60
Car-less households	.42	− .18	− .52
Two or more cars	− .46	.11	.56

Source: Keys and Wilson (1984).

Key Informant Interviews

Our initial aim was to bring together a number of people who, in the course of their employment, voluntary work or other community involvement, used Macedonian or German or who had extensive contact with Macedonian or German speakers. These people were to be considered key informants, in critical social locations, who could give us specific advice from their perception of linguistic needs. Interestingly, there were far fewer people falling into this category than we had anticipated. Except for the area of social work and the 'ethnic schools', we were unable to draw upon other professionals who used Macedonian or German language in the course of their work or were from Macedonian or German background themselves and serviced people of their own linguistic group. As a consequence, the contributions to the discussions were more in the nature of personal opinions. The notion of 'key informant' obviously became problematic for us.

Information was elicited from our German and Macedonian informants in two ways: (1) a formal survey questionnaire; and (2) relatively unstructured discussion/interview groups. The information from the group discussions was recorded on tape and transcribed. Some groups were held in English and some in German/Macedonian, depending on the group's choice. Most chose English, despite the fact that in every instance there were group leaders available for additional Macedonian/German groups. This might partly be explained as a desire to give opinions directly to the principal researchers.

Formal Attitudes Survey Questionnaires

In formulating a formal questionnaire to survey attitudes we faced two immediate difficulties. First, there were very few models to go by internationally, let alone for the Australian context. The O'Bryan *et al.* Canadian survey was one of the few that covered the sorts of areas we wished to study. Second, we felt that the methodological assumptions of most surveys of attitudes to languages were problematic. We have already made reference to the O'Bryan *et al.* survey in this regard. As an introductory rationale to the survey structure and its place in our overall research strategy, we will develop these arguments further.

In a major overview of the study of attitudes to languages, Lewis states the usual frame of reference for language attitude surveys:

> Attitudes either are, or help create, mental sets. These mental sets often constitute a cluster of preconceptions that determine the evaluation of a task, a situation, an institution, or an object before one actually faces it . . . . Attitude is determined . . . [not only] by the ob-

jective situation, its complexity, or its novelty, but just as much by a desire for approval or the avoidance of disapproval, among other needs.

... [A]ttitudes are an important dimension in the structure of a society as are other more tangible forces — like the size of the language group, age distribution, and so on. Many would say that the import-ance of a particular language in society derives in a very large part from the attitudes which are adopted toward it. The structure of a hetero-geneous society, whether that heterogeneity is ethnic, linguistic, religious or socio-economic, is largely the result of the conflict or the convergence of attitudes to the various components of social diversity. (Lewis, 1981: 262–3)

It is precisely this methodological assumption about the role of subjectivity, which underlies all the surveys of attitudes to language maintenance we could find, that we thought questionable. First, it neglects the fact that attitudes are themselves shaped in contexts. Arguably, the flowering of 'ethnic politics' is not simply the product of feelings welling up in people, but is as much the result of spaces having been made through officially instituted policies of pluralism, and funding for pluralism. In other words, it is important to view the attitudes under review as much as products of social, structural and institutional circumstances, as they are spontaneous demands. For example, current attitudes to first language maintenance cannot be measured and viewed as social absolutes but have to be seen in the context of policies which have constructed cultural plural-ism and which have thus given attitudes a particular space, shape and form.

Second, a methodology which examines attitudes in relative isolation is likely to assume that attitudes are reality, simply and unproblematically. On the contrary, attitudes are often distortions or partial misapprehensions of reality. It is the task of social science to work beyond the assumptions of opinion polls, to suggest and test social strategies for their effectiveness rather than their popu-larity. This is not because effectiveness and popularity are polar opposites. Indeed, the ineffective will soon become unpopular, and the immediately un-popular might become popular once its effectiveness is demonstrated. A strict reliance on attitudes assessment presupposes that no one is ever in a position to educate. The only role of the social scientist, it is presupposed, is to record opinions.

For example, 'communities' might perhaps immediately like small, one-off, first language maintenance programmes. But it would be very dubious research finding if such programmes were known to be, or proved to be, ineffect-ive in terms of a number of broad social and educational goals. In the short run such programmes could possibly be an ideological one. But in the long run, the role of following demonstrable ineffectiveness, their initial popularity might wane. Rather than research simply reflecting perceived needs, specialist, scientific study of the situation is required with a view to relating real and perceived needs through social and educational practice.

Accordingly, the attitudinal survey instruments we devised measure perceptions as other surveys in the field conventionally do. But crucially, we also attempted to link attitudes to the social circumstances created by official policies of, and funding for, cultural pluralism. This linkage was tested against an objective assessment of needs by means of language proficiency tests, and within a sociological assessment of the types of language needs of speakers of English as a second language (of which such speakers are sometimes not in a specialist position to be fully aware). So it is absolutely critical that the attitudes surveys not be regarded as a separate or discrete part of this research project. That would be to misinterpret both our overall intentions and the internal structure of the questionnaires.

The Key Informants' Discussion Groups: German Language Background

The participants in the German group dicussions were almost all involved in the German 'ethnic' school that runs on a part-time basis outside day school hours. Those interested enough to join the discussions included parents, teachers, organizers and their friends. It is, in our view, extremely significant that we could not interest other professionals (health, legal and so on) to participate. Apparently language maintenance was not a sufficiently important priority for such service deliverers to choose to join in a discussion to voice their opinions.

During the discussions the reasons frequently given for the value of maintaining German language across generations included a concern that children understand their parents, a statement that German was an important international language in its own right, and a belief that language learning in general is worthwhile. For example, it was argued that another language is handy for travel. Arguments about the cognitive benefit of bilingual teaching were not countenanced (except by one teacher in one of the discussion groups). There was a general consensus that children should not be cushioned from the necessity of having to adapt to English and the mainstream education system as it stands. The specific practical usefulness of German was broached by all the participants. In local factories it was claimed that workers had occasionally found it helpful to be able to read German technical instructions, and that German was a minor *lingua franca* in the steelworks among Germans, Poles, Hungarians and Turks, many of whom had either been guestworkers or had learnt some German for various other reasons before migration to Australia.

There was also a general agreement by the participants that their German language background had not been met with significant prejudice in Australia. There were no cases reported of being ostracized or victimized for speaking a language other than English in public. It was claimed that taunts they had suffered as children or as younger people about Hitler and the war had subsided and, in any case, these were simply made in relation to the war and not as an expression of racism. The hardships they had encountered during the period of initial adjustment they considered predictable: loss of family connections, difficulties in getting things done and so on. They felt all of these had become less problematic as time went on. No one perceived that they had experienced employment difficulties as a result of their having to learn a new language of daily social interaction as an adult.

This optimism was consistent with a philosophical commitment to what might once have been called 'assimilation', as reflected in their attitudes to learning English. Children, it was claimed, picked up English quickly, and 'naturally'. Also there were assertions that adult Germans were better educated than other immigrants and, it was said facetiously, were more intelligent and therefore picked up English more quickly. It was frequently commented that living in Wollongong tended to obscure slightly the necessity of learning English. An immigration officer had warned one of the group members that Wollongong is not the real Australia and that if he wanted to adjust quickly into the real Australia, maybe he should go to Goulburn. Another woman said she would not live in Oak Flats because there were too many Germans there and she wanted her family to become part of the wider community as quickly as possible.

English was viewed as vital. Except for several teachers in the group, it was also thought that special classes — bilingual or English as a Second Language — were unnecessary. For all, including adults, it was considered that the best way to learn was simply to mix as much as possible with the wider community. None of the members of the groups was interested in continuing their education in German (such as in technical courses with instruction in German which might be offered in TAFE), although there were calls for the introduction of German language and literature at Wollongong University which at present only teaches the Romance languages.

On strategies and emphases for teaching German, the attitudes of the groups were extremely contradictory. No one wanted to say that ethnic schools did not have a role to play, and many said that additional funding would be preferable. For mainstream schooling, a clear majority said that second language teaching was not necessary until the secondary school. Some were concerned that ethnic schools should not become a substitute for formal language teaching in mainstream schools. About half said that language learning — any language — was an important part of education, while others said that they viewed German specifically as important to them. Contradicting this view of the general educational importance of language learning was another frequently voiced opinion (consistent with those about the importance of English) that German was a private concern and responsibility and that English was the critical language in the public domain.

One person (as mentioned above) was aware of cognitive arguments for transitional bilingualism. She was herself a teacher and had learnt English in a bilingual school in Germany and found the experience worthwhile. But this person also viewed the ultimate responsibility for language maintenance as resting with the family.

On what to do and where, there was no clear overall pattern to the responses. The following are paraphrases of some of the more regularly repeated comments: 'Short courses, no matter how minor, were better than nothing at any stage.' 'German should not begin until secondary school, when it can be taught properly as a foreign, academic language.' 'German should be taught in pre-school.' 'Ethnic schools and the Department of Education's Saturday morning schools taught for too short a period to be adequate.' 'Full foreign language teaching in mainstream primary schools was too much to expect of the system.' 'It is counter-productive to offer languages before secondary school as this leads children to rebel; they want to be like everyone else and only voluntarily begin to appreciate their parents' language at secondary school age.' 'German is best introduced in the primary school; secondary school is too late.'

Faced with the question of which languages, in terms of policy priorities, should be taught, the groups showed that they had not thought through the issue. Here is a representative sample of opinions. 'In Europe, people learnt English as a second language because English was so important internationally; here, where there are so many other languages (and we all already have to know English), it is hard to know which other languages to promote.' 'Perhaps second language learning is not so critical here and there is certainly no need for it to be compulsory as it frequently is in Europe.' 'The larger languages (in terms of international trade and so on) should certainly be promoted, and this obviously includes German; for this reason, German is equally worthy of study for all students.' A significant proportion thought that learning another (any other) language was important, and were happy, for example, to see some of the local primary schools teaching Italian or Spanish.

There was no real awareness that deciding which language to teach might be a problem. The immediate issue was usefulness (and German happened to be viewed, as it is conventionally, as internationally useful) and that usefulness meant that learning any other international language was generally worthwhile. The groups were reluctant to make any comment on numerically smaller languages, or languages viewed as minor ones in the international scene.

As for personal experiences of language, the overall picture matched well with the group members' general attitude to the learning of English in Australia. They regarded concentrations of German speakers in one area as a bad thing, and as hampering progress in English. It was considered that having compatriots already settled in Australia might have been comforting at first, but one had to be careful not to let this slow down integration into Australian society which, critically, involved knowing English well. All agreed that their children had no problems with language in relation to schooling. Often they claimed children refused to learn German, but that they picked up a passive knowledge of the language anyway, which then became the foundation for further learning on trips to Germany or as something in which they took a greater interest as they grew up.

In sum, the first thing we have to note is a lack of clarity on issues about which policy-makers need direction, such as strategies and sites for language teaching. Second, there was a lack of awareness of academic arguments for particular strategies in language teaching (such as transitional bilingualism to maintain and develop lines of cognition). Third, we noted a lack of concern, explicable for the German language, about the politics of which languages are to be taught. Fourth, and most importantly, there was a simultaneous expression of arguments about language and usefulness (as rationales for learning both English and German or other languages) and relatively weak expressions of 'ethnic' language politics in terms of maintaining home culture and institutional respect. On this some resentment was expressed about Italians or Greeks getting special treatment. On polling days, for example, there were no instructions in German. Although it was agreed by the participants that most people of German language background could read English they nevertheless felt that they would like to see their language represented, at least as a symbol of its existence and worth.

The Key Informants' Discussion Groups: Macedonian Language Background

The key informants we got together for group discussion from the Macedonian community came from more diverse sources than was the case with the Germans. There were, among others, church organizers, university students, welfare workers, teachers and people who worked in the steelworks. But there still was not the range available to make key informant techniques methodologically useful as the principal strategy of the research project. Except for people involved in the 'ethnic school' and several welfare workers, we were unable to find professionals or voluntary workers for whom Macedonian language maintenance was perceived to be a critical issue in their work. We also had a problem about the attendance of rival groups. The main thing that became immediately clear was that the politics of mother tongue language maintenance was not only more crucial to the Macedonian participants in these discussions than it was for the German group, but that it was articulated more broadly — through the church and voluntary organizations, as well as through education.

At first glance it appeared that linguistic continuity defined an amalgam of church, ethnic schools and voluntary organizations as a 'community', and that language was central to the politics of 'ethnic communty'. The notion of such a linguistically defined community, however, soon presented itself as problematic, as local Macedonians were divided between Eastern Orthodox (80 per cent), Jewish (10 per cent) and Moslem (10 per cent), for whom, it was claimed (but disputed), that the Eastern Orthodox group was most committed to Macedonian language maintenance. But even here there were problems, as it was claimed that because young people were having difficulties with the language used by the church, some attempt was being made to simplify or modify the script and linguistic forms. Furthermore, some of the older priests sometimes still used Serbo-Croatian, which complicated even further the issue of what the linguistic community was.

Against this factual complexity there was considerable dispute about the role of the church in language maintenance. Some said that the church was a minor factor in social life and that the Macedonian language was not essential to it. Others said that Macedonian was critical in the socialization process and that the church had a crucial role both in bringing people together in this process and as an expression of community in its own right.

Participation in organized sport was presented as another crucial arena that drew together the Macedonian community. According to group members, the importance of the Macedonian language varied according to the length of residence of individual members in Australia. It was claimed that Macedonian, when it was spoken at sporting venues, was almost invariably mixed with English. It was further claimed that the younger generation (those born in Australia or brought to Australia as young children) generally communicated with each other solely in English. Three-quarters of one of the Macedonian soccer teams, said one of its players, did not speak Macedonian with any fluency at all.

In home life it was generally said that English was being used more and more. This was not viewed as detrimental but, against this, there was the claim that personal relationships and involvement in the community would be extended if young people made a point of speaking Macedonian. The general maintenance of the language was seen as the prime responsibility of the community itself.

To the question of the ultimate purpose of learning Macedonian, the main response was to preserve culture and preserve the language. As an instance of culture, one person described how certain children's stories simply would not 'work' in English. Culture, in this context of maintenance, meant specifically parent-child socialization (basically a desire that children are socialized to value the things that their parents value) and also the cohesion of the 'community'. Both of these notions had only been weakly expressed by our German informants.

A significant rationale given for the importance of maintaining Macedonian stemmed from the concern that the language was under threat and had a long history of being under threat in the homeland. It was explained with some intensity that Macedonian only became an official and written language in the post-war period and in some places, northern Greece for example, its use was still not encouraged.

Despite the enormity of this concern, there was some disagreement about which form of Macedonian should be taught and, in particular, whether there was a standard Macedonian language or not. Some said standard Macedonian was spoken in Macedonia but not here. Others said standard Macedonian was the language formalized in grammar texts. Dialect was not regarded as a problem, as it was claimed that all forms of Macedonian were mutually comprehensible. But it was also somewhat contradictorily claimed that books are written in standard Macedonian, yet only the educated could use and understand this language adequately. After one of the key informant evenings, we received the following letter.

We are writing to you on behalf of the Macedonian Welfare Association in response to your Language Maintenance Survey that was held on the 19/6/1984.

We are of the opinion that you of the Centre for Multicultural Studies may be at this stage confused as to whether or not there is in fact a 'standard' Macedonian Language. This confusion may have been prompted because of the varying opinions at the above-mentioned meeting. Let us assure you that the language that we all speak, whether it be colloquial or literal, is 'standard' Macedonian.

Through observation from our welfare standpoint, the Macedonian clientele use a colloquial form. This is not to say however, that literary works such as prose, poetry and drama are not in the same language. Consider the comparison between Shakespearean English and English used in Australia. The former is quite acceptable to study and use at intellectual levels but the Australian attempting to use such language in everyday speech would be ridiculed, yet it is still the English language.

As you are aware, languages are dynamic and such is the case with Macedonian. Inclusions through usage and acceptance are common place. The particular social environment has necessitated local injection (of terms peculiar to that environment) quite valid here in Australia while not necessarily accepted on university campuses in Skopje or other parts of Macedonia.

If a programme, such as described at the meeting, were to be initiated here, it follows that the language used should be drawn from the majority of Macedonians here in Australia.

We commend the Centre for its consideration of such an important topic as the Macedonian language.

We seem to be left with division about the Macedonian that should be taught. At the one extreme it is claimed, as in the second paragraph of this letter, that there is a single Macedonian language. So there is no problem about what is to be taught. At the other extreme there is a view that the Macedonian language has both a standard literary form and significant dialect and Australian variations. Children must be taught the former 'properly', even though this would not necessarily be the best way of helping students relate to their family and 'community'. Often, as in the letter, these two views sat rather uneasily together in our discussions.

One severe practical problem, it was generally felt, was the availability of trained people who knew written Macedonian well enough to be able to teach it. (Even after getting letters and questionnaires translated into Macedonian by interpreters or welfare workers for whom English–Macedonian translation was a central part of their job, we received complaints about spelling, grammar and meaning.)

There was no consistent agreement about how and where Macedonian should be taught. Some thought that more resources should be put into the state Department of Education Saturday morning schools; others, the 'ethnic schools'. In opposition, some of the younger participants of the group discussion recounted experiences of disliking Macedonian language classes outside school hours and with pedagogically conservative teaching. Many thought that the real effort should go into teaching Macedonian as a 'proper' subject in mainstream schools. Of those who held this view, some were of the opinion that this was to be left to secondary school while others thought it should be an offering throughout schooling. The possibility of bilingual education was generally thought to be unnecessary as the children picked up English readily, except perhaps where Macedonians were a very substantial proportion of the school population. There was universal agreement that learning another language was a valuable exercise in its own right.

On the subject of who to service with what language, some suggested that it should be the majority group in each area, and a few thought it should be all or any languages for which there was demand. Others thought that if different schools specialized in different languages, parents could choose which school they sent their children to. The particular difficulties of Macedonian as a language were also brought up. Against a view that it should be like any other language in the secondary school, it was pointed out that there is only a small body of Macedonian literature, few qualified teachers and inadequate available teaching resources. A lot of funding and effort would be needed before it would have the prestige of some of the other foreign languages.

There was also quite a contradictory negative general view of the 'ethnic schools'. While all agreed that they were better than nothing, they claimed that the children generally disliked them, partly because they 'don't want to be different'. Some thought that Macedonian teaching in mainstream schools was much more effective in this respect, in that this made the language respectable. Nevertheless, the group members by and large wanted 'ethnic schools' maintained and additional funding made available to them.

In terms of factors such as employment, Macedonian was not regarded as a useful language. For example, they argued that the necessary technical jargon of work was only known in English. It was unanimously thought that TAFE should not run technical courses in 'community languages'. Many English technical words, it was claimed, were used even in Macedonia and, in any event, English is the main language of work — a fact from which, it was thought, no one should shelter themselves. A motor mechanic explained how he could only explain the working of a car using English terminology.

One key informant was a Macedonian exchange teacher who not only had spent some months teaching in Australia by the time of our survey, but had had experience of teaching returned Australian-Macedonians in Macedonia. She was very critical of what she viewed as an excessively liberal Australian education system, not just in terms of the teaching of Macedonian, but also the teaching of English (which she taught in Macedonia). She said that returned Australian-Macedonians almost always did very poorly at school in Yugoslavia, even including English taken as a foreign language.

The Questionnaire: Background Information

Table 5.2 provides details of our sample. At some points the size of sub-groups of the samples are too small to be useful. There were, nonetheless, some strong trends coming through, even though we were not able to exploit all of the stat-

Table 5.2 The Overall Sample

	Male	Female	Total
Macedonian adults	36	13	49
children	28	22	50
German adults	26	34	60
children	12	7	19
Control adults	6	15	22
children	18	25	42
Total	126	116	242

istical possibilities in the survey instruments. One factor of immediate note in Table 5.2 is the male/female ratios. The adult questionnaires were sent home to parents, through children involved in the testing in each school, and issued to those interested enough to attend one of the key informant evenings. The German female response rate was 56.7 per cent, Macedonian 26.5 per cent and control 68.2 per cent. Apart from being an indicator of who the household opinion-broker on language maintenance is, it will be important to bear the relative male-female weightings in mind when interpreting some of the subsequent statistics.

Table 5.3 Place of Birth

	Australia	East/West Germany Austria	Yugoslavia	Other	Total
Macedonian adults	4		45		49
children	33		17		50
German adults	4	54			60
children	15	4		2	19
Control adults	19			3(UK)	22
children	40			2(UK)	42
Total	115	58	62	7	242

Background statistics from the questionnaire give us some information about German and Macedonian migration, which is also useful in interpreting the results (see Table 5.3).

Table 5.4 shows a much higher proportion of overseas-born Macedonian children and adults than German children and adults. This reflects the more recent nature of Macedonian migration. A crucial, related statistic from the census gives us information about rates of intermarriage: 60 per cent of people with one parent born in Germany have two parents born in Germany, while 85 per cent of people with one parent born in Yugoslavia have two parents born in

Table 5.4 Date of Arrival in Australia

	Born in Australia	Arrived 1949–59	Arrived 1960–69	Arrived 1970–79	Arrived since 1980
Macedonian	43	3	18	33	2
	43.4%	3.0%	18.2%	33.3%	2.0%
German	18	38	14	7	2
	22.8%	48.1%	17.7%	8.9%	2.5%
Control	58	2	1	2	0
	98.1%	3.2%	1.6%	3.2%	0

Yugoslavia (ABS, 1983: 3). This is reflected in our sample: 96.0 per cent of the Macedonian background children had a Macedonian-speaking father and 92.0 per cent a Macedonian-speaking mother. This compares with 84.2 per cent of the German-speaking background children with a German-speaking father and 73.7 per cent with a German-speaking mother.

Our hypothesis on household size was that Macedonian households would generally be larger than those of the control group. This did not prove to be the case (see Table 5.5).

Table 5.5 Household Size

Number of people	2	3	4	5	6	7	8 or more	Total
Macedonian	2	9	45	18	6	2	1	83
	2.4%	10.8%	54.2%	21.7%	7.2%	2.4%	1.2%	
German	20	10	26	9	4	1	0	70
	28.6%	11.3%	37.1%	12.9%	5.7%	1.4%	0	
Control	0	6	28	14	4	1	0	53
	0	11.3%	52.8%	26.4%	7.5%	1.9%	0	
								206
								(+36 N/a)

A strong Macedonian-control parallel is immediately obvious, indicating that Macedonian families are probably no more likely to be extended families living within a single household than Australians of English-speaking background. Indeed, the predominance of households of four and five members must lead one to infer that the nuclear family structure prevails for both groups. The German group, however, follows a different pattern, with a much smaller family size than either of the other two groups. This, read beside the figures in Tables 5.3 and 5.4, shows that the Germans in the Wollongong-Shellharbour region are (relatively) an ageing group, as a result of the timing of the principal wave of German migration.

A question in the children's questionnaire elicited information about whether they have their own bedroom: 81.0 per cent of the control group children have their own bedroom, 84.2 per cent of the German group, but only 56.0 per cent of the Macedonian group. Given Macedonian-control parallels in household size, this has to be taken as a socio-economic indicator — of smaller houses for the Macedonian group.

Our statistics relating to educational qualifications show strong parallels between the groups and occupation across the range of no tertiary qualifications, college certificate, technical courses, apprenticeship, trade course or university degree. This, we felt, was more a reflection of who were willing and able to answer that questionnaire than a useful background statistic. We also felt the relatively high female response rates in German and control groups probably affected this statistic. Likewise, the employed, unemployed or not in workforce statistics proved to be very much a function of male/female response rates.

Of employed German adults 70 per cent said they liked their job, as did 75.5 per cent of employed Macedonian adults; 83.3 per cent of German adults said they liked Australia, and 79.6 per cent of Macedonians. Written comments to this question included (for the German adults) frequent positive comments about the climate: 'The whole country is easy-going, nice people, beaut country', 'It's not so crowded here, there's more open space'; 'It's a good place for children; there's more freedom and more housing opportunities. The Macedonian adults were also generally very positive about Australia, apart from one complaint that it's 'very, very, very boring'.

Of the German children 84.2 per cent said they liked school, 68 per cent of the Macedonian children and 71.4 per cent of the control group children. Year 10 children were asked when they intended to leave school. The ratios of those intending to leave in year 10 and those intending to leave in year 12 were roughly the same for the Macedonian, German and control groups, but enrolment figures suggest that, for the Macedonian group at least, these expectations are ill-founded. Similarly, job expectations between the groups show striking parallels.

Linguistic Backgrounds

Of the Macedonian adults 95.9 per cent claimed that their first language was Macedonian; 96.7 per cent of German adults claimed their first language was German; and 95.5 per cent of the control group adults claimed their first language was English. Of Macedonian children 99 per cent claimed their first language was Macedonian, and 100 per cent of the control group claimed to speak English as their first language. However, only 68.4 per cent of the German children claimed that German was their first language, indicating lower levels of mother tongue language maintenance, most probably related to length of family residence in Australia and rates of intermarriage.

There appeared to be quite a high degree of confusion, particularly in the Macedonian group, as to whether they spoke a dialect or standard form of the language (see Table 5.6)

Table 5.6 Language Type Spoken

	No answer	Dialect	Standard	Both	Total
Macedonian	52 52.5%	18 18.2%	8 8.1%	21 21.2%	99
German	20 25.3%	3 3.8%	36 45.6%	20 25.3%	79

The non-response rates shown in Table 5.6 are unusually high. The very limited claims among the Macedonians to speak a standard form of the language relate both to their pre-migration socio-economic position and to the relatively recent formalization and standardization of Macedonian. Germans, while admitting the existence of dialect, strongly claimed to be capable in 'standard' German. We must stress that these statistics are a matter of subjective self-appraisal around categories commonly used to differentiate language types, and not objective indicators of objective categories.

Fewer German adults claimed to be able to speak their mother tongue as well as they had before migration (56.7 per cent) than Macedonian adults (73.5 per cent). Of Macedonian children 86 per cent claimed they could speak their mother tongue, while 31.6 per cent of German children answered 'yes' to this question, 26.3 per cent 'no' and 36.8 per cent 'a little'. (The Macedonian 'no' and 'a little' responses had been negligible, at 4 per cent and 8 per cent respectively.) Splitting the total non-Australian-born German and Macedonian sample by date of arrival in Australia, there were extremely strong claims to speaking the mother tongue as well as pre-migration in the (small) group who had arrived since 1980 (100 per cent) and in 1970–79 (82.6 per cent). The claim weakened, however, for the 1960–69 period (51.6 per cent), but firmed slightly for the 1949–59 period (62.8 per cent). This need not be an objective indicator, and minimally shows a commitment to language maintenance remaining steady after an initial weakening.

However, when adults were asked which languages their children spoke, more Germans claimed their children spoke English only (28.3 per cent) than did Macedonians (6.1 per cent). This is related to length of residence (see Table 5.7). The longer the period of residence in Australia, the stronger the tendency for parents to perceive that their children speak English only.

Table 5.7   *Children's Language by Family's Length of Residence*

Date of arrival	No answer	English only	Mother tongue only	English plus mother tongue	Total
1949–59	2 4.7%	12 27.9%	0 0	29 67.4%	43
1960–69	5 16.1%	4 12.9%	0 0	22 71.0%	31
1970–79	2 8.7%	3 13.0%	0 0	18 78.3%	23
1980–	1	0	2	0	3

About equal numbers of Macedonian (81.6 per cent) and German (78.3 per cent) parents claimed to be able to understand their mother tongue as well as they had before migration. In the case of the Germans, the figure is noticeably stronger than the self-assessment of speaking skill figures, indicating a greater fall-off in active speaking skills than the more passive understanding (principally listening) skills. Similarly, 82 per cent of Macedonian children claimed they could understand their mother tongue (roughly parallel to their speaking self-assessment), while, at 47.4 per cent, more German children claimed to be able to understand their mother tongue than to be able to speak it. Breaking up overall adult mother tongue understanding self-assessment by length of residence, there appears to be a drop-off into the pre-1970 arrivals (1980– : 100 per cent; 1970–79: 95.7 per cent; 1960–69: 77 per cent), but no drop-off for the 1949–59 period of arrival (79.1 per cent). These claims were all stronger than the claims to speaking skills.

Claims to reading skills among parents were higher than claims to speaking skills, but lower than understanding skills among both Macedonian and German groups. This is explicable in terms of reading being a more passive skill than speaking. Again, viewing reading figures by length of residence, there is a strong drop-off at about fifteen years of residence, but stabilizing beyond that point. There were parallel claims among Macedonian and German parents about their children's mother tongue reading abilities, with perceived children's reading ability tapering off by length of residence in Australia.

Of Macedonian adults 70 per cent claimed to be able to write as well as they did before migration, as did 66.7 per cent of German adults. Of Macedonian children 36.0 per cent answered 'yes' to the question of whether they were able to write Macedonian, 30 per cent 'a little' and 30 per cent 'no'. For the Germans, the result was 21.1 per cent 'yes', 46.8 per cent 'no' and 26.6 per cent 'a little'. Apart from factors such as length of residence, the relatively strong Macedonian showing here might well be a quirk of script. Macedonian children might have registered mere knowledge of the Cyrillic alphabet as a writing skill, whereas, for Germans, with the same script as English, writing might have been interpreted as a higher-order activity. Interestingly, almost the same percentage of Macedonian parents claimed that their children were able to write their mother tongue as German parents. Writing skills taper off as length of residency increases, but, as with speaking, understanding and reading, this tapering-off tends to stabilize in the longer term. According to parents' perceptions, children's writing skills, however, consistently diminish across length of residency in Australia.

Of Macedonian adults 22.4 per cent said they thought mainly in English, compared with 38.3 per cent of Germans; 49.0 per cent of Macedonian adults said they thought both in English and their mother tongue, and 36.7 per cent of Germans. Only 24.5 per cent of Macedonians and 23.3 per cent of German adults said they thought mainly in their mother tongue. The move to thinking in English is strongly correlated to length of residency in Australia.

Of Macedonian adults 34.7 per cent said they spoke English very well, and 48.3 per cent of Germans. There is a steady improvement in self-assessed English-speaking skills across length of residency in Australia. Of Macedonian adults 42.9 per cent claimed to understand English very well, and 68.3 per cent of Germans. The strength of these claims, compared with claims to speaking skills, reflects the nature of the skill. Again, there is steady improvement in self-assessed English-speaking skills across length of residency in Australia.

Of Macedonian adults 38.8 per cent said they read English very well, and 58.3 per cent of the Germans. These results must be in part related to the literacy levels of those inclined to answer the questionnaire or attend the key informant discussion groups, even though questionnaires, discussion groups and invitations to the discussion groups were presented both in English and Macedonian or German. Of Macedonian respondents 34.7 per cent said they were able to read English poorly or not at all, compared with only 3.4 per cent of the German sample. Figures for adult English writing across length of residency in Australia indicate that the longer the residency, the better the self-assessment of ability in the skill.

Of Macedonian adults 36.7 per cent said they wrote English very well, compared with 38.3 per cent of Germans. The strong drop-off of Germans claiming good writing ability, compared to their previous claims to reading ability, is of note here. Of the Germans 20 per cent said they did not write well, wrote poorly or did not write at all, and 44.9 per cent of Macedonians. The reading and writing self-assessment of the Macedonian adults reinforces the finding of Morrissey and Palser (1983) that Macedonian adults scored relatively poorly in ASLPR ratings of literacy skills. Compared with the German group, this is to be seen in the context of socio-economic factors before and after migration, length of residence in Australia and the fact that the same script is used for both English and German which makes things easier for the Germans. Across length of residence there is a general improvement in self-assessed writing skills, but even in the 1949–59 (combined Macedonian and German) group, only 37.2 per cent felt they could write English very well, as opposed to a 65.1 per cent self-assessment of understanding.

Of Macedonian adults 46.9 per cent said they had attended English classes, as did 45 per cent of German adults. Fewer of the longer established Australian residents had attended English classes (34.9 per cent of the 1949–59 group) than the more recently established residents (56.5 per cent of the 1970–79 group). Of those who had attended formal English classes, almost all of the Macedonian adults had attended in Australia, while almost half the Germans had undertaken at least some of their formal English learning before arrival in Australia. This is an indicator of the pre-migration educational background of each group. Although Macedonian English class attendance rates are roughly the same, the Germans attended for significantly longer periods than the Macedonians.

Of Macedonian parents 42.9 per cent said their children were learning their mother tongue at school, as did 58.3 per cent of Germans (a result of the subject offerings in the schools we surveyed). Only two Macedonian families had home tutors for Macedonian. Of Macedonian parents 16.3 per cent sent their children to language classes outside day school hours, against 31.7 per cent of Germans.

Of Macedonian children 68.0 per cent felt no need to improve their mother tongue, as did 73.7 per cent of German children. This is rather a crude indicator of lack of interest in mother tongue language learning, either in terms of feeling that their mother tongue language ability is adequate to needs or a general lack of interest.

When parents were asked about their perception of their children's best language, only 6.1 per cent of Macedonians and 5.0 per cent of Germans claimed it was the mother tongue; 26.5 per cent of Macedonian parents and 5.0 per cent of German parents claimed their children were equally proficient in English and the mother tongue; 49.0 per cent of Macedonian parents and 83.3 per cent of German parents claimed that English was their children's best language. Again, this reflects the comparative general length of residence of the two groups. For both groups the trend towards English as the child's perceived best language is strongly correlated with length of residency in Australia.

Parental assessment of children's preferred language strongly parallels their assessment of best languages: 6.1 per cent of Macedonian parents claimed their children preferred to use their mother tongue and 6.7 per cent of Germans. Preference for English was 30.6 per cent for Macedonians and 60.0 per cent for Germans. Equal favour to the two languages was registered as 46.4 per cent for Macedonians and 25.0 per cent for Germans. The German/Macedonian variation is explicable in the same terms as previously. One has to wonder, however, at the extent to which parents' perceptions of child preference are so subjective a measure as to allow significant projection on the part of the parent. The perceived non-preference for mother tongue among children is, nonetheless, striking.

Sites of Mother Tongue and English Language Usage

At a number of points in each of the questionnaires information was elicited about sites of mother tongue and English language usage. Of the Macedonian adults surveyed 95.9 per cent said they used Macedonian at home, compared with 81.7 per cent of German adults using German. There was a very strong drop-off rate for the German children, of whom only 36.8 per cent used German at home, but not for the Macedonians, of whom 92.0 per cent used their mother tongue at home. This is probably mainly a function of length of family residency in Australia. There was, however, a very strong disjunction between these results and parent reports on children's usage of the mother tongue at home. For the two groups, children's use of mother tongue at home decreases with increasing length of family residency in Australia: 75.5 per cent of Macedonian parents said their children used Macedonian at home (significantly down on the children's report), while 66.7 per cent of Germans said their children used German at home (significantly up on the children's report). We can hypothesize a number of explanations for this discrepancy, which problematize the whole methodology of opinion surveys. Contradictorily, the Macedonian parents might have been making a negative projection, and the German parents a positive, wish-fulfilling one. Or what constitutes using a language at home might be viewed very differently by parents and children, or by different linguistic groups. In short, the possible variables are so unpredictable in subjective self-assessment as to make an opinion survey into language usage a very shaky exercise.

Of Macedonian adults 40.8 per cent use English at home, compared with 68.3 per cent of German adults. For the two groups, this increases substantially with length of residency in Australia (26.1 per cent for 1970–79 arrivals to 64.5 per cent for 1960–69 arrivals), but levels off for the 1949–59 group (at 60.5 per cent). One assumes that the levelling is for first generation migrants, and that no conclusion should be drawn about levelling off of home language use patterns across generations. (Indeed, the evidence elsewhere points to another significant intergenerational change).

Of Macedonian adult respondents 83.7 per cent claimed to speak their mother tongue with relatives, as did 50.0 per cent of Germans. This probably reflects the fact that fewer Germans had relatives in Australia, as well as changing patterns of language usage. Roughly the same percentages of children (respectively) use their mother tongue in interaction with relatives. This seems to decrease with length of family residence in Australia for children, but not for adults. This confirms our hypothesis that the decisive point of language maintenance or non-maintenance is intergenerational.

Of German adults 56.7 per cent use English with relatives, but only 26.5 per cent of Macedonians. This increases substantially with length of residency in Australia (17.4 per cent for 1970–79 arrivals; 38.7 per cent for 1960–69 arrivals; and 55.8 per cent for 1949–59 arrivals), indicating that, while mother tongue language usage stabilizes within first generation migrant groups, English language usage continuously increases.

Of adult Macedonians 81.6 per cent use their mother tongue with friends, compared with 63.3 per cent of adult Germans. Of Macedonian children 78.0 per cent use their mother tongue with friends, in contrast to only 15.8 per cent of the children in the German sample. The high Macedonian showing is probably related both to recency of family arrival and to the relative concentration of Macedonian language background children in a few schools in the Wollongong-Shellharbour region. Children of German background, as we pointed out in Chapter 2, are geographically very much more dispersed. Parent perception of their children's mother tongue usage is worth mentioning here as it is under-estimated by the Macedonian parents and overestimated by the German parents. A number of constructions could be put on this statistic (including the methodological ones we mentioned above). Again, we should stress that parental projection must itself be seen as an unpredictable variable in the politics of language maintenance.

Of Macedonian adults 59.2 per cent use English with friends, compared with 75.0 per cent of German adults. For the two groups, the tendency to use English with friends increases with length of residence in Australia.

Of the Macedonian adults 42.9 per cent reported using their mother tongue at work, as did 15 per cent of German adults. This is probably a fairly unusual result in the Australian context, being related to BHP policy of grouping work-gangs by language, the very nature of the steelworks and asso-ciated industries in terms of migrant labour, and German (as discussed in Chapter 2) being a minor *lingua franca* in steelworks. Use of mother tongue at work decreases steadily across length of residence in Australia.

Of Macedonian children 72.0 per cent claimed they used their mother tongue at school, compared with 36.8 per cent of German students. The latter figure, given geographical dispersal and low claims by children to using German with friends, must be related to taking German as a school subject or attending 'ethnic' or Saturday morning language school. Only 34.7 per cent of Macedonian parents thought their children used Macedonian at school, indicating a revealing misconception about playground usage, and confirming their negative projections about their children's Macedonian usage elsewhere. (Only one of the schools we surveyed taught Macedonian.)

Of Macedonian adults 59.2 per cent said they use their mother tongue with neighbours, compared with only 18.3 per cent of Germans. This pattern of language usage is clearly a function of geographical dispersion. Of Macedonian children 52 per cent said they used Macedonian with neighbours, against no German children at all.

Of Macedonian adults 61.2 per cent use English with neighbours, compared with 80 per cent of German adults. Rates of usage increase with increasing length of residency in Australia.

Of Macedonian adults 34.7 per cent use their mother tongue while shopping, compared with 10 per cent of the German adult sample. No Macedonian or German children said they use their mother tongue shopping. Of Macedonian adults 85.5 per cent use English in shopping, compared with 95.9 per cent of German adults.

Of Macedonian adults 32.7 per cent use their mother tongue in clubs, compared with 45 per cent of German adults. The figures for English usage in clubs are 59.2 per cent and 61.7 per cent respectively.

Of Macedonian adults 36.7 per cent use Macedonian at the cinema but only 6.7 per cent of German adults use German. The children's figures are quite similar at 34 per cent and 5.3 per cent respectively. Macedonian films are frequently shown in clubs in the region.

Of Macedonians 30.6 per cent use their mother tongue to watch TV or videos, and 20 per cent of Germans. As the multilingual television channel 0 was not available in the Wollongong-Shellharbour region in 1984, this was almost entirely the result of the availability of videos. There is a Macedonian video shop in the area. While only one German language background child said they used German for watching TV or videos, 62 per cent of the children of Macedonian language background said they used Macedonian for this purpose. This very strong showing is a combination of home video usage and videos shown during Macedonian language teaching.

Of the Macedonian adults 75.5 per cent use their mother tongue to listen to the radio, compared with 48.3 per cent of German adults. The figures for children are 62 per cent and 21.1 per cent respectively. Adult usage tapers off with increasing length of residence in Australia.

Of Macedonian adults 67.3 per cent use Macedonian to read newspapers. Both Australian and Yugoslav Macedonian papers are available. Of German adults 53.3 per cent read German language newspapers. The figures for children show a strong drop-off to 26 per cent and 15.8 per cent respectively. Mother tongue newspaper reading reduces with length of residency in Australia.

Of Macedonian adults 63.3 per cent read magazines in their mother tongue, compared with 68.3 per cent of Germans. These figures reduce dramatically for children to 22 per cent and 21.1 per cent respectively. The strong German showing for mother tongue magazine reading compared to mother tongue newspaper reading is in part attributable to the quality of available German language magazines such as *Der Spiegel* and *Stern*.

Of Macedonian adults 59.2 per cent use their mother tongue to sing, compared with 46.7 per cent of Germans. For children these figures are 50 per cent and 26.3 per cent respectively. Of Macedonian adults 87.8 per cent use their mother tongue to write letters, compared with 78.3 per cent of Germans. These figures drop off with length of residency in Australia, and presumably the maintenance of fewer contacts with people in the country of origin. Among children these figures have reduced to 48 per cent and 15.8 per cent respectively.

Of Macedonian adults 75.5 per cent use their mother tongue at church, compared with 15.0 per cent of Germans. Use of mother tongue at church drops off significantly with length of residence in Australia. For children this reduced to a surprising 8 per cent and zero respectively. Of Macedonian adults 18.4 per cent use English at church, compared with 45 per cent of German adults. In speaking to priests 71.4 per cent of Macedonian adults use their mother tongue, as do 18.3 per cent of Germans. For children this was 6 per cent and zero respectively.

Attitudes to Language Maintenance

Of Macedonian adults 81.6 per cent said they would like to continue learning their mother tongue, compared with 50 per cent of the German adults. This response is most probably related to adult Macedonian literacy levels. This desire increased with length of residency in Australia. Of Macedonian children 70 per cent expressed a desire to continue learning their first language formally, compared with 52.6 per cent of German children. This question, however, was repeated in different ways in the questionnaire and was not answered consistently. Most of the children said they would like to see their mother tongue offered as a language at school, but many were ambivalent about studying it themselves.

German and Macedonian children and adults were asked about the importance of mother tongue maintenance (see Table 5.8). The data in the table indicate a stronger commitment to mother tongue maintenance among Macedonians than Germans and among adults than children.

Of Macedonian adults 87.8 per cent think it is as important to read their mother tongue as to speak it, as do 88.3 per cent of German adults, but only 60 per cent of Macedonian children and 47.4 per cent of German children. The

Table 5.8 Opinions on Mother Tongue Maintenance

	Essential	Very important	Not important	No answer	Total
Macedonian adults	24	22	3	–	49
	49%	44.9%	6.1%		
Macedonian children	16	24	8	2	50
	32%	48.0%	16%	4%	
German adults	18	31	8	3	60
	30%	51.7%	13.3%	5%	
German children	3	8	7	1	19
	15.8%	42.1%	36.8%	5.3%	
					178

relative importance attributed to reading in relation to speaking tends to decrease among adults with increased length of residence in Australia.

Of Macedonian adults 83.7 per cent and 75.5 per cent of German adults thought mother tongue maintenance was important to family unity, but only 36 per cent of Macedonian children and 42.1 per cent of German children.

Of Macedonian adults 79.6 per cent thought mother tongue maintenance was important for personal identity, compared with 66.7 per cent of German adults. Only 22.7 per cent of the control adults agreed. Only 24.0 per cent of Macedonian children and 15.8 per cent of German children agreed. One cannot but help infer that mother tongue maintenance is considered important for reasons of personal identity when it is already a critical part of one's personal identity. Generally, as came out very strongly in the open-ended comments in the questionnaire, the children were much more sanguine about the usefulness of language. An aspiring receptionist thought Macedonian might be a useful language. Positive comments about languages were mostly centred on jobs, education or travel.

Of Macedonian adults 83.7 per cent considered maintenance of culture to be an important reason for mother tongue maintenance, compared with 83.3 per cent of German adults. Of the control adults 45.5 per cent agreed, and 53.3 per cent of German children answered this question positively.

Relatively few adults considered mother tongue maintenance to be a human right (38.8 per cent of Macedonians and 11.7 per cent of Germans). Only one Macedonian child and one German child thought mother tongue maintenance was a human right.

Of Macedonian adults 20.4 per cent, of German adults 5 per cent and of control adults 18.2 per cent thought mother tongue maintenance might be useful for work, while 18.4 per cent of Macedonian adults and 6.7 per cent of German adults thought that mother tongue maintenance had an adverse effect on one's abilities in English. While 18 per cent of Macedonian children agreed, there was a strong 'unsure' response to these questions, indicating that neither a positive nor a negative link immediately suggests itself.

Macedonian, German and control adults were in basic agreement that Australians respected languages other than English, at least more so now than in the past. Children, however, were not so sure. One comment frequently appearing in open-ended parts of the children's questionnaire was about racism in school. In defence, a number of children said that the beauty of knowing a language other than English was that one could talk with friends without being understood. One of the control children listed languages he would like to learn 'so the Australian kids could know what the others were saying about them'.

Of Macedonian adults 81.6 per cent, of German adults 90 per cent and of control adults 77.3 per cent thought that mother tongue maintenance was a family responsibility. Only 62 per cent of Macedonian children, 47.4 per cent of German children and 26.4 per cent of control children agreed. (These and subsequent sites of responsibility for language maintenance were not framed as mutually exclusive in the questionnaire, so the figures have to be seen in an overall comparative context.)

Of Macedonian adults 55.1 per cent, of German adults 43.3 per cent, but only 13.6 per cent of control adults thought that responsibility for mother tongue language maintenance lay with the school; 22.0 per cent of Macedonian children, 26.3 per cent of German children and only three control children agreed.

Of Macedonian adults 42.9 per cent thought mother tongue maintenance was a government responsibility, as did 20 per cent of German adults, and 4.1 per cent of control adults. Only 8 per cent of Macedonian children, two German children and no control children agreed.

Of Macedonian adults 40.8 per cent thought the church had some responsibility for mother tongue maintenance, but only 5 per cent of German adults did. This reflects the place of religion in the Macedonian community.

When asked which language was most important, German and Macedonian adults strongly disagreed. Only 26.5 per cent of Macedonians thought English was unequivocally the most important language in Australia, compared with 56.7 per cent of German adults; 30.6 per cent of Macedonians considered Macedonian more important, against 13.3 per cent of Germans; 42.9 per cent of Macedonian adults against 26.7 per cent of German adults thought English and the mother tongue to be equally important. With increasing length of residence, English is considered more important. However, both Macedonian and German adults almost universally thought that a knowledge of more than one language is essential or very important.

Contradicting (to a degree) some statements made on this subject at the key informant evenings, there was some interest among the adult respondents in continued training in their mother tongue. The relatively high showing for German is probably related to German being a language of technology and science (see Table 5.9).

Table 5.9 Preferred Language for Further Training

	No answer	English	German	Macedonian	English and mother tongue	Total
Macedonian	2	30	1	5	11	49
	4.1%	61.2%	2.0%	10.2%	22.4%	
German	6	27	20	0	7	60
	10.0%	45.0%	33.3%	0	11.7%	

When questioned about the teaching of various subjects to children in school in the mother tongue, very few adults considered music to be one such subject. More considered art a possibility (32.7 per cent of Macedonians and 16.7 per cent of Germans). History rated 49 per cent for the Macedonians and 33.3 per cent for the Germans, with children mostly disagreeing at 22.0 per cent and 5.3 per cent respectively. Geography and social studies figures broadly paralleled those for history for all sub-samples. Science and mathematics, however, were not considered suitable subjects to be taught in the mother tongue. One can only conclude that the respondents were more concerned about 'cultural' appropriateness than the technical arguments about the benefits of bilingualism.

A number of questions in the survey had strikingly high non-response rates. Those relating to alternative language policy options are cases in point. The contrast with the very high response rate on most of the other questions constitutes an important research finding in its own right. Of Macedonian adults 65.3 per cent and of German adults 25 per cent did not reply to the question of whether they thought mother tongue maintenance contributed to intellectual development. This points to the fact that many of the most difficult educational and policy questions cannot be answered by reference to public opinion or simply in deference to the wishes of 'ethnic politics'. There are many extremely difficult, technical and logistical questions which can only be answered in tandem with hard research.

The non-response rate to technical and policy-oriented questions increased dramatically with relative recency of migration. We suggest that an important role of those concerned about the question of languages other than English in the Australian context is to research and educate the community. Even if we had received clear and statistically viable responses to those questions, the policy questions raised there would still be very much matters for debate. There were, however, interesting responses to the open-ended part of these questions which form no very consistent pattern other than to indicate (understandably) relatively little awareness of the fine points and linguistic consequences of different language policy alternatives.

Among statements by Macedonian adult respondents about usefulness of knowing more than one language were claims that this 'broadens the mind and perhaps leads to a reduction in prejudice', that this would 'enhance Australian culture', that it 'increased job possibilities', that it 'enhances one's learning and understanding capacity', that it 'aids intellectual development' and that it 'helps in communication in a multicultural nation'. There were also some very general statements such as 'he who knows two languages is worth two people' and that learning another language 'offers a different perception to the interpretation of our ephemeral existence'. Language acquisition was frequently classed as desirable in terms of 'culture' in the sense of 'civilization' and 'science'. There were only a few comments about mother tongue language learning as a means to maintain 'customs and traditions', or as a means to the affirmation of personal identity. There was the occasional comment that English was the only language of relevance or importance to the Australian situation.

There were comments by Macedonian adults about language teaching in Australia, but they do not form any consistent pattern. 'A foreign language should only be learnt as a foreign language and should not be used [e.g. bilingualism] to teach other subjects.' 'All subjects should be in English.' 'Bilingual education would make it easier for some children.' 'Children who use their mother tongue at home already know it and should learn other languages at school.' There was a comment that teacher training and inadequate resources were problems for Macedonian language teaching. In response to the last series of questions, one respondent wrote to the questioners that they would know the answers better.

The German adults, commented *inter alia* that 'parents have prime responsibility for teaching children their mother tongue'. 'Language learning is generally advantageous, but there is no need for it in Australia.' 'Knowledge of different languages enables cultural insight, promotes better understanding of non-English-speakers or poor English-speakers, enriches daily life and helps eliminate racism.' 'Language learning is more an academic skill than an emotional tie or necessity.' 'At present, another language doesn't open many doors, but it is a mental stimulus.' Language learning was also seen to be useful to 'foreign travel' and in creating a 'better world view'. As with the Macedonian adults less concern was expressed for mother tongue language maintenance, with just a few comments about 'ancestors', 'heritage', 'dignity' and 'family culture'. One person, on the other hand, said that the acquisition of an Australian identity, including learning English, was a first priority.

If one takes the Macedonian and German responses to the open-ended questions about varieties of language teaching, there seemed, overall, to be a greater concern for the goals traditionally associated with 'foreign' language teaching than with the goals of linguistic and cultural maintenance which are commonly the basis of 'community' language programmes.

Amongst the control adults there was a division of opinion, ambivalence and a degree of confusion. The following statements represent one strand of opinion: 'To be accepted in Australian culture, one should speak English as a first language.' 'Funding such a programme [bilingual education] would deprive other students of a fair allocation of funds for their education. Also, if all children speak or are spoken to in English, they assimilate much better.' 'All persons who migrate to this country should be taught English before they arrive in our country.' 'Mother tongue maintenance should be presented at other institutions, so that the precious little time our students have at school is spent perfecting English. We are an English speaking country. This is what our schools should therefore perfect.' The same person who made this last comment was not opposed to traditional foreign language teaching however: 'It makes you more aware of the workings of your own language and sometimes the meanings of words (e.g. Latin, French). Other people don't seem so "foreign".'

The place for mother tongue maintenance, some other control parents firmly felt, was in the home. 'In my opinion, English isn't taught properly in schools today. I would rather more time spent teaching grammar, spelling, etc. than another language. If migrant parents want children to be taught their mother tongue, it should be done in their own time.' 'The non-English language can be learned at home and spoken there. Otherwise, English should be learned as the common or national language.' 'It is the first obligation of migrants to learn English as they are naturalized.'

On the other hand, some control adults had quite a different view of the situation. 'Language in general', one said, in a view that was echoed by others, was for 'enlightenment, enrichment of our culture and enhanced communication prospects.' It was also useful for study and travel. Moving away from conventional assumptions about 'foreign' languages and towards the notion of 'community' languages, some said that 'exposure to local cultures other than Anglo-Saxon' was important. 'Bilingualism seems a good idea if it helps rectify language deficiency.' Our society is too multicultural for English to be the only language taught.' In this situation 'greater understanding of language and grammar brings about a better understanding of people.'

Among the children of German language background few responded to the open-ended interviewers' questions beyond making general statements about the usefulness or non-usefulness of languages other than English in general and German in particular. One year 10 child thought that learning more than one language was too confusing. The Macedonian children, however, had more to say. A year 10 boy, who wanted to be a panel beater, said that languages were too hard and that there was 'no use of them'. Another child studied Macedonian for a year at the 'ethnic school' and dropped out because she found it too hard. One student put down his dislike for the 'ethnic school' to 'too much mucking about'. Several boys said they got into trouble a lot at school, and a teacher commented that Macedonian language background girls were generally much quieter and more withdrawn. Both of these responses could possibly be language-related, in terms of frustration at the registration of language difficulties as academic underachievement. Several students complained about having difficulties with 'hard words' in English. Several girls, however, said they liked school and wanted to go to university. One said that Macedonian language was 'of limited use and not personally important', and another that friends influenced her to stop learning Macedonian at 'ethnic school' — a decision which she now regrets. Finally, the control students displayed the same division of opinion as their parents. Comments ranged from 'If people come here they should be able to speak English', to wanting to learn 'foreign languages', to wanting to learn 'Yugoslavian so I can understand my friends across the road'.

Language Proficiency Evaluation: Results

The following presentation of results has to be prefaced with some comments about their statistical strength. While our overall sample size was healthy, we needed to cross-tabulate numerous factors to make any meaningful comments on an exceedingly complex, multifaceted situation. At some points it has proved that subsets of the total sample are small. Nevertheless, at many other points subsets are statistically strong, and even when they are not, some strong tendencies still show through which are of hypothetical usefulness for any subsequent, more detailed research. Given the limitations of time and funding and the expense of mounting a valid assessment procedure, nothing more could be done in our study. We view it primarily as a tentative step in a very thorny area. The problems we encountered and the mistakes we stumbled into were as instructive as the results. The following are generalizations emerging from the results. A full statistical report is to be found in the original report to the Australian Department of Immigration and Ethnic Affairs (Kalantzis, Cope and Slade, 1986).

Mother tongue language proficiencies: the overall picture

More children of Macedonian background have a working knowledge of their mother tongue than children of German background. The few of German background who did have a working knowledge of their mother tongue were generally a little more proficient in it. This applied particularly to high school children, and might be explained by the fact that (1) these children studied German in the high school, and (2) they did not find the formal evaluation procedures unusual in German.

Total language proficiency in English was poorer than the control group for both samples of children of Macedonian and of German background. The difference is significant enough to reaffirm concern about underachievement of children from non-English-speaking backgrounds. Considerable further research is required to account for this difference. We do not think that these results point to the bilingual experience as being the cause of underachievement at school. We feel that what needs to be investigated are the ways these children acquire language proficiency: both for their mother tongue and, specifically, the sort of curriculum, instruction and environment they experience at school and how this might not be suitable to their particular needs. It was not within the scope of our brief to investigate such issues. Our results, therefore, cast no light on causal factors. They simply indicate some trends that warrant further investigation into language and schooling and their relation to equality of opportunity.

Socio-economic factors

When we selected our mother tongue sample, we asked for all of the children with Macedonian or German backgrounds in years 5 and 10. In the schools of high socio-economic background the numbers from these categories were very small; whereas in the low socio-economic areas the samples were large, particularly for Macedonians at the primary school level. There was also a trend indicating that the sample from the low socio-economic background made more use of their mother tongue than those of high socio-economic background. This is not to imply any necessary socio-economic to linguistic chain of causation, as these linguistic and socio-economic factors coincide with a range of factors such as recency of settlement and geographical concentration. The Macedonian and German groups represented the total population in years 5 and 10 in each school. The control group of English-speaking background was selected by teachers to represent the spectrum of abilities in each year in the school.

Though the statistics are not conclusive, there appears also to be a trend for the English proficiency of those of non-English-speaking background in low socio-economic areas to be somewhat lower than for those of high socio-economic background. A similar trend appeared for the control English language background group.

High school–primary school sifferentials

High school students of Macedonian background appeared to have a higher level of mother tongue proficiency than those of German background. In both cases, though, it was significantly lower than their level of English proficiency, which appeared roughly equal. The control English language background group in the same school as our German sample appear to have a larger spread over lower language proficiency levels than the control group in the school from which we drew our Macedonian sample. This can be explained in part by the fact that one of the high socio-economic background schools for the Macedonian sample happened to be the one that was a selective school until recently. The result for the control group from this school was markedly superior to all other schools. Nonetheless, the combined English language proficiency levels for the control samples were higher than for the children of Macedonian or German background.

A similar picture emerged for primary school English only, despite the fact that in one of the schools from which we drew our major Macedonian sample the English language proficiency level was generally low for the very few English language background students there. There was also some indication that mother tongue proficiency was higher for both Macedonians and Germans in the primary school than in the secondary school.

Sex differentials

It appeared that female levels of proficiency were higher than for males in the mother tongue. This was so for both the Macedonian and the German sample, though Macedonian female levels of proficiency were comparatively higher than for those of German background.

There was no significant difference in overall levels of English proficiency for males and females of Macedonian background. There was, however, some difference in English proficiency levels for male children of German background and females of German background, with females scoring higher than males. The female German background sample had similar results to the English language background control female sample. In both cases (German female and control female) results were significantly higher than both Macedonian male and female scores. There was no significant difference between the male and female scores of the English only control samples.

Language skills differentials

One of our methodological problems was that it was not possible to draw upon a group of mother tongue speakers as a control. To draw upon criteria suitable for native speakers in their homeland would have obviously been inappropriate. To draw upon a group that studied Macedonian at an ethnic school or German as a foreign language day school also would have posed comparability problems. We were thus left in a quandary over how to standardize results. Essentially it was the modified ratings criteria for English proficiency generally that the interviewers were supplied with, and their own knowledge of the language, that guided their scoring. Despite this methodological situation, certain general tendencies were discernible. For the Macedonian background sample, levels of proficiency for speaking appeared to be higher than for listening or reading. Writing in Macedonian was the most poorly performed skill.

Socio-economic differentials and language skills differentials

There appeared to be a tendency for lower levels of proficiency in speaking and writing of the mother tongue for those from higher socio-economic background. While there is no control with which to compare mother tongue proficiency, if the overall results are contrasted to the control English language background proficiencies, they are clearly at opposite ends of the ratings scale from both low socio-economic background and high socio-economic background. It could be suggested that the proficiencies in mother tongue are not comparable to native-like proficiency of a language in general, with the academic skills of reading and writing scoring the lowest.

The English only control sample tended to score better in all areas than Macedonian and German background samples, but there was no overall significant difference between higher and lower socio-economic background. This reflects in part the limited number of our sample and the fact that they were chosen selectively to represent the range of abilities in each school. There seems to be some difference, however, between mother tongue speakers' proficiency in English from different socio-economic backgrounds, with those of high socio-economic backgrounds appearing to score higher. This seems to correlate with poorer mother tongue proficiency, but again one needs to be wary about what causes this apparent link.

For the German background group, speaking and writing tended to score the lowest, followed by listening and reading. This indicates possibly a higher passive knowledge of the language, linked to the fact that, for half the sample, German was studied at both primary and secondary school. In the case of the Macedonian background sample, the larger spread over the middle range of ratings for speaking indicates possibly a higher active use of the language at home. (Only one primary school and no high schools offered Macedonian. Also no high school student attended ethnic afternoon school.) In the case of the primary school particularly, additional factors, such as whether the child was born in Australia or born in Macedonia, and in all schools generally, a return trip to Macedonia and the extent of social contact in the Macedonian community affected active use of Macedonian and thereby altered results. It would be possible from the mountain of data collected to make such correlations, but financial and time factors limited our sample and our ability to exploit the data and the survey instruments fully.

The control English language background speaking and reading scores tended to be mostly at higher levels of proficiency than their listening and writing scores. The spread over the range in writing reflects the fact that the control sample was chosen in such a way that it drew a balanced number of high, middle and low school achievers. This was not the case, however, for our Macedonian sample (which consisted of all available students in a given year at a given school). Here most of the students were rated by their class placement and school assessment as low school achievers. Given the language problem clearly evidenced by our tests, it is difficult to conclude that the children's assessment by their school as low achievers actually reflects their intellectual or academic potential. The German background sample is small and therefore limited in its significance, but the trend in our results indicates a closer correlation in proficiency at all levels with the English only control sample than the Macedonian background sample.

Sex differentials and language skills differentials

The main difference of any significance in mother tongue proficiency between males and females was in reading. Both Macedonian and German females appeared to score higher in this area. The Macedonian background females seemed to score a little higher in speaking, writing and listening also. The sample was too small to make any generalizations about German background students. The females tended to score at the higher levels in writing than males for all samples, whereas more males from the Macedonian and the control samples tended to score higher ratings for speaking. For the other language areas, the results are uneven and do not reflect any significant trend based on male/female divisions.

Primary/high school and language skills differentials

There seemed to be no improvement in speaking scores in Macedonian from primary school to high school. There was only some improvement in listening scores, which might indicate an increase in passive knowledge through longer exposure to the language. Writing skills scored less in the high school. The German sample was too small in the primary school to provide information for valid generalizations. At high school German seems generally to be more of a foreign language experience for those in our sample.

In the English tests, the Macedonian background sample showed no significant difference in their speaking scores from primary to high school. The order of improvement in scores was listening, reading and, lastly, writing. For the German background sample, speaking and listening scores tended to be higher in the primary schools and reading and writing seemed higher in the high schools. But, again, the sample was too small to make generalizations, particularly for the primary school. When taken together, the control English language background samples showed no significant difference between primary school language proficiency and high school language proficiency, in all areas.

The average total scores for language proficiency clearly put the control group ahead of both Macedonian and German background samples. Mother tongue proficiency scores were far below English proficiency scores. The Macedonian sample did declare that they used their mother tongue at home and occasionally with friends at school, and one primary sample studied it at school. Yet, despite this, there is some evidence building up that the sort of Macedonian these children had acquired or currently used was deficient in terms of the particular communicative and analytical skills the tests set out to evaluate.

Language proficiency differentials by place of birth

A result also worthy of note, is the inverse scoring for mother tongue and English proficiency, depending on whether children were born in Australia or not, for children of both Macedonian and German background.

Primary Schools Interview and Evaluation Reports: English

The whole school average language ability appears to be very low in School A. The Macedonian background children appear to operate with a very mechanical use of English. They display problems with mass and unit distinctions, tense, word sense, sentence structure and word order, and have problems with punctuation. Many children are not fluent in English, and the irregularities that appeared in their writing seem to indicate serious phonetic problems. There were only two English-only speakers in year 5 at one school, and their English proficiency scores were not significantly higher than the Macedonian background sample.

Average total scores for English proficiency were higher for School B.

Macedonian is not taught at School C, and Macedonian proficiency scores generally were very low for the Macedonian language background children there. There was a widespread discrepancy at this school in the scores of the control group, but those who scored highly had an impressive command of English. In fact, only one student from School C displayed serious language difficulties. Most wrote extensively, correctly and set out their writing well. Speaking, listening and reading were also very competent. The writing of the Macedonian language background sample at this school, in contrast, was very limited in expression and remained at a concrete level. Most used only short factual sentences with few descriptive devices. Spelling and punctuation were also irregular. In speech, sentences were truncated and repetitive. The children kept to what was familiar and were hesitant. Students at this school were less willing to use Macedonian.

The primary school from which our German background sample was drawn (School E) had a German language programme. However, our German background sample came mostly from households where only one parent was German. All scores except reading were very low, perhaps indicating that children had only a very limited passive knowledge of the language. In writing, they were quite happy to write extensively even if many words were English instead of German. The range of scores between the English only control sample and the German background sample for English proficiency was not significantly different.

High Schools Interview and Evaluation Reports: English

All Macedonian students in our sample from School D were born in Australia. Two-thirds had expectations to go on to year 12 and had as their career goals jobs like sales assistants, shopkeepers, pilots and engineers. Most did not complain or admit to any problems with English. They mostly used Macedonian at home with their families. Their passive knowledge of Macedonian seemed greater than their active proficiency. Their Macedonian scores were uneven in their range but, generally, overall proficiency seemed very limited.

The English results of the Macedonian background children of this school were higher than the high school from which we drew our larger sample and which has a larger percentage of students from non-English-speaking backgrounds (School B). Reponses were again uneven. There was some indication of a wide vocabulary, but some students were handicapped by inflexible structures and grammatical irregularities. Listening and writing had the lowest scores.

The control English language background group in School D, in contrast, was very articulate and used complex structures. They were more able to move between formal and colloquial expression with ease. The most notable feature was the vocabulary range of these students and the mixture of register that they utilized. For example, 'obtain', 'receive' and 'get' all appeared in one student's writing. Similarly, 'finish', 'complete' and 'cease' appeared in another. Fewer of these students contemplated going on to year 12 than those from the Macedonian background group. Their career goals were generally in the direction of jobs like teaching, nursing or journalism.

The Macedonian background students from School D displayed a very wide range of ability. The listening exercise proved one of the most difficult, with most children able to relay details of casual conversation but not the gist. Those students who scored better listened for meaning rather than detail and were able to retell the conversation in their own words. In free conversation some children who were obviously very confident sometimes were frustrated in expressing their meaning by an inability to find the right words or use appropriate grammatical structures. Utterances of the order of 'what language are you' and 'can't hear very clear' occurred frequently. Colloquial expression was also limited. At this school very few of the children of Macedonian background continued into years 11 and 12.

The results of the German background group were uneven in both Schools F and G. The results of the control sample at one of the schools were particularly high, with the children able to build arguments well, point by point. In the writing they varied their style, and their sentences built upon each other. Their vocabulary was extensive in all the areas evaluated.

It would be useful to establish the parameters of native-like proficiency in English for school purposes and then to assess how children of non-English-speaking backgrounds arrive at native-like proficiency, or the extent of the need to have native-like proficiency for schooling. Our findings only skim the surface of the issue, but we hope they provide pointers to work that still needs to be done in this area.

Interview and Evaluation Reports: Macedonian

Macedonian proficiency scores were lower than English, despite Macedonian being the children's mother tongue and being taught in one of the schools. Pronunciation appeared again to be a serious problem. One interviewer called this 'Macedonified English', incorporated into Macedonian interchanges. The children were taught the Cyrillic script of School A but not all were able to read it and many used both Cyrillic and Latin script in their writing. The children across the schools appeared to have a very limited vocabulary in Macedonian. It seemed that Macedonian was used mostly with parents, but English was the norm among siblings. The range of oral competency appeared limited to the home sphere. In conversation the children seemed to use English as a supplement to complete Macedonian sentences and expressions. Reading was word-for-word, rather than reading for sense. Punctuation cues were also missed in reading. The Macedonian background sample from School A was more relaxed about using Macedonian than the samples from other schools.

The children spoke in dialect and had difficulty coping with the formal evaluation situation. They had little familiarity with letter writing forms (how to start a letter, etc.). Spelling irregularities are frequent because:

1. Children wrote as they spoke. This produced some confused results particularly with regard to voiced and unvoiced consonants at the end of words.

2. Children produced their own spelling based on English orthography. This was common to all students because, for example, Macedonian vowels are pure, at least in comparison to English, and the children confused and mixed them. For example:

    (a) 'o' is written 'or'
    'a' is written 'ar' or 'or'
    'u' is written 'oo'

and

    (b) 'ck' is used rather than just 'k' as it should be for /k/.
    As in English, 'y' is used instead of 'j' for /j/; 'sh' instead of 's' /s/; and, 'ch' instead of 'c' /c/.

    (c) Not many students knew of the existence of the palatal /k/ and /g/. Perhaps this was because they do not use them properly when speaking. Very few children used k or g in their writing, and (palatal n) was not used at all.

    (d) Many problems arose with the use of consonantal clusters. In Macedonian there are consonantal clusters with mostly rolled 'r' in between. When trying to write words with these features, children often put in redundant vowels. For example, 'smrdi' became 'smerdi' (stinks). It was interesting that a large number of children used the same deviate spelling.

(e) Another problem children had was with double vowels. In Macedonian a double vowel in spelling expresses a longer vowel. However, when writing a double vowel, children either added /j/ or ignored the pronunciation and left one vowel out. For example, 'ziveeme' was incorrectly written as 'zivejme' or 'ziveme'.

(f) Another significant problem was the large number of children who were not sure whether certain syllables were one word or two. Often a word would be separated into two or more syllables and then written as two or more discrete words. Others wrote what should have been two or more words as one. For example, 'izubdivme' was written as 'iz gubivme'.

(g) Most children wrote 'sh' instead of 'z' because they were unable to distinguish 's' from 'z'.

In situations where a lack of vocabulary became problematic, a common strategy was to borrow an English word, modify its spelling and add legitimate suffixes.

The majority of children in School A wrote Cyrillic well, although they could only print it. In School B the Latin script was generally used to write Macedonian. Overall, writing levels were better for the primary school children.

According to their own reports, the School B children rarely write in Macedonian, and this was reflected in the fact that their writing would be hard to interpret for someone who read Macedonian but who knew little English. There was little 'stylistic' variation apparent in the writing. No individuality was displayed; students used only a few simple 'standardized' sentences to construct their answers, even though one text was meant to be a personal letter.

Most School A children could read Cyrillic. However, no School B, C or D children could. Some were not even aware of the existence of the Cyrillic script. In the high schools there were various problems.

1. Double vowels — 'voopstena' — caused problems. Many children did not know how to sound out a word. Most words with double vowels are compound words used only in literary levels of language.
2. There were many problems with vowels, which were often pronounced as in English rather than Macedonian.
3. Children had problems sounding out consonant clusters.
4. There were problems with palatals which were almost universally absent from the readings.
5. Only two or three of the high school children read with any sense of in-

tonation, punctuation or communicative intent. Mostly they read by sounding out each syllable. The primary school children in School A largely read with a good sense of intonation, punctuation and communicative intent.

6. Many high school children did not want to attempt the reading exercise, saying that they could not read Macedonian. Many had read little or nothing in Macedonian before. Those who read, and often wrote well, said they wrote regularly to relatives overseas. Most expressed the opinion that this was the only use for reading or writing in Macedonian.

To make a broad generalization, the children were better at conversation and following what was said (Speaking A) than they were in the comprehension (Listening B). This was partially due to the comprehension (Listening B) involving the idea of a 'test'. However, for those who were successful in the comprehension, there was another factor involved. The test was taken from 2EA radio announcements of dances and other social functions. Those students who usually attended such functions were already familiar with the names of places, groups, etc.

Generally, the children preferred to talk in Macedonian about things to do with the home, family, overseas, etc. When the conversation shifted to school or sport, for example, the children would hesitate until they found the appropriate Macedonian words, or they would use an English word.

Most children at all schools were good at listening, even when they could not speak well. In the lower proficiency cases comprehension abilities were restricted to domestic topics.

All children spoke in the dialect form of the language used by their parents. An exception was a child from School A, who had been in Australia only one or two years and had attended school in Macedonia. Although he was a shy boy, he was very good at the standard form of Macedonian.

A problem with some children in the Speaking A test was that they were shy and not talkative. One interviewer put the children at ease by telling jokes, etc., and they responded to the task better, thinking of it as a game. When performing the task, it was interesting to note that the things some children built were a lot easier to describe than others.

A large number of children stated that they wished they could choose Macedonian language classes as part of their electives. The main reason given was that when they travel overseas to Macedonia, they would be able to communicate properly with relatives.

Some children had attended 'ethnic schools' run by the ethnic community, but most children in high school were not currently attending or did not want to attend. The reasons for this were stated as follows: too time consuming; boring;

no materials; teachers too strict; inconvenient location of class; often children 8–16 years in one group; taught history and geography of Macedonia or other literature they think is irrelevant to their present experiences.

Children at School A mostly attend the departmental Saturday school and like it. The reasons were stated as follows: the school is close to where the children live; all their friends go; attendance is encouraged by the school because it reinforces the Macedonian taught in the regular classes. Due to the encouragement of School A's principal, the teachers of the Saturday school are making attempts to reduce the rote learning method of teaching and to introduce a variety of new teaching practices.

Interest in learning Macedonian depended on a number of factors, the principal one being its utility for individual students. Thus in the case of School A many children indicated that they had spent long holidays overseas, frequently of several months' duration. The parents of these children were often undecided about which country they would ultimately choose to live in.

In general, those children whose Macedonian was extensive and who indicated that they would like to learn more, had Macedonian friends both inside and outside school. They socialized at Macedonian dances, or were themselves performers in one of the five or six dance groups in the area. They usually spoke Macedonian at home to parents who had very limited English language skills.

Those students who thought Macedonian was irrelevant had friends of many nationalities other than Macedonian. They were disinterested in or disliked, Macedonian music, dancing and other organized social activities.

It is perhaps significant that none of the high school students was studying any non-English language at school. This may have been due to a lack of opportunity for language study. Nevertheless, the students stated that they saw no need for language studies.

In the primary schools children said that they did want to learn other languages. The main reasons given were that they wanted to learn about others, or that their friends spoke a particular language.

Peer group pressure played some part. For example, two particular boys, when together, said that they hated learning Macedonian. However, when interviewed separately, one said he would like to learn standard Macedonian because he had been overseas and would like to speak 'properly'. This student also used significantly more English in his speech when performing the task exercise with the first boy than he did when alone in the interview.

In general, therefore, it seems that student interest in learning Macedonian depends on the value placed on the language in family situations, whether students have friends who mainly speak Macedonian and whether or not the student is interested in, or attends, Macedonian community functions.

Interview and Evaluation Reports: German

Most of the comments about German proficiency involved the children's reluctance to use it and the incorporation of many English words and structures. The curriculum, teaching methods, teacher attitudes and the whole school atmosphere have to be considered as factors influencing the results. A detailed consideration of these issues lies outside our brief.

The interviews and tests performed at High Schools F and G were performed under almost identical conditions. Only one or two students at either school achieved results that demonstrated an average or above-average knowledge or use of the German language. The tests were found difficult by most students, even those who have been residents in Australia for only a short time (one boy had only been here since 1980).

Some students still spoke or listened to their parents speak German at home, and most of these students communicated reasonably well in German. A student's comprehension and communication skills were ascertained almost immediately in the ten-minute interview session at the beginning of each interview. It should be noted, however, that nearly all the students interviewed responded only to those questions put to them. In fact, none volunteered any information other than that asked for, and their responses, although in German, in the case of a number of students prohibited any analysis of how extensive their German may have been. Perhaps this was due to the circumstances of the interview, a test situation, even though they had been assured otherwise.

The tape recorded segment of the interview certainly separated those with little or no knowledge of German from those who had some. Yet this part of the test also highlighted some of the discrepancies of the testing. That is, the dialect of the speaker on the tape was a very refined type of German, and a number of students who had come through the first part of the test demonstrating reasonable communication skills found it very difficult to understand the speaker on the tape recording. In one instance a boy who had answered all the questions put to him in the initial interview with very few difficulties complained about the accent of the speaker and said he had trouble understanding what was being said. Yet the last passage on the tape made use of a slang word which was crucial to the passage, and this boy had no trouble at all in answering this question. This boy was one of two students able to answer this question correctly. The boy in question spoke with a Bavarian accent and used a number of Bavarian words and expressions. At first glance the results of the tests would show that many children born in Germany or born to German-born parents in our sample could not read, write or think extensively in German.

The interviewer was able to adapt the oral questionnare/interview to the level of individuals, extending them where possible, but the difficulty was that most students are not used to conversing at length in what is, in most cases, effectively a foreign language. Also for some students it was an interviewer/teacher-student type situation where students are often loathe to take the initiative. Apart from the interviewer trying to put the students at ease, this is a situation that probably cannot be overcome. Most performed well in the oral interaction task. However, students generally could not express ideas such as box/square, circle. Most found the listening test on tape quite a difficult test. Some students understood none of it; a few performed quite well at it.

As would be expected, it is writing skills that are least practised in community languages, as they are often the least needed. At one of the high schools (where there is no German class) this created an insurmountable barrier (except for the student who came to Australia four years ago). Some of the students could write no German at all, others did make an attempt but it was merely an English spelling for German sounds and English word order.

Some found the reading evaluation difficult. However, multiple-choice questions did assist the students a lot (whereas they would have faced more difficulty in comprehension with open-ended questions).

A year 10 German class exists at one of the high schools only. The German teacher there had a very brief look at some of the evaluation instruments and thought they might be a bit difficult for students at her school; however, the better students, she felt, should have been able to handle them. Students participating in the German survey were reassured that results certainly did not affect their school reports, but there remained some unease. One student was rather unwilling to participate in the survey because she felt German was not one of her stronger points. At the second high school there was no year 10 German class. One student here was very unwilling to participate in the survey (he had no writing or reading skills in German).

The School E tests had an outcome very similar to that of the high schools. The primary school also contained only one or two children with any working knowledge of German, and this was mainly due to the children's parents speaking German at home either to the children or to each other. The children who attended the German class at the school had some knowledge of German. They knew the names of common everyday items but they were by no means proficient at the language.

The evaluation procedure once again demonstrated that most children, even those comfortable with the speaking, had difficulty reading, writing and thinking in German. It was quite difficult to elicit extended answers from the students in the year 5 oral interview. Students did not generally have an extensive knowledge of position words for the task, although they could often improvise with names of objects.

Students experienced a lot of difficulty with the listening tape. Some problems were to do with memory (when we asked them Set A and Set B questions). We changed the format of this test in that we gave the students the questions so they could focus their attention while they heard it being read. They were also allowed to make notes if they wanted to (which, interestingly, they did in German, not English). Writing is the area where students showed the least competence. Reading aloud was generally performed well by the students.

At the primary school the German teacher was present for some of the evaluations as she was keen to know what the survey entailed. She did feel, however, that some of the tasks were not appropriate to the level of her students, e.g. the writing requirements. The reason was that in her language programme she places little emphasis on writing skills (they write in an English/German mixture), as she believes writing is not one of the skills needed to such an extent when learning a community language. She considers the speaking and listening skills to be of more importance.

The German teacher's method of teaching the children was to encourage them to use German as much as possible, without making it difficult for them. She allowed then to use an English word if they were at a loss for the German word, and placed little emphasis on grammar or correct spelling. Her aim appears to be to teach the children to communicate in German, with the other skills coming once this has been achieved.

Further, it was relayed by a teacher at the school that the German class was not viewed favourably by the staff; one teacher thought it was a nuisance. This teacher suggested that everything revolved around these lessons and that they disrupted the efficient running of the school. The German teacher was asked about the attitude of the staff to her lessons, and she remarked that she was very aware that teachers of the school considered her lessons to be a nuisance and a disruption to the school.

6
Summary and Conclusions

The 'Culture' of Multiculturalism

To contribute to the formulation of clear social and language policy, we have examined a range of possible premises in the terminology of 'multiculturalism' and 'multilingualism'. As these have meanings which are very much contested, we have worked through the alternative policy consequences of the alternative meanings.

In elaborating upon the sociological and historical roots of the language question, we posit two powerful tendencies in the modern world: to cultural unification and universalization, and at the same time to the placement of people of diverse historical and linguistic origins in close relation and the reproduction of that diversity. Policies equivalent to multiculturalism have been established, particularly in those emerging nation states where these two great historical tendencies are most acutely juxtaposed. Whether in the various forms to be found in Australia, the USA, Canada or Sweden for example, the historical impetus has been the same: to integrate peoples of diverse origin into a singular social structure of industrialism.

Yet against this fundamental process of integration there is a level of diversity that continues. Indeed, diversity can be a rationale for reproducing unequal social relations (classically, as in South Africa), a concession to the rigours of unification, or a positive vibrancy integral to the cosmopolitan, dynamic culture of industrialism itself. Diversity of origin is a logistical challenge for the unifying force of modernity that cannot be ridden over roughshod. Yet the structures of industrialism limit the spaces available to cultural variety.

A simple pluralist conception of culture for multiculturalism busies itself with the celebration and maintenance of only such variety as can easily exist in diversity in industrialism. In so doing, it often tends to neglect the wider structural context limiting that diversity, to trivialize the content of culture, to want to conserve tradition uncritically, to patronize other cultures by fostering for others practices one might not wish upon oneself, and overwhelmingly to assume in practice that culture and traditionalism are equivalent and that the cultural phenomena of this order are principally the preserve of minorities or recent immigrants. An alternative to simple pluralist multiculturalism is an holistic view of culture, more in line with the use to which the term 'culture' is put by cultural anthropologists.

The subject matter that simple pluralism considers its own is very worthy of emphasis. Variety is very important: one's ancestral language, for example, can be an important fulcrum of communality, a rallying point for political and social solidarity, of psychological comfort in the home, of heartfelt aesthetic power or a conveyor of specific meanings related to self-identity (level three in the theoretical schema). But cultural and linguistic maintenance is never an unproblematic continuation of ancestral forms. Critically, it occurs within changing structural contexts which limit and influence its continuation. Although there is a level of cultural diversity in modern Australian industrial society, there is another level of a structural cultural singularity. We have called this cultural singularity 'Western industrialism'. For Aborigines and many immigrants, cultural maintenance in an anthropological sense simply has not occurred, or there is a certain phenomenal cultural continuity at one level (level three in the theoretical schema), but only in the context of structural cultural break at another (level two).

Within a language, according to historical and social context, there is often considerable variety of register, genre, syntax or semantic field. Socio-linguistically, some language forms (such as those of peasant-agrarian contexts) do not have the same functional efficacy as others (such as those of educated, middle-class city dwellers) for Western industrialism in Australia. There is a practical inevitability to English being the common language of social understanding and effective participation in Australia today. The particular geographical origin of this language may well have been an historical accident, and English has no special virtue as a language. Nonetheless, it is today more than just one piece in the Australian mosaic of 'community' languages. It is also a crucial means to social power and self-determination (level two in the theoretical schema).

Language policy cannot simply orient itself towards maintenance for maintenance's sake or for sentimental reasons; at least, this is only a sub-consideration. First and foremost, language is an open, dynamic communicative tool and, as such, common to all human cultures and in the nature of culture itself (level one in the theoretical schema). We are not duty-bound to conserve any ancestral characteristics that do not perform a useful purpose for us. On the other hand, we should not be pressured to reject ancestral characteristics because they do not prove to be structurally useful to us.

As there is a difference between simple pluralist multiculturalism and an holistic view of culture in Australia, so there is also a difference between language policy whose principal orientation is maintenance and language policy which is also concerned more broadly with social empowerment. The simple pluralist proponents of maintenance might well denounce possible assimilationist intent in English as a second language or transitional bilingual programmes. But the pedagogical and social consequences, even in the teaching of languages other than English, can be very different according to policy rationales which view language as a tool of self-determination and social access and those which view language mainly as a symbol and means of maintaining cultural diversity. We need means of fostering languages other than English which will lead to profound and cost-effective consequences, not just in the space left for cultural and linguistic diversity in Australia's Western industrialism (level three of the schema), but also in terms of access to the structures of power and participation (level two).

Issues and Debates: International Perspectives

An examination of three case studies of language policy and practice, in Sweden, Canada and the USA, reveals points of similarity and difference relevant to our Australian practice.

In Sweden a theoretical and political tension, parallel to the one described above, exists between emphases on language teaching in the name of cultural diversity or the reproduction of ethnicity and a proposition that 'semilingualism' was an object to be overcome in order to improve the access of linguistic minorities to social goods. Monolingual minority language teaching and long-term transitional bilingual programmes are a specific feature of Swedish approaches to the language question, related both to the particular nature of the welfare state and to a perceived need to guarantee 'freedom to return', given the geographical proximity of places of origin and the current economic situation.

The same tension exists in Canada between arguments that emphasize tolerance and cultural diversity as a rationale for language teaching and arguments about the long-term cognitive and educational benefits of bilingualism. Important research findings show that balanced coordinate bilingualism might produce some such benefits, but compound bilingualism (which is most frequently the process of language acquisition for people of non-English-speaking background in Australia) can have detrimental effects on children's cognitive and linguistic development. But the research also signals that such generalizations cannot be made independently of wider contextual factors such as socioeconomic status. The strength of the Canadian literature and the particular results of seminal experiments such as the St Lambert's project have to be related to the peculiar linguistic and political situation of French and English.

In the United States the tension has been represented historically in a political movement over the past three decades from desegregation and the goal of ensuring that educational outcomes were not hindered by inappropriate language instruction, then to pluralism ('rights of maintenance and difference') and more recently returning to strident and unsubtle arguments about basics and American society. Some of the most recent research in the field works with an understanding of linguistic realms along the lines of the cultural levels schema we have presented.

The Empirical Research

Our first methodological decision was to select one decisive site where evidence of maintenance or non-maintenance of first languages other than English would most clearly be found. It was decided that we should examine intergenerational changes by surveying school children in years 5 and 10 along with their parents. The surveys were to register attitudes, self-assessment of language proficiency and, using more objective techniques, to assess and compare school students' first and second language proficiency. This site was not selected for its representativeness in terms of the whole spectrum of places where languages other than English are maintained in Australia. Rather, the intergenerational nexus was selected because it is possibly the most decisive of all sites in terms of language maintenance or non-maintenance and the one most open to government assistance. Year 5 sits in the middle of the compulsory phase of education, at a stage where linguistic-cognitive foundations are being laid. Year 10 is at the end of the compulsory phase, preparatory to workforce entry or further education. On this basis, adults and children of Macedonian, German and English (control) language backgrounds were surveyed in a number of local settings in the Wollongong-Shellharbour region, selected because they showed significant statistical variation of socio-economic level.

The German and Macedonian groups surveyed proved to be clearly differentiated. The German background group was longer settled in Australia, more geographically dispersed, displayed a higher rate of interethnic marriage and was socio-economically diverse. The Macedonian background group was more recently settled, relatively concentrated geographically, with a lower rate of intermarriage and was socio-economically more homogeneous (at a comparatively lower level).

Almost all the German and Macedonian parents claimed that German or Macedonian was their first language. But, while all Macedonian children claimed that Macedonian was their first language, only 68 per cent of German children made this claim for German. Parallel to this, 86 per cent of Macedonian children claimed they could speak their mother tongue well, compared with only 32 per cent of German children.

Across adult length of residence in Australia, it was perceived that mother tongue language abilities initially decreased. After a few decades of residence, however, this claim stabilized to indicate a perception that mother tongue abilities were no longer reducing. Alongside this stabilization there were statements that thinking in English, and English language skills, increased continuously over length of residence.

When we compared the different language skills between generations and across an individual's whole length of residence, there was a general drop-off in perceived mother tongue abilities. This tendency was greater for the productive skills of speaking and writing, and also more marked for literacy than oracy in general.

A parallel pattern of reponses arose in the analysis of different sites of language use and language maintenance. In the domestic area, for example, there was more mother tongue language usage among the Macedonians than among the Germans, and more among adults than among children. Language usage patterns tended to change initially in the direction of less mother tongue usage, but then stabilized over length of residence within a generation.

While there was quite strong advocacy of the value of language maintenance, this was less strong on the part of the Germans than the Macedonians and weakened across generations. There was a decreasing emphasis on the importance of language in maintaining family unity. Language was linked less to identity by the control adults than by the Germans, by the Germans less than by the Macedonians, and generally by the children less than by the adults.

There seemed to be a general lack of awareness among the respondents of possible alternative models of language policy and practice. The most popular rationale and suggestion appeared to be language teaching along traditionally conceived 'foreign language' lines.

Language maintenance occurs either strongly, weakly, or fails to occur at all, in a complex social situation, involving generational changes, length of residence of an individual in Australia, socio-economic factors, gender, the experience of school and so on. One of the general pitfalls in the literature in this area, not just in Australia but internationally, is that valid analysis requires independent control of each of a number of contributing factors.

In the evaluation of mother tongue maintenance, the children of Macedonian background retained higher levels of usage on the whole than the children of German background. This would seem to be related to relative recency of arrival and geographical dispersal.

For both the German and Macedonian groups, English language skills were below those of the control group. The difference is significant enough to reaffirm concern about underachievement of children from non-English-speaking backgrounds. Considerable further research is required to account for this difference. We do not think that these results point to the bilingual experience as being the cause of underachievement at school. We feel that what needs to be investigated are the ways these children acquire language proficiency, both the mother tongue and second language, and specifically the sort of curriculum, instruction and environment they experience at school, and how this might not be suitable to their particular needs.

Policy Directions

Ideally, multiculturalism can be a policy for social participation and equity. Just as the modern world has simultaneously unified humankind structurally and made a level of cultural plurality an integral feature of everyday life, so policymakers need to consider whether that unificaton is equitable and whether diversity, while being a right, is without prejudice to equity.

Various policy directions can follow from differing rationales for language maintenance. For example, there is a danger that language programmes emanating from a poorly thought out simple pluralist position might end up being short-term, poorly funded exercises in 'community' relations. There are also methodological dangers with the notion of 'community languages', if 'community languages' imply preparing children only for the language as it is used in the place of origin. Furthermore, if the goal is the production of inter-ethnic understanding, limited language programmes are not necessarily the most effective way of achieving this. There needs to be an urgent general assessment of current practices in order to establish the extent to which outcomes relate to goals.

On the other hand, language programmes consistent with the goal of social participation would consider languages primarily as tools of communication and assess their requirements with this end in view. This would include early language education programmes that continued and developed a child's first language while simultaneously establishing English. It would also involve teaching languages other than English to a standard and degree of intellectual seriousness similar to that traditionally expected in foreign language teaching (without necessarily being traditional in terms of pedagogy), beginning as early in schooling as possible and sustained over a number of years. For students of non-English-speaking background, teaching to these ends will help ensure that there is not a linguistic and cognitive break on entry to school. For all students, language learning that provides a genuine intellectual challenge can aid not only linguistic development but also the growth of wider intellectual abilities.

Bibliography

ADELMAN, Clem (1981) 'Language, Culture and Bilingual Study: Reflections after a Case Study of Schools', *Journal of Multilingual and Multicultural Development*, Vol. 2, No. 4, pp. 259–68.

AFFRENDRAS, Evangelos E. (1981) 'An Outsider Comes Inside: The Views of a Greek Sociolinguist Visiting Australia', in *Community Languages: Their Role in Education*, GARNER, Mark (ed.), Melbourne, River Seine Publications.

ALDERSON, J.C. (1981a) 'Reaction to the Morrow Paper and Report of the Discussion on Communicative Language Testing', in *ELT Documents III, Issues in Language Testing*, London, British Council.

ALDERSON, J.C. (1981b) 'Report of the Discussion on Testing English for Specific Purposes', in *ELT Documents III, Issues in Language Testing*, London, British Council.

ALDERSON, J.C. (1981c) 'Report of the Discussion on Communicative Language Testing', in ALDERSON and HUGHES (1981).

ALDERSON, J.C. and HUGHES, A. (1981) *Issues in Language Testing*, ELT Documents III, London, British Council.

ALDERSON, J.C., CANDLIN, C.N., CLAPHAM, C.M., MARTIN, D.J. and WEIR, C.J. (1986) *Language Proficiency Testing for Migrant Professionals: New Directions for the Occupational English Test*, Report submitted to the Council on Overseas Professional Qualifications by the Tertiary and Evaluation Consultancy Institute for English Language Education, University of Lancaster.

ALLEN, H.B. and CAMPBELL, R.N. (eds) (1961) *Teaching English as a Second Language*, New York, McGraw-Hill.

AMERICAN INSTITUTES FOR RESEARCH (AIR) (1977) *Evaluation of the Impact of ESEA Title VII Spanish/English Bilingual Education Program*, Los Angeles: National Dissemination and Assessment Center, California State University, 1978.

AMODEO, Luiza B. and ARNBERG, Lenore (1983) *Issues in Early Childhood Bilingualism: Pros and Cons*, New Mexico.

ARTHUR, B., *et al.*, (1980) 'The Register of Impersonal Discourse to Beginners: Verbal Adjustments to Foreign Accent', in *Discourse Analysis in Second Language Research*, LARSEN-FREEMAN, D. (ed.), Rowley, Mass., Newbury House.

AUSTRALIAN BUREAU OF STATISTICS (1983) 'Cross-classified Characteristics of Persons and Dwellings, 1981', *Census of Population and Housing*, Catalogue No. 245.0, Canberra, Australian Government Publishing Service.

AUSTRALIAN INSTITUTE OF MULTICULTURAL AFFAIRS (1985) *Reducing the Risk: Unemployment and Labour Market Programs*, Melbourne, AIMA.

AUSTRALIAN INSTITUTE OF MULTICULTURAL AFFAIRS (1986) *Migrant Unemployment*, Melbourne, AIMA.

BAKER, Catherine A. (1983) 'Bilingual Education: "Que Pasce?"', *Contemporary Education*, Vol. 54, No. 2, Winter 1983, pp. 105–8.

BALL, Martin J. and MUNRO, Sian M. (1981) 'Language Assessment Procedures for Linguistic Minorities: An Example', *Journal of Multilingual and Multicultural Development*, Vol. 2, No. 4, pp. 231–41.

BANKS, J. (1983) 'Cultural Democracy, Citizenship Education, and the American Dream', National Council for the Social Studies Presidential Address, *Social Education*, Vol. 47, pp. 222–32.

BARIK, Henri C. and SWAIN, M. (1975) 'Three Year Evaluation of a Large Scale Early Grade Immersion Program: The Ottawa Study', *Language Learning*, No. 25, pp. 1–30.

BARIK, Henri C. and SWAIN, Merrill (1978) 'A Longitudinal Study of Bilingual and Cognitive Development', *International Journal of Psychology*, Vol. II, No. 4, pp. 251–63.

BEN-ZEEV, Sandra (1977) 'Mechanisms by Which Childhood Bilingualism Affects Understanding of Language and Cognitive Structures', in *Bilingualism*, HORNBY, P. (ed.) New York, Academic Press, pp. 29–55.

BHATNAGAR, J. (1970) *Immigrants at School*, London, Cornmarket Press.

BHATNAGAR, J. (1980) 'Linguistic Behaviour and Adjustment of Immigrant Children in French and English Schools in Montreal', *International Review of Applied Psychology*, No. 29, pp. 141–59.

BHATNAGAR, J. (ed.) (1981) 'Introduction, in *Educating Immigrants*, London, Croom Helm.

BHATNAGAR, J. (1982) 'Language and Culture Maintenance Programs in Canada', in *Self-Concept, Achievement and Multicultural Education*, VERMA, G. and BAGLEY, C. (eds), London, Macmillan.

BHATNAGAR, J. (1983) 'Multicultural Education in a Psychological Perspective', in *Multicultural and Multilingual Education in Immigrant Countries*, HUSEN, T. and OPPER, S. (eds), Oxford, Pergamon Press, pp. 59–76.

BIBEAU, Gilles (1984) 'No Easy Road to Bilingualism', *Language and Society*, No. 12, pp. 44–7.

BIRRELL, R. (1987) 'The Educational Achievement of Non-English Speaking Background Students and the Politics of the Community Languages Movement', Mimeo, Canberra, ANU Centre for Economic Policy Research Conference: The Economics of Migration.

BLANCO, George M. (1978) 'The Implementation of Bilingual/Bicultural Education Programs in the United States', in *Case Studies in Bilingual Education*, SPOLSKY, B., *et al.*, (eds), Rowley, Mass., Newbury House.

BLANCO, George (1979) 'The Education Perspective', *Center for Applied Linguistics*, Vol. 4, pp. 1–66.

BOSTOCK, William W. (1973) 'Monolingualism in Australia', *Australian Quarterly*, Vol. 45, No. 2, pp. 39–52.

BOSTOCK, William W. (1977) 'Alternatives of Ethnicity', *Immigrants and Aborigines in Anglo-Saxon Australia*, Hobart, Cat and Fiddle Press.

BOURHIS, Richard Yuon, *et al.* (1981) 'Notes on the Construction of a "Subjective Vitality Questionnaire" for Ethnolinguistic Groups', *Journal of Multicultural and Multilingual Development*, Vol. 2, No. 2, pp. 145–55.

BRADLEY, Lynette (1980) *Assessing Reading Difficulties: A Diagnostic and Remedial Approach*, London, Macmillan.

BRATT, Paulston C. (1982) 'Problems in the Comparative Analysis of Bilingual Education', in *Multicultural and Multilingual Education in Immigrant Countries*, HUSEN, T. and OPPER, S. (eds), Oxford, Pergamon Press, pp. 115–22.

BRINDLEY, G. (1986) *The Assessment of Second Language Proficiency: Issues and Approaches*, Australia, NCRC.

BROWN, P. and LEVINSON, S. (1978) 'Universals in Language Usage: Politeness Phenomena', in *Questions and Politeness*, GOODY, E.W. (ed.), Cambridge, Cambridge University Press.

BRUCK, M., JAKIMIK, J. and TUCKER, G.R. (1971) 'Are French Immersion Programs Suitable for Working-class Children? A Follow-up Investigation', *Word*, 27, pp. 311–14.

BRUCK, M., LAMBERT, W.E. and TUCKER, G.R. (1974) 'Bilingual Schooling through the Elementary Grades: The St. Lambert Project at Grade Seven', *Language Learning*, 24, pp. 183–204.

BRUMBY, E. and VASZOLYI, E. (eds) (1977) *Language Problems in Aboriginal Education*, Perth, Mt Lawley CAE.

BRUMFIT, C.J. (1984) *Communicative Methodology in Language Teaching: The Roles of Fluency and Accuracy*, Cambridge, Cambridge University Press.

BULLIVANT, Brian (1986) 'Are Anglo-Australian Students Becoming the New Self-Deprived in Comparison with Ethnics?: New Evidence Challenges Conventional Wisdom', Mimeo, Melbourne, Australian Association for Research in Education Annual Conference, November.

BULLIVANT, B. (1987) 'Getting a Fair Go', *Occasional Paper No. 13*, Canberra, Human Rights Commission.

BULLOCK, A. (1975) *A Language for Life: Report of Committee of Inquiry for the Department of Education and Science*, London, HMSO.

BURGESS, Roberta, PARKER, Claudia and RICKERT, Maria (1985) 'The Educational Needs of Non-English Speaking Background Girls in Secondary Schools in NSW', Mimeo, NSW Ministry of Education, Social Policy Unit.

BURKE, Gerald and DAVIS, Denis (1985) 'Ethnic Groups and Post-Compulsory Education with Particular Reference to TAFE', Mimeo, Melbourne, AIMA.

BUSCHENHOFEN, P. (1983) 'Current Emphases in the Nothern Territory Department of Education's Bilingual Education Program for Aboriginal Children', *Journal of Intercultural Studies*, Vol. 4, No. 2, pp. 3–11.

CAHILL, D., *et al.* (1984) *Review of the Commonwealth Multicultural Education Program*, Canberra, Commonwealth Schools Commission.

CAMPBELL, R. and WALES R. (1970) 'The Study of Language Acquisition', in *New Horizons in Linguistics*, LYONS, J. (ed.), Harmondsworth, Penguin Books.

CAMPBELL, W.J., BARNETT, J., JOY, B. and MCMENIMAN, M. (1984) *A Review of the Commonwealth English as a Second Language (ESL) Program*, Canberra, Commonwealth Schools Commission.

CANALE, M. (1983a) 'On Some Dimensions of Language Proficiency', in *Issues in Language Testing Research*, OLLER, J.W. (ed.), Rowley, Mass., Newbury House.

CANALE, M. (1983b) 'From Communicative Competence to Communicative Language Pedagogy,' in *Language and Communication*, RICHARDS. J.C. and SCHMIDT, R. (eds), London, Longman.

CANALE, M. and SWAIN, M. (1980) 'Theoretical Bases of Communicative Approaches to Second Language Teaching and Testing', *Applied Linguistics*, 1(1) Vol. 1, pp. 1–47.

CARROLL, B.J. (1961) 'Fundamental Considerations in Testing for English Language Proficiency of Foreign Students', in *Teaching English as a Second Language*, ALLEN, H.R. and CAMPBELL, R.N. (eds), New York, McGraw-Hill.

CARROLL, B.J. (1968) 'The Psychology of Language Testing', in *Language Testing Symposium*, DAVIES, A. (ed.), Oxford University Press.

CARROLL, B.J. (1980) *Testing Communicative Preformance: An Interim Study*, Oxford, Pergamon Press.

CARROLL, B.J. (1981) 'Specifications for an English Language Testing Service', in *ELT Documents III, Issues in Language Testing*, London, British Council.

CASHDAN, A. and GRUGEON, E. (eds) (1972) *Language in Education: A Source Book*, London, Routledge and Kegan Paul.

CASTILLO, E.S. (1980) 'A Test of Communicative Competence in Philipino', in *Direction in Language Testing*, Anthology Series 9, Seamoo, Singapore University Press.

CASTLES, Stephen, COPE, Bill, KALANTZIS, Mary and MORRISSEY, Michael (1988) *Mistaken Identity: Multiculturalism and the Demise of Nationalism in Australia*, Sydney, Pluto Press.

CASTLES, Stephen, MORRISSEY, Michael and LEWIS, Don (1987) *Patterns of Disadvantage amongst the Overseas Born and Their Children*, Research Report, University of Wollongong, Centre for Multicultural Studies.

CHIPMAN, Lauchlan (1980) 'The Menace of Multiculturalism', *Quadrant*, Spetember, pp. 3–6.

CHIPMAN, Lauchlan (1985) 'A National Language(s) Policy?: Snowing the Senate Committee', *Quadrant*, March, pp. 16–17.

CHOMSKY, C. (1964) *The Acquisition of Syntax in Children from Five to Ten*, Cambridge, Mass., MIT Press.

CHOMSKY, N. (1965) *Aspects of the Theory of Syntax*, Cambridge, Mass., MIT Press.

CHRISTIE, F. (1986) 'Setting the Context: Language in Education', Paper presented at a Conference on ESL in Mainstream Education, Canberra.

CLARK, J.L.O. (1978) *Foreign Language Testing: Theory and Practice*, Philadelphia, Pa., Center for Curriculum Development.

CLIFT, Dominique (1984) 'Towards the Larger Community', *Language and Society*, No. 12, pp. 65–8.

CLYNE, Michael (1970) 'Migrant English in Australia', in *English Transported: Essays on Australian English*, RAMSON, W.S. (ed.), Canberra, Australian National University Press, pp. 123–35.

CLYNE, Michael G. (1972) *Perspectives on Language Contact*, Melbourne, Hawthorn Press.

CLYNE, Michael G. (1976) *Australia Talks*, Canberra, Pacific Linguists 23.

CLYNE, Michael G. (1977) 'Bilingual Education: Past and Present', Richmond, Victoria, Chomi Reprint.

CLYNE, Michael G. (1981a) 'Community Languages and Language Policy: A Demographic Perspective', in *Community Languages: Their Role in Education*, GARNER, Mark (ed.), Melbourne, River Seine Publications, pp. 13–36.

CLYNE, Michael G. (1981b) 'Primary School Languages and Bilingual Education: Some Overseas Research and Legends', in *Community Languages: Their Role in Education*, GARNER, Mark (ed.), Melbourne, River Seine Publications, pp. 135–44.

CLYNE, Michael G. (1982) *Multilingual Australia: Resources, Needs, Policies*, Melbourne, River Seine Publications.

CLYNE, Michael G. (1983) 'Bilingual Education as a Model for Community Languages in Primary Schools', *Journal of Intercultural Studies*, Vol. 4, No. 2, pp. 23–36.

COHEN, Andrew D. and SWAIN, Merrill (1976) 'Bilingual Education: The "Immersion" Model in the North American Context', *TESOL Quarterly*, Vol. 10, No. 1, pp. 45–53.

COHEN, D. (1970) 'Immigrants and the School', *Review of Educational Research*, No. 40, pp. 13–27.

COMMONWEALTH DEPARTMENT OF EDUCATION (1982) *Towards a National Language Policy*, Canberra, Australian Government Publishing Service.

COMMONWEALTH SCHOOLS COMMISSION (1985) *Quality and Equality*, Canberra Publishing and Printing Co., Canberra.

COPE, Bill (1987) 'Racism, Popular Culture and Australian Identity in Transition: A Case Study of Change in School Textbooks Since 1945,' in *Prejudice in the Public Arena: Racism*, RASMUSSEN, Radha and MARKUS, Andrew, Melbourne, Monash University, Centre for Migrant and Intercultural Studies, pp. 73–92.

COPE, Bill (1988a) 'Facing the Challenge of "Back to Basics": An Historical Perspective', *Social Literacy Monograph No. 28*, Sydney, Common Ground (forthcoming in *Curriculum Perspectives*, 1989).

COPE, Bill (1988b) 'Traditional versus Progressivist Pedagogy', *Social Literacy Monograph No. 11*, Sydney, Common Ground.

COPE, Bill and KALANTZIS, Mary (1988a) 'Cultural Differences and Self-Esteem: Alternative Curriculum Approaches', in *Hearts and Minds: Self-Esteem and the Schooling of Girls*, KENWAY, Jane and WILLIS, Sue (eds), Canberra, Department of Employment, Education and Training, pp. 151–66.

COPE, Bill and KALANTZIS, Mary (1988b) 'Hacking into the Social Forest with Ideological Choplogic: Bullivant Runs across Some "Ethnocultural Diacritica" ', *Journal of Intercultural Studies*, Vol. 9, No. 2, pp. 80–3.

COPE, Bill and MORRISSEY, Michael (1986) 'The Blainey Debate and The Critics of Multiculturalism', Paper for the AIMA National Research Conference, University of Melbourne.

COPE, Bill and POYNTING, Scott (1989) 'Class, Gender and Ethnicity as Influences on Australian Schooling: An Overview', in *The Social Contexts of Schooling*, COLE, Mike (ed.), Basingstoke, Falmer Press.

CORNELL, W.F., *et al.* (1975) *12–20 Studies of City Youth*, Sydney, Hicks Smith.

CUMMINS, J. (1976) 'The Influence of Bilingualism on Cognitive Growth: A Synthesis of Research Findings and Explanatory Hypotheses', *Working Papers on Bilingualism 9*, Toronto, Ontario Institute of Studies in Education, pp. 1–43.

CUMMINS, J. (1977) 'Psycholinguistic Evidence', *Center for Applied Linguistics*, Vol. 4, pp. 78–89.

CUMMINS, J. (1979) 'Linguistic Interdependence and the Educational Development of Bilingual Children', *Review of Education Research*, Vol. 49, No. 2, Spring, pp. 223–51.

CUMMINS, J. (1980a) 'The Cross-Lingual Dimensions of Language Proficiency: Implications for Bilingual Education and the Optimal Age Issue', *TESOL Quarterly*, Vol. 14, No. 2, pp. 175–85.

CUMMINS, J. (1980b) 'Psychological Assessment of Immigrant Children: Logic or Intuition?', *Journal of Multilingual and Multicultural Development*, Vol. 1, No. 2, pp. 97–111.

CUMMINS, J. (1981) *Bilingualism and Minority Language Children*, Toronto, OISE Press.

CUMMINS, J. (1984) *Bilingualism and Special Education: Issues in Assessment and Pedagogy*, Clevedon, England, Multilingual Matters.

CUMMINS, J. and GULUTSAN, M. (1974a) 'Bilingual Education and Cognition', *Alberta Journal of Education Research*, Vol. 20, No. 3, September, pp. 259–69.

CUMMINS, J. and GULUTSAN, M. (1974b) 'Some Effects of Bilingualism on Cognitive Functioning', in *Bilingualism, Biculturalism and Education*, CAREY, S. (ed.), Edmonton, Alta., University of Alberta Press.

CUMMINS, J. and SWAIN, M. (1986) *Bilingualism in Education*, London, Longman.

DAVIES, A. (ed.) (1968) *Language Testing Symposium*, Oxford, Oxford University Press.

DAVIES, A. (1978) 'Language Testing: Survey Article', *Language Teaching and Linguistics Abstracts*, Vol. 2, No. 3/4, Part 1: pp. 145–59, Part 2: pp. 215–31.

DAVIES, A. (1983) 'The Validity of Concurrent Validation' in *Current Developments in Language Testing*, HUGHES, A. and PORTER, D. (eds), London, Academic Press.

DAVIES, A. (1984) 'Validating Three Texts for English Language Proficiency', *Language Testing*, Vol. 1, No. 1, pp. 50–69.

DAWE, Lloyd (1980) 'Bilingualism and Mathematical Reasoning in English as a Second Language', *Educational Studies in Mathematics*, 14, pp. 325–53.

De LEMOS, M. (1975) *Study of the Educational Achievement of Migrant Children*, Melbourne, Australian Council of Educational Research.

De LEMOS, M. and Di LEO (1978) 'Literacy in Italian and English of Italian High School Students', *Ethnic Studies*, Vol. 2, No. 2, pp. 1–12.

DEOSARAN, R. (1976) *The 1975 Every Student Survey: Research Report No. 140*, Toronto, Toronto Board of Education.

DEPARTMENT OF IMMIGRATION AND ETHNIC AFFAIRS (1985) *A Review of the Experiences of Migrants in the Labour Market*, Canberra, DIEA.

DEPARTMENT OF RESEARCH AND EVALUATION. BOARD OF EDUCATION — CITY OF CHICAGO (1976) *Short Tests of Linguistic Skills*, Chicago, Ill., Department of Research and Evaluation.

DONOHUE, Thomas S. (1982) 'Towards a Broadened Context for Modern Bilingual Education', *Journal of Multilingual and Multicultural Development*, Vol. 3, No. 2, pp. 57–87.

DOUGLAS, D. and SELINKER, L. (1985) 'Principles for Language Tests within the ''Discourse Domains'' Theory of Interlanguage: Research, Test Construction and Interpretation', *Language Testing*, Vol. 2, No. 2, pp. 205–26.

DRAKE, Diana (1979) 'Empowering Children through Bilingual Bicultural Education', in *Bilingual Multicultural Education and the Professional: From Theory to Practice*, TRUEBA, Henry T. and BARNETT-MIZRAHI, Carol (eds) Rowley, Mass., Newbury House.

DUFFY, A. and PHILLIPS, J. (1983) 'Language Tests: a Review of Recent Developments', Mimeo.

EDWARDS, John (1981) 'The Context of Bilingual Education', *Journal of Multilingual and Multicultural Development*, Vol. 2, No. 1, pp. 25–44.

EDWARDS, John (1982) 'Bilingual Education Revisited: A Reply to Donohue', *Journal of Multilingual and Multicultural Development*, Vol. 2, No. 2, pp. 89–101.

EKSTRAND, L. (1981) 'Unpopular Views on Popular Beliefs about Immigrant Children: Contemporary Practices and Problems in Sweden', in *Educating Immigrants*, BHATNAGAR, J. (ed.), London, Croom Helm.

EKSTRAND, L.H. (1982) 'Maintenance or Transition — or Both? A Review of Swedish Ideologies and Empirical Research', in *Multicultural and Multilingual Education in Immigrant Countries*, HUSEN, T. and OPPERS, S. Oxford, Pergamon Press, pp. 141–59.

ELLIS, Rod (1984) 'Communication Strategies and the Evaluation of Communicative Performance', *ELT Journal*, Vol. 38, No. 1, January, pp. 39–44.

FEENEY, J. and HARTMANN, N. (1977) *Learning Oral French: A Study of English-Speaking Elementary School Students*, Toronto, Metropolitan Separate School Board.

FELDMAN, G. and SHEN, M. (1971) 'Some Language Related Cognitive Advantage of Bilingual Five Year Olds', *Journal of Genetic Psychology*, Vol. 118, pp. 234–44.

FELKER, Donald W. (1979) 'Building Positive Self-Concepts', in *Bilingual Multicultural Education and the Professional: From Theory to Practice*, TRUEBA, Henry and BARNETT-MIZRAHI, Carol (eds), Rowley, Mass., Newbury House, pp. 215–27.

FISHMAN, Joshua A. (1967) 'Bilingualism with and without Diglossia; Diglossia with and without Bilingualism', *Journal of Social Issues*, Vol. 23, No. 2, pp. 23–38.

FISHMAN, Joshua A. (1972a) 'Varieties of Ethnicity and Varieties of Language Consciousness' in *Essays by Joshua A. Fishman*, DIL, Anwar S., (ed.), Stanford, Calif., Stanford University Press.

FISHMAN, Joshua A. (1972b) 'Language in Sociocultural Change', in *Essays by Joshua A. Fishman*, DIL, Anwar S. (ed.), Stanford, Calif., Stanford University Press.

FISHMAN, Joshua A. (1972c) 'Societal Bilingualism: Stable and Transitional', in *Language in Sociocultural Change*, DIL Anwars., (ed.), Stanford, Calif., Stanford University Press.

FISHMAN, Joshua A. (1976) *Bilingual Education: An International Sociological Perspective*, Rowley, Mass., Newbury House.

FISHMAN, Joshua A. (1977) 'The Social Science Perspective', in *Bilingual Education, Current Perspectives*, Vol. 1, S. Arlington, Va., Centre for Applied Linguistics, pp. 1–49.

FISHMAN, Joshua A. (1979a) 'Some Basic Sociolinguistic Concepts', in *Bilingual Multicultural Education and the Professional: From Theory to Practice*, TRUEBA, Henry T. and BARNETT-MIZRAHI, Carol (eds), Rowley, Mass., Newbury House.

FISHMAN, Joshua A. (1979b) 'Linguistics: The Scientific Study of Language', in *Bilingual Multicultural Education and the Professional: From Theory to Practice*, TRUEBA, Henry T. and BARNETT-MIZRAHI, Carol (eds), Rowley, Mass., Newbury House.

FISHMAN, Joshua A. (1980) 'Bilingualism and Biculturalism as Individual and as Societal Phenomena', *Journal of Multilingual and Multicultural Development*, Vol. 1, No. 1, pp. 3–15.

FISHMAN, Joshua A. (1982) 'Sociolinguistic Foundations of Bilingual Education', *Bilingual Review*, Vol. 9 (Eastern Michigan University Press).

FORSTER, Charles R. (1982) 'American Bilingualism: The Need for a National Language Policy', in *Issues in International Bilingual Education*, HARTFORD, B.S. *et al.* (eds), New York, Plenum Press.

FOSTER, L., LEWIS, R. and RADO, M. (1980) *Exploring Students' Attitudes in Australia towards Ethnic Language Maintenance and Bilingual Education*, Research Report, La Trobe University.

FOSTER, L., LEWIS, R., RADO, M. and ROWLEY, G. (n.d.) *Evaluating Bilingual Education*, Richmond, Victoria, Chomi.

FRIED, L. (1983) 'On the Validity of Second Language Tests', in *Modelling and Assessing Second Language Acquisition*, HYLTENSTAM, K. and PIENEMANN, M., Clevedon, England, Multilingual Matters.

GAARDER, A. Bruce (1975) 'Bilingual Education: Central Questions and Concerns', *New York University Education Quarterly*, Vol. 6, No. 4, pp. 2–6.

GAARDER, A. Bruce (1977) *Bilingual Schooling and the Survival of Spanish in the United States*, Rowley, Mass., Newbury House.

GARDENER, R.C. (1979) 'Attitudes and Motivation: Their Role in Second-Language Acquisition', in *Bilingual Multicultural Education and the Professional: From Theory to Practice*, TRUEBA, Henry T. and BARNETT-MIZRAHI, Carol (eds), Rowley, Mass., Newbury House, pp. 319–27.

GEFFERT, Hanna N., *et al.* (1975) *The Current Status of U.S. Bilingual Education Legislation*, CAL-ERIC/CLL Series on Languages and Linguistics, No. 23.

GENESEE, F. (1978–79) 'Scholastic Effects of French Immersion: An Overview after Ten Years', *Interchange*, No. 9, pp. 20–9.

GILES, Howard, MILES, Hewstone and BALL, Peter (1983) 'Language Attitudes in Multilingual Settings: Prologue with Priorities', *Journal of Multilingual and Multicultural Development,* Vol. 4, Nos. 2–3, pp. 81–100.

GILHOTRA, M.S. (1984) 'Language Maintenance among the Sikhs of Woolgoolga', *Journal of Intercultural Studies*, Vol. 5, No. 1, pp. 22–30.

GOODENOUGH, W.H. (1976) 'Multiculturalism as the Normal Human Experience', *Anthropology and Education Quarterly*, Vol. 8, No. 4, pp. 4–7.

GRAY, M. (1984) 'Encouraging Debate', *Interchange*, September, pp. 5–6.

GREENE, J. (1977) *Thinking and Language*, London, Methuen.

GRENIER, Gilles and VAILANCOURT, Francois (1983) 'An Economic Perspective on Learning a Second Language', *Journal of Multilingual and Multicultural Development*, Vol. 4, No. 6, pp. 471–83.

HALLIDAY, M.A.K. (1975) *Learning How to Mean*, London, Edward Arnold.

HALLIDAY, M.A.K. (1978) *Language as a Social Semiotic*, London, Edward Arnold.

HALLIDAY, M.A.K. (1985a) *An Introduction to Functional Grammar*, London, Edward Arnold.

HALLIDAY, M.A.K. (1985b) *Spoken and Written Language*, Geelong, Deakin University Press.

HALLIDAY, M.A.K. and HASAN, R. (1985) *Language Content and Text: Aspects of Language in a Social-Semiotic Perspectives*, Geelong, Deakin University Press.

HANSEGARD, Nils E. (1979) *Tvasprakighet Eller Halvsprakighet* (Bilingualism or Semilingualism), Stockholm, Akadelmilitteratur.

HARLEY, B. and SWAIN, M. (1977) 'An Analysis of Verb Form and Function in the Speech of French Immersion Pupils', *Working Papers on Bilingualism*, 14, pp. 31–46.

HARTFORD, Beverly S. (1982) 'Issues in Bilingualism: A View to the Future', in *Issues in International Bilingual Education*, HARTFORD, B.S. *et al.* (eds), New York, Plenum Press.

HEATON, J.J. (1975) *Writing English Language Tests*, London, Longman.

HENRY, Colin and EDWARDS, Brian (1986) *Enduring a Lot: The Effects of the School System on Students of Non-English Speaking Backgrounds*, Canberra, Human Rights Commission.

HERBERT, Charles H. (1979) 'Natural Language Assessment', in *Bilingual Multicultural Education and the Professional: From Theory to Practice*, TRUEBA, Henry T. and BARNETT-MIZRAHI, Carol (eds), Rowley, Mass., Newbury House, pp. 397–401.

HOLLISTER, P. (1984a) 'The Language Dimension, Case Study 1: Individuals' Characteristics', *Department of Immigration and Ethnic Affairs Statistical Development and Analysis*, Canberra, Australian Government Publishing Service.

HOLLISTER, P. (1984b) 'The Language Dimension, Case Study 2: Geographical Patterns', *Department of Immigration and Ethnic Affairs Statistical Development and Analysis*, Canberra, Australian Government Publishing Service.

HORNBY, P. (ed.) (1977) *Bilingualism*, New York, Academic Press.

HORVATH, B.M. (1980) *The Education of Migrant Children: A Language Planning Perspective*, ERDC Report No. 24, Canberra, Australian Government Publishing Service.

HORVATH, B.M. (1981) 'Community Languages in the Schools: Linguistic and Cultural Dilemmas', in *Community Languages: Their Role in Education*, GARNER, Mark, Melbourne, River Seine Publications, pp. 37–54.

HORVATH, B.M. (1986) 'An Investigation of Class Placement in New South Wales Schools', Mimeo, NSW Ethnic Affairs Commission/Sydney University.

HUGHES, A. and PORTER, D. (eds) (1983) *Current Developments in Language Testing*, London, Academic Press.

HUGO, Graeme (1987) *Australia's Changing Population: Trends and Implications*, Melbourne, Oxford University Press.

HULSTIJN, J.H. (1980) 'Testing Second Language Proficiency with Direct Procedures', in *Modelling and Assessing Second Language Acquisition*, HYLTENSTAM, K. and PIENEMANN, M. (eds.), Clevedon, England, Multilingual Matters.

HUSBAND, Charles and KHAN, Verity Saifullah (1982) 'The Viability of Ethnolinguistic Vitality: Some Creative Doubts', *Journal of Multicultural and Multilingual Development*, pp. 193–205.

HUSEN, Torsten and OPPER, Susan (1983) *Multicultural and Multilingual Education in Immigrant Countries*, Oxford, Pergamon Press.

HYLTENSTAM, K. and STROUD, C. (1982) *Invandrare och Minoriteter*, No. 9, pp. 190–213.

HYMES, Dell (1972) 'Models of the Interaction of Language and Social Life', in *Directions in Sociolinguistics: The Ethnography of Communication*, GUMPERZ, J. and HYMES, Dell (eds), New York, Holt, Rhinehart and Winston.

IANCO-WORRALL, A.D. (1972) 'Bilingualism and Cognitive Development', *Child Development*, Vol. 43, pp. 1390–1400.

ILYIN, Donna (1969) *Ilyin Oral Interview*, Rowley, Mass., Newbury House.

INGRAM, D.E. (1984) *Introduction to the A.S.L.P.R.*, Canberra, Australian Government Publishing Service.

INGRAM, D.E. and WYLIE, Elaine (1983) 'Australian Second Language Proficiency Ratings' (*ASLPR*), Sydney, D. West Government Printers.

INNER LONDON EDUCATION AUTHORITY, EDUCATION COMMITTEE (1987) 'Ethnic Background and Examination Results', Mimeo.

JAMES, Charles J. (1985) *Foreign Language Proficiency in the Classroom and Beyond*, Skokie, Ill., National Textbook Company.

JAYASURIYA, Laksiri (1988) *Language and Culture in Australian Public Policy*, Occasional Paper, New Series No. 4, University of Western Australia, Department of Social Work and Social Administration.

KALANTZIS, Mary (1986) 'Community Languages: Politics or Pedagogy?' *Australian Review of Applied Linguistics*, Series S, No. 2, pp. 168–79.

KALANTZIS, Mary (1987) 'From First Language Illiteracy to Second Language Literacy: NESB Adult Learning', *Prospect: Journal of Adult Migrant Education Program*, Vol. 3, No. 1, pp. 34–44.

KALANTZIS, Mary (1988a) 'Aspirations, Participation and Outcomes: From Research to a Curriculum Project for Reform', in *Including Girls: Curriculum Perspectives on the Education of Girls*, FOSTER, V. (ed.), Canberra, Curriculum Development Centre, pp. 37–46.

KALANTZIS, Mary (1988b) 'The Cultural Deconstruction of Racism: Education and Multiculturalism', in *The Cultural Construction of Race*, De LEPERVANCHE, Marie and BOTTOMLEY, Gillian (eds), Sydney, Sydney Association for Studies in Society and Culture, pp. 90–8.

KALANTZIS, Mary (1989) 'Ethnicity Meets Class Meets Gender in Australia', in *Australian Feminist Interventions*, WATSON, Sophie (ed.), London, Verso.

KALANTZIS, Mary and COPE, Bill (1981) *Just Spaghetti and Polka? An Introduction to Australian Multicultural Education*, Sydney, Common Ground.

KALANTZIS, Mary and COPE, Bill (1984) 'Multiculturalism and Education Policy', in *Class, Gender and Ethnicity in Australia*, BOTTOMLEY, Gillian and de LEPERVANCHE, Marie (eds) Sydney, George Allen and Unwin, pp. 82–97. Reprinted in RIZVI, Fazal (ed.) (1986) *Ethnicity, Class and Multiculturalism*, Geelong, Deakin University Press, pp. 73–85.

KALANTZIS, Mary and COPE, Bill (1987a) 'Gender Differences and Cultural Differences: Towards an Inclusive Curriculum', *Curriculum Perspectives*, Vol. 7, No. 1, pp. 64–8.

KALANTZIS, Mary and COPE, Bill (1987b) *An Overview: Teaching/Learning Social Literacy*, Sydney, Common Ground.

KALANTZIS, Mary and COPE, Bill (1988) 'Why We Need Multicultural Education: A Review of the "Ethnic Disadvantage" Debate', *Journal of Intercultural Studies*, Vol. 9, No. 1, pp. 39–57.

KALANTZIS, Mary and COPE, Bill (1989a) 'Literacy in the Social Sciences', in *A Fresh Look at the Basics*, CHRISTIE, Frances (ed.), Melbourne, Australian Council for Educational Research.

KALANTZIS, Mary and COPE, Bill (1989b) 'Pluralism and Equitability: Multicultural Curriculum Strategies for Schools', *Curriculum and Teaching*, Vol. 4, No. 1, forthcoming.

KALANTZIS, Mary, COPE, Bill and HUGHES, Chris (1985) 'Pluralism and Social Reform: A Review of Multiculturalism in Australian Education', *Thesis Eleven*, No. 10/11, pp. 195–215.

KALANTZIS, Mary, COPE, Bill and ISSARIS, Maria (1988) 'Culture and Merit', *Journal of Intercultural Studies*, Vol. 9, No. 2, pp. 65–79.

KALANTZIS, Mary, COPE, Bill and SLADE, Diana (1986) *The Language Question: The Maintenance of Languages Other Than English, Vol. 1: Research Findings; Canberra, Australian Government Publishing Service*.

KALANTZIS, Mary, SLADE, Diana and COPE, Bill (1986) *The Language Question: The Maintenance of Languages Other than English, Vol II: Methodology and Empirical Results*. Canberra, Australian Government Publishing Inc.

KALANTZIS, Mary, SLADE, Diana and COPE, Bill (1989) 'Minority Languages and Mainstream Culture: Problems of Equity and Assessment', in *Individualising the Assessment of Language Abilities*, DE JONG, John H.A.L. and STEVENSON, Douglas, K. (eds) Clevedon, England, Multilingual Matters.

KELLY, Gail P. (1981) 'Contemporary American Policies and Practices in the Education of Immigrant Children', in *Educating Immigrants*, BHATNAGAR, J. (ed.), London, Croom Helm.

KELLY, R. (1978) 'On the Construct Validation of Comprehensive Tests: An Exercise in Applied Linguistics', Ph.D. thesis, University of Queensland.

KESSLER, Carolyn and QUINN, Mary Ellen (1982) 'Cognitive Development in Bilingual Environments', in *Issues in International Bilingual Education*, HARTFORD, B.S., *et al.*, (eds), New York, Plenum Press.

KEYS, C.C. and WILSON, M.G.A. (1984) *The Urban Illawarra: A Social Atlas*, Wollongong, Illawarra Regional Information Service.

KINGAS, C. (1981) 'A Rationale for Bilingual Education in Australia', in *Community Languages: Their Role in Education*, GARNER, Mark (ed.), Melbourne, River Seine Publications.

KINGMAN, Sir John (1988) *Report of the Committee of Inquiry into the Teaching of English Language*, London, Her Majesty's Stationery Office.

KJOLSETH, Rolf (1972) 'Bilingual Education Programs in the United States: For Assimilation or Pluralism?' in *The Language Education of Minority Children*, SPOLSKY, B., (ed.), Rowley, Mass., Newbury House, pp. 94–121.

KLARBERG, M. (1983) 'Diglossic Education: The Jewish Tradition, Some Australian Manifestations and Their Implications', *Journal of Intercultural Studies*, Vol. 4, No. 2, pp. 55–6.

KLEINFELD, J.S. (1979) *Eskimo School on the Andreafsky*, New York, Praeger.

KRASHEN, Stephen D. (1984) 'Immersion: Why It Works and What It Has Taught Us', *Language and Society*, No. 12, pp. 61–4.

KUUSINEN, J., *et al.* (1982) *Research Reports, No. 53*, University of Jyvaskyla, Department of Education.

LADO, R. (1961) *Language Testing: The Construction and Use of Foreign Language Tests*, London, Longman.

LAMBERT, W.E. (1983) 'Deciding on Languages of Instruction: Psychological and Social Considerations', in *Multicultural and Multilingual Education in Immigrant Countries*, HUSEN, Torsten and OPPER, Susan, Oxford, Pergamon Press, pp. 93–104.

LAMBERT, W.E. and TUCKER, G.R. (1972) *Bilingual Education of Children: The St. Lambert Experiment*, Rowley, Mass., Newbury House.

LAPIN, Sharon and SWAIN, Merrill (1984) 'Research Update', *Language and Society*, No. 12, pp. 48–54.

LARSEN-FREEMAN, D. (1980) *Discourse Analysis in Second Language Research*, Rowley, Mass., Newbury House.

LEE, V. (1979) *Language Development*, Milton Keynes, Open University.

LEE, Y.P., FOK, C.C.Y., LORD, R. and LOW, G. (eds) (1985) *New Directions in Language Testing*, Oxford, Pergamon Press.

LEOPOLD, W.F. (1961) 'Patterning in Children's Language Learning', in *Psycholinguistics*, SAPOTA, S. (ed.), New York, Holt and Rinehart and Winston.

LEWIN-POOLE, Sonia, *et al.* (1981) 'So Who Wants Bilingual Teachers?', in *Community Languages: Their Role in Education*, GARNER, Mark (ed.), Melbourne, River Seine Publications.

LEWIS, E. Glyn, (1981) *Bilingualism and Bilingual Education*, London, Pergamon Press.

LITTLEWOOD, W. (1981) *Communicative Language Teaching: An Introduction*, Cambridge, Cambridge University Press.

LO BIANCO, Joseph (1987) *National Policy on Languages*, Canberra, Australian Government Publishing Service.

LURIA, A.R. (1976) *Cognitive Development: Its Cultural and Social Foundations*, Cambridge, Mass., Harvard University Press.

MACKEN, M. (1989) 'Assessment of Student's Writing: A Linguistic Approach' MEd. dissertation, Deakin University.

McLEAN, Barbara (1982) *Languages Other Than English in the Primary School: Six Case Studies*, Canberra, Commonwealth Schools Commission.

MACNAMARA, J.P. (1967) 'The Effects of Instruction in a Weaker Language', *Journal of Social Issues*, Vol. 23, No. 2. pp. 121–35.

MACNAMARA, J.P. (1970) 'Bilingualism and Thought', in *Bilingualism and Language Contact: Anthropological, Linguistic, Psychological and Sociological Aspects*, ALATIS, J. (ed.), Washington D.C., Georgetown University Press, pp. 25–40.

MACNAMARA, J.P. (1977) (ed.) *Language Learning and Thought*, New York, Academic Press.

MACNAMARA, John (1979) 'The Cognitive Strategies of Language Learning', in *Bilingual Multicultural Education and the Professional: From Theory to Practice*, TRUEBA, Henry T. and BARNETT-MIZRAHI, Carol (eds), Rowley, Mass., Newbury House.

MAGISTE, E. (1979) 'The Competing Language Systems of the Multilingual: A Development study of decoding and encoding processes' in *Journal of Verbal Learning and Verbal Behaviour*, Vol. 18, No. 1, pp. 73–8.

MARJORIBANKS, Kevin (1979) *Families and Their Learning Environments: An Empirical Analysis*, London, Routledge and Kegan Paul.

MARSHALL, G. (1977) 'Investigation into the Present State of Language Proficiency Tests and the Possible Use and Development of Communicative Tests for English as a Second Language', Minority Group Support Service, Coventry, Coventry Education Authority.

MARTIN, Jean and MEADE, Phil (1979) *The Educational Experience of Sydney High School Students*, Canberra, Australian Government Publishing Service.

MARTIN, John Stanley (1981) 'Community Languages in Swedish Schools', in *Community Languages: Their Role in Education*, GARNER, Mark (ed.), Melbourne, River Seine Publications.

MARTIN, J.R. (1985) 'Process and Text: Two Aspects of Human Semiosis', in *Systemic Perspectives on Discourse: Selected Theoretical Papers from the 9th International Systemic Workshop*, BENSON, J.D. and GREAVES, W.S. (eds), Norwood, N.J., Ablex.

MARTIN, J.R. and ROTHERY, J. (1981) *Writing Project Report, No. 2*, Working Papers in Linguistics, Linguistics Department, University of Sydney.

MARTIN, J.R. and ROTHERY, J. (1986) *Writing Project Report No. 4*, Working Papers in Linguistics: Linguistics Department, University of Sydney.

MARTIN, J.R., CHRISTIE, F. and ROTHERY, J. (1987) 'Social Processes in Education: A Reply to Sawyer and Watson (and others)', in *The Place of Genre in Learning: Current Debates*, REID, I. (ed.), Geelong, Deakin University.

MATTHEWS, Julie (1986) *Education Needs of Young Refugees: Strategies to Assist*, Sydney, ICRA.

MESTRE, J.P. and GERACE, W.J. (1981) 'The Interdependence of Mathematical Skills, G.P.A. and Language Proficiency for Hispanic College Students', *ERIC, ED. 204*, p. 150.

MILLER, Jane (1983) *Bilingualism, Culture and Education*, London, Routledge and Kegan Paul.

MISTILIS, Nina (1986) 'Destroying Myths: Second Generation Australians' Educational Achievements', Mimeo, Centre for Migrant and Intercultural Studies, Work in Progress Seminar, 30 June.

MORRISSEY, M.J. and PALSER, J.M. (1983) *English Language Learning in the Illawarra*, Canberra, Australian Government Publishing Service.

MORRISSEY, M.J., *et al*. (1984) 'English Language Training and Labour Market Programs', A Position Paper for the Committee of Review on Labour Market Programs.

MORROW, K. (1979) 'Communicative Language Testing: Revolution or Evolution, in *The Communicative Approach to Language Teaching*, BRUMFIT, C.J. and JOHNSTON, K. (eds), Oxford, Oxford University Press.

MORROW, K. (Project Leader) (1980) *Examinations in the Communicative Use of English as a Foreign Language: Specifications and Specimen Papers*, Kent, England, Royal Society of Arts Examination Board.

MORROW, K.E. (1986) 'The Evaluation of Tests of Communicative Performance', in *Innovations in Language Testing*, PORTAL, M. (ed.), Windsor, NFER/Nelson.

MOURGEON, R., BRANT-PALMER, C., BELANGER, M. and CHICHOCKI, W. (1980) *Le Francaise Parlé en Situation Minoritaire*, Toronto, Ministry of Education.

MOUTSOS, B. (1982) Learning in the Mother-Tongue: the Richmond Collingwood Greek Bilingual Pilot Project, *Polycom*, No. 31, pp. 6–8.

MUNBY, J. (1978) *Communicative Syllabus Design*, Cambridge, Cambridge University Press.

NATIONAL LANGUAGE POLICY CONFERENCE REPORT (1982) Canberra, Australian National University.

NEW SOUTH WALES DEPARTMENT OF EDUCATION (1976) *Enquiry into Literacy and Numeracy*, Sydney, NSW Department of Education.

NEW SOUTH WALES DEPARTMENT OF EDUCATION (1980) *Survey of Students from Non-English Speaking Backgrounds*, Sydney, NSW Department of Education.

NEW SOUTH WALES DEPARTMENT OF EDUCATION (1983) Survey of Class Placement in New South Wales Schools, Unpublished report, Sydney, NSW Department of Education.

O'BRYAN, K., REITZ, J. and KUPLOWSKA, O. (1976) *Non-Official Languages. A Study in Canadian Multiculturalism*, Ottawa, Printing and Publishing Supply and Services, Canada.

OHMAN, S. (1981) *Att Leva Med Mangfalden*, Stockholm, Department of Labour.

OKSAAR, E. (1979) 'Tvasprakighet', in *Papers from the Second Nordic Conference on Bilingualism, Stockholm, 1978*, STEDJE A. and TRAMPE, P. (eds) Stockholm, Akadel-militteratur, pp. 51–65.

OKSAAR, E. (1982) 'Multilingualism and Multiculturalism from the Linguist's Point of View', in *Multicultural and Multilingual Education in Immigrant Countries*, HUSEN, T. and OPPER, S. (eds.), Oxford, Pergamon Press, pp. 17–35.

OLLER, J.W. (1971) 'Dictation as a Device for Testing Foreign Language Proficiency' in *English Language Teaching*, Vol. 25, No. 3, pp. 254–9.

OLLER, J.W. (1979) *Language Tests at School*, London, Longman.

OLLER, J.W. (1980) 'Communicative Competence: Can It Be Tested?' in *Research in Second Language Acquisition*, SCARCELLA, R.C. and KRASHEN, D. (eds), Rowley, Mass., Newbury House.

OLLER, J.W. (1982) 'Evaluation and Testing in Vernacular Languages', in *International Bilingual Education*, HARTFORD, B.S. *et al.* (eds) New York, Plenum Press.

OLLER, J.W. (1983) 'Evidence for a general language proficiency factor: an expectancy grammar' in *Issues in Language Testing Research*, OLLER, J.W. (ed.) Rowley, Mass., Newbury House.

OLLER, J.W. and KHARY, F. (1980) 'Is There a Global Factor of Language Proficiency', in *Directions in Language Testing Anthology*, Series 9, Seameo, Singapore University Press.

OPPER, Susan (1983) 'Multiculturalism in Sweden: A Case of Assimilation and Integration', *Comparative Education*, Vol. 19, No. 2, pp. 193–212.

OZOLINS, Uldis (1984) 'A Language Policy for Australia', *Aboriginal Child at School*, Vol. 12, No. 2, pp. 34–44.

PALMER, A.S. and BACHMAN, C.F. (1981) 'Basic Exams in Test Valuation' in *Issues in Language Testing*, ALDERSON, J.C. and HUGHES, A. (1981), ELT Documents IU, London, British Council.

PAULSTON, Christina B. (1974) 'Implications of Language Learning Theory for Language Planning: Concerns of Bilingual Education', *Papers in Applied Linguistics; Bilingual Education Series 1*, Arlington, Va., Center for Applied Linguistics.

PAULSTON, Christina B. (1977) *Research*, Vol. 2, Arlington, Va., Center for Applied Linguistics, pp. 87–151.

PAULSTON, Christina B. (1978) 'Bilingual/Bicultural Education', *Review of Research in Education*, American Educational Research Association.

PAULSTON, Christina B. (1979) 'Communicative Competence', in *Bilingual Multicultural Education and the Professional: From Theory to Practice*, TRUEBA, Henry T. and BARNETT-MIZRAHI, Carol (eds), Rowley, Mass., Newbury House.

PEAL, E. and LAMBERT, W. (1962) 'The Relation of Bilingualism to Intelligence', *Psychological Monographs*, Vol. 76, No. 27, pp. 1–23.

PICKERING, Des (1971) 'An Examination of the Psycholinguistic Abilities and Disabilities of Grade Two Children of Differing Socio-economic Status and Ethnic Background — Greek and Australian, *Research Report 10/71*, Melbourne, Victorian Education Department, Curriculum and Research Branch.

PORTAL, Matthew (ed.) (1986) *Innovations in Language Testing*, Windsor, NFER Nelson.

POWIERZA, L.M. (1983) *Languages: The Dilemmas*, Melbourne, AIMA.

QUINN, T.J. (1980) 'Language and Culture Teaching in Australia', *CDC Occasional Paper, No. 4*, Canberra, Curriculum Development Centre.

QUINN, T.J. (1981) 'Establishing a Threshold-Level Concept for Community Language Teaching in Australia', in *Community Languages: Their Role in Education*, GARNER, Mark, (ed.), Melbourne, River Seine Publications, pp. 79–96.

RADO, Marta (1975) 'Bilinguals in Monolingual Schools', *Journal of the Association of Teachers of English as a Foreign Language of NSW*, pp. 27–42.

RADO, Marta (1976) 'Language Use of Bilingual Adolescents: Self-appraisal', in *Australia Talks*, CLYNE, M.G. (ed.) Canberra, Pacific Linguistics 23, pp. 187–200.

RADO, M. and FOSTER, C. (1984) 'Implications of Language Use and Language Policy for Members of Non-English Speaking Families in Australia', *Proceedings, Policies and Families*, Melbourne, Institute of Family Studies.

REA, P.M. (1985) 'Language Testing and the Communicative Language Teaching Curriculum', in *New Directions in Language Testing*, LEE, Y.P., *et al*, Oxford, Pergamon Press.

REID, I. (ed.) (1987) *The Place of Genre in Learning: Current Debates*, Geelong, Deakin University.

RENARD, H.G. (1980) *Bilingualism Brings Light*, Frankston, Victoria, Buccaneer Press.

RICHARDS, J.C. (1974) *Error Analysis: Perspectives on Second Language Acquisition*, London, Longman.

RIGG, Pat and KAZEMEK, Francis E. (1985) '23 Million Illiterates? By Whose Definition?' *Journal of Reading*.

RIONDA, C.S.A. (1980) 'Research in Language Based Evaluative Measures of Communicative Competence', *Directions in Language Testing*, Anthology Series 9, Seameo, Singapore University Press.

RIST, R.C. (1978a) *Guestworkers in Germany: The Prospect for Pluralism*, New York, Praeger.

RIST, R.C. (1978b) 'The Education of Guestworker Children: Federal Republic of Germany', *Integrated Education*, Vol. 16, No.3, pp. 14–24.

RIST, R.C. (1983) 'The Social Context of Multicultural and Multilingual Education in Immigrant Countries: Some Program and Policy Considerations', in *Multicultural and Multilingual Education in Immigrant Countries*, HUSEN, Torsten and OPPER, Susan, (eds), Oxford, Pergamon Press, pp. 39–52.

RIVERA, Charlene (1984) (ed.) *Language Proficiency and Academic Achievement*, Clevedon, England. Multilingual Matters.

ROBINSON, Gail L. (1978) *Language and Multicutural Education: An Australian Perspective*, Sydney, Australia and New Zealand Book Company.

ROBINSON, Gail L. (1981) 'Bilingual Education in Australia and the United States', in *Community Languages: Their Role in Education*, GARNER, Mark (ed.), Melbourne, River Seine Publications, pp. 55–78.

ROTBERG, I.C. (1982) 'Some Legal and Research Considerations in Establishing Federal Policy in Bilingual Education', *Harvard Education Review*, Vol. 52, No. 2, pp. 149–68.

RUBICHI, R. (1983) 'Planning and Implementation of a Bilingual Program: Italian in South Australia', *Journal of Intercultural Studies*, Vol. 4, No. 2, pp. 21–34.

SAVILLE-TROIKE, Muriel (1979a) 'Culture, Language, and Education', in *Bilingual Multicultural Education and the Professional: From Theory to Practice*, TRUEBA, Henry T. and BARNETT-MIZRAHI, Carol (eds), Rowley, Mass., Newbury House.

SAVILLE-TROIKE, Muriel (1979b) 'First and Second Language Acquisition', in *Bilingual Multicultural Education and the Professional: From Theory to Practice*, TRUEBA, Henry T, and BARNETT-MIZRAHI, Carol (eds), Rowley, Mass., Newbury House.

SENATE STANDING COMMITTEE ON EDUCATION AND THE ARTS (1984) *Report on a National Langauge Policy*, Canberra, Australian Government Publishing Service.

SHARPE, Margaret C. (1977) 'Alice Springs Aboriginal English', in *Language Problems in Aboriginal Education*, BRUMBY, E. and VASZOLYI, E. (eds), Mt Lawley CAE, Perth. pp. 45–50.

SHOHAMY, Elena (1983) 'The Stability of Oral Proficiency Assessment on the Oral Interview Testing Procedures', *Language Learning*, April, pp. 33–4.

SIMOES, Antonio (1976) *The Bilingual Child: Research and Analysis of Existing Educational Themes*, New York, Academic Press.

SINILLIE, B.A. (1978) 'Testing the English Ability of Adult Migrants and Overseas Students', *3rd ALAA Congress*, August 1979.

SKUTNABB-KANGAS, T. (1983) 'Research and Its Implications for the Swedish Setting: An Immigrant's Point of View', in *Multicultural and Multilingual Education in Immigrant Countries*, HUSEN, Torsten and OPPER, Susan (eds), Oxford, Pergamon Press, pp. 127–40.

SKUTNAB-KANGAS, T. (1988) 'Multilingualism and the Education of Minority Children', in *Minority Education: From Shame to Struggle*, SKUTNABB-KANGAS, T. and CUMMINS, J. (eds), Clevedon, England, Multilingual Matters.

SKUTNABB-KANGAS, T. and RAHBECK, S. (1981) 'Guestworker or Immigrant: Different Ways of Reproducing an Underclass', *Journal of Multilingual and Multicultural Development*, No. 2, pp. 89–115.

SKUTNABB-KANGAS, T. and TOUKOMAA, P. (1976) 'Teaching Migrant Children's Mother Tongue and the Language of the Host Country in the Context of the Socio-Cultural

Situation of the Migrant Family', *Tutkimsuksia Research Report, No. 15*, University of Tampere, Finland.

SLADE, D.M. (1983) 'Drama and Theme in Language Teaching', MA thesis, University of London.

SLADE, D. (1988) 'Discourse Analysis of Spoken English: What Can Generic Analysis Offer to the Description of Spoken Interaction', Unpublished paper presented at Australian Association of Applied Linguistics, Launceston, Tasmania, August.

SLADE, D.M. and GARDNER (1985) 'Interactional Skills in Casual Conversation: Discourse Analysis and the Teaching of Conversational Skills to Adult E.S.L. Learners', *Australian Review of Applied Linguistics*, Vol. 8, No. 1, pp. 105–121.

SLADE, D. and GIBBONS, J. (1988) 'Testing Bilingual Proficiency in Australia: Issues, Methods, Findings', *Evaluation and Research in Education*, Clevedon, England, Multilingual Matters.

SLADE, D. and NORRIS, L. (1986) *Teaching Casual Coversation: Part One: Strategies Component (with accompanying tape) Part Two: Topic Component (with accompanying tape)*, Adelaide, South Australia, National Curriculum Resource Centre.

SMOLICZ, G. (1981) 'The Three Types of Multiculturalism', in *Community Languages: Their Role in Education*, GARNER, Mark (ed.), Melbourne, River Seine Publications.

SMOLICZ, G. (1982) 'Who's Afraid of Bilingualism?' *Education News*, Vol. 18, No. 5, pp. 16–18.

SMOLICZ, J.J. and SECOMBE, M.O. (1988) *Community Language Education in Australia*, Policy Option Paper, Canberra, Department of Prime Minister and Cabinet, Office of Multicultural Affairs.

SNODGRASS, John C. (1972) 'Correlates of Academic Achievement amongst Migrant Adolescent Boys of Southern European Descent', Unpublished ME thesis, University of Sydney.

SPOLSKY, Bernard (ed.) (1972) *The Language Education of Minority Children*, Rowley, Mass., Newbury House.

SPOLSKY, Bernard (1974) 'Speech Communities and the Schools', *TESOL Quarterly*, Vol. 8, No. 1, pp. 17–26.

SPOLSKY, Bernard (1975) 'Language Testing: Art or Science?, Paper presented at the 4th AILA International Congress, Stuttgart.

SPOLSKY, Bernard (1978) 'American Indian Bilingual Education', in *Case Studies in Bilingual Education*, SPOLSKY, B., *et al.* (eds), Rowley, Mass., Newbury House.

SPOLSKY, Bernard (1982) 'Sociolinguistics of Literacy, Bilingual Education and TESOL', *TESOL Quarterly*, Vol. 16, No. 2, pp. 141–51.

SPOLSKY, Bernard and COOPER, Robert L. (1977) *Frontiers of Bilingual Education*, Rowley, Mass., Newbury House.

SPOLSKY, B., MURPHY, P., HOLM, W. and FERRELL, A. (1980) 'Three Functional Tests of Oral Proficiency', *TESOL Quarterly*, Vol. 6, No. 3, pp. 221–35.

STERN, H.H. (1984) 'The Immersion Phenomenon', *Language and Society*, No. 12, pp. 4–7.

STRONG, Charles (1983) 'Two Decades Later: Nine Commissioners Review Key Language Issues in Canada', *Language and Society*, No. 11, Autumn, pp. 3–7.

STURMAN, Andrew (1986) *Immigrant Australians and Education: A Review of Research*, Melbourne, ACER.

SWAIN, M. (1974) 'French Immersion Programs across Canada', *The Canadian Modern Language Review*, No. 31, pp. 117–28.

SWAIN, M. (1982) 'Immersion Education: Applicability for Nonvernacular Teaching to Vernacular Speakers', in *Issues in International Bilingual Education*, HARTFORD, B.S. *et al.* (eds) New York, Plenum Press.

SWAIN, M. (1985) 'Large-Scale Communicative Language Testing', in *New Directions in Language Testing*, LEE, Y.P. *et al.* (eds), Oxford, Pergamon Press.

SWAIN, M. and BARIK, Henri (1978) 'Bilingual Education in Canada: French and English', in *Case Studies in Bilingual Education*, SPOLKSY, B. *et al.* (eds), Rowley, Mass., Newbury House.

TAFT, Ronald (1975a) 'The Career Aspirations of Immigrant Schoolchildren in Victoria', *La Trobe Sociology Papers, 12*, Melbourne La Trobe University.

TAFT, Ronald (1975b) 'Secondary Scholarship Holders in Victoria and Their Background', *Sociology in Australian Education: A Book of Readings*, EDGAR, Donald F., Sydney, McGraw-Hill, pp. 14–25.

TAFT, Ronald (1983) 'The Social and Ideological Context of Multicultural Education in Immigrant Countries', in *Multicultural and Multilingual Education in Immigrant Countries*, HUSEN, Torsten and OPPER, Susan (eds), Oxford, Pergamon Press, pp. 1–13.

TAFT, R. and CAHILL, D. (1978) *Initial Adjustment to Schooling of Immigrant Families*, Canberra, Australian Government Publishing Service.

TAFT, R. and CAHILL, D. (1981) 'Education of Immigrants in Australia', in *Educating Immigrants*, BHATNAGAR, J. (ed.), London, Croom Helm.

TENEZAKIS, Maria (1975) 'Lingusitics Subsystems and Concrete Operations', *Child Development*, Vol. 46, pp. 430–6.

TENEZAKIS, Maria (1977) 'Later Development of English with and without Another Language: Evidence from Testing Monoglot and Greek-speaking Children in Sydney', *Research Report*, Sydney, Macquarie University, School of Education.

TKALCEVIC, Mato (1980) 'Macedonians in the Australian Society', 2nd ed., Melbourne, Government Press.

TOUGH, J. (1977) *The Development of Meaning*, London, George Allen and Unwin.

TROIKE, Rudolph C. and SAVILLE-TROIKE, Muriel (1982) 'Teacher Training for Bilingual Education: An International Perspective', in *Issues in International Bilingual Education*, HARTFORD, B.S. *et al.* (eds) New York, Plenum Press.

TROYNA, B. (1988) 'Paradigm Regained: A Critique of the "Cultural Deficit" Perspectives in Contemporary Educational Research', *Comparative Education*, Vol. 24, No. 3, pp. 273–83.

TRUEBA, Henry T. (1979) 'Implications of Culture for Bilingual Education', in *Bilingual Multicultural Education and the Professional: From Theory to Practice*, TRUEBA, Henry T. and BARNETT-MIZRAHI, Carol (eds), Rowley, Mass., Newbury House.

TUCKER, G.R. (1975) 'The Acquisition of Knowledge by Children Educated Bilingually', in *Georgetown University Round Table on Languages and Linguistics*, DATO, D.P. (ed.), Washington, DC, Georgetown University Press, pp. 267–77.

TUCKER, G.R. (1980) 'Implications for U.S. Bilingual Education: Evidence from Canadian Research', *Focus*, *No. 12*, Ottawa, NCBE.

TUCKER, Richard G. (1977) 'The Linguistic Perspective', *Centre for Applied Linguistics*, Vol. 2, pp. 1–40.

UNESCO (1953) 'The Use of Vernacular Languages in Education', *Monographs on Fundamental Education*, 8, Paris, UNESCO.

URE, Jean (1980) 'Bilingualism and Achievement in School', *Journal of Multilingual and Multicultural Development*, Vol. 1, No. 3, pp. 253–60.

VALLETTE, R. (1977) *Modern Language Testing: A Handbook*, New York, Harcourt Brace Jovanich.

VAN EK, J. (1976) *The Threshold Level for Modern Languages Learning in Schools*, London, Longman.

VAN EK, J.A. and TRIM, J.L.M. (eds) (1984) *Across the Threshold*, New York, Pergamon Press.

VERNON, Phillip E. (1977) 'Measuring Abilities of Persons of Different Cultures', *Forum of Education*, Vol. 36, No. 3, pp. 24–52.

VICTORIAN ETHNIC AFFAIRS COMMISSION (1984a) Division of Research and Policy, *Migrants and the Workforce, 1. Unemployment Trends*, August.

VICTORIAN ETHNIC AFFAIRS COMMISSION (1984b) *Language Use in Australia*, July.

VILLIERS, De, P.A. and VILLIERS, J.G. (1979) *Early Language*, London, Fontana.

VYGOTSKY, L.S. (1962) *Thought and Language*, Cambridge, Mass., MIT Press.

VYGOTSKY, L.S. (1978) *Mind in Society*, Cambridge, Mass., Harvard University Press.

WEIR, C.J. (1981) 'Reaction to the Morrow Paper (1)', in *Issues in Language Testing*, London, British Council.

WIDDOWSON, H.G. (1984) *Explorations in Applied Linguistics 2*, Oxford, Oxford University Press.

WIDDOWSON, H.G. and BRUMFIT, C.J. (1981) 'Issues in Second Language Syllabus Design', in *The Second Language Classroom: Directions for the 1980's*, ALATIS, J.E., ALLMAN, H.B. and ALATIS, P.M. (eds), Oxford, Oxford University Press.

WIECZERKOWSKI, W. (1971) *Erwerb einer Zweiten Sprache Im Unterricht*, Hamburg, Schroedelverlag.

WIGNELL, P., MARTIN, J.R. and EGGINS, S. (1987) The Discourse of Geography: Ordering and Explaining the Experiential World. *Writing Project, No. 5,* Working Papers in Linguistics, University of Sydney, Linguistics Department.

WILLIAMS, R. and SWALES, J. (eds) (1984) *Common Ground: Shared Interests in ESP and Communicative Studies*, ELT Documents, Oxford, British Council/Pergamon Press.

WILLIAMS, Trevor (1987) *Participation in Education*, Research Monograph No. 30, Hawthorn, Victoria, Australian Council for Educational Research.

WRIGHT, E. (1975) *Programme Placement Related to Selected Countries of Birth and Selected Languages*, Toronto, Toronto Board of Education.

ZIRKEL, Perry A. (1979a) 'A Method for Determining and Depicting Language Dominance', in *Bilingual Multicultural Education and the Professional: From Theory to Practice*, TRUEBA, Henry T. and BARNETT–MIZRAHI, Carol (eds), Rowley, Mass., Newbury House.

ZIRKEL, Perry A. (1979b) 'The Whys and Ways of Testing Bilinguality Before Teaching Bilingually', in *Bilingual Multicultural Education and the Professional: From Theory to Practice*, TRUEBA, Henry T. and BARNETT-MIZRAHI, Carol (eds.), Rowley, Mass., Newbury House.

Index